NOTHING LEFT TO LOSE

ALSO BY PHILIP SLAYTON

Lawyers Gone Bad: Money, Sex and Madness in Canada's Legal Profession (2007)

Mighty Judgment: How the Supreme Court of Canada Runs Your Life (2011)

Bay Street: A Novel (2013)

Mayors Gone Bad (2015)

How To Be Good: The Struggle Between Law and Ethics (2017)

The Future of Tennis (2018)

NOTHING LEFT TO LOSE

An Impolite Report on the
State of Freedom in Canada

PHILIP SLAYTON

TORONTO, 2020

For Rodger Beehler (1938–2006)

Sutherland House
416 Moore Ave., Suite 205
Toronto, ON M4G 1C9

First edition, March 2020

If you are interested in inviting one of our authors to a live event or
media appearance, please contact publicity@sutherlandhousebooks.com
and visit our website at sutherlandhousebooks.com for more
information about our authors and their schedules.

Manufactured in Canada
Cover designed by Lena Yang
Book composed by Karl Hunt
Cover photo courtesy of Getty Images

Library and Archives Canada Cataloguing in Publication
Title: Nothing left to lose : an impolite report on
the state of freedom in Canada / by Philip Slayton.
Names: Slayton, Philip, author.
Description: Includes index.
Identifiers: Canadiana 20200156136 | ISBN 9781989555224 (hardcover)
Subjects: LCSH: Civil rights—Canada. | LCSH: Canada—Politics and
government—1945- | LCSH: Canada—Civilization—1945- | LCSH: Liberty.
Classification: LCC JC599.C3 S53 2020 | DDC 323.0971—dc23

ISBN 978-1-989555-22-4

TABLE OF CONTENTS

FOREWORD

A GOLDEN AGE

I've lived in a golden age, in a golden place.

In 1954, when I was ten years old, my family immigrated to Canada. I have spent most of my life in this beautiful country, living in a democratic society, during a peaceful and prosperous time, a time marked, above all, by freedom. How lucky can you get?

But now, as my life enters its last phase, I am afraid. Things are changing, and changing fast. The golden age is coming to an end. Almost certainly, my children and grandchildren will not have the kind of life I have enjoyed. Freedom, which requires so many particular circumstances to flourish, and is essential to almost everything that is worthwhile, is in serious jeopardy, even in Canada, the most blessed of countries. We have lost much already. And time is running out. In this book I try to explain what has happened and why, before suggesting what we might do to salvage something before there is nothing left to lose.

A POINT OF VIEW

Everyone is a creature of their time, circumstances, and history. Everyone has a point of view that incorporates and expresses these constraints. Many strive to transcend their point of view, conscious of its limitations. They try to be "objective." They try to understand other perspectives. They try to be balanced, fair, and respectful. They recognize that a majority point of view can become a minority point of view as history shifts. They know that what is regarded as legitimate and acceptable in one age can become illegitimate and unacceptable as society's thinking changes. They understand that paying attention to others, particularly to the pain that others experience, is part of leading a moral life. They try to understand other points of view because we have a moral obligation to try and be as intelligent and informed as possible.

The duty to understand other points of view, the requirement to be intelligent and informed, is supremely important in a highly diverse country such as Canada where there are many perspectives and where social peace and progress depend upon as much understanding and tolerance across groups as possible. But there are limits to what is attainable. No one can transcend their personal identity completely. No one can abandon their point of view without a trace. There should not be criticism of this failure. No one should be asked to apologize for being what they are.

It is sometimes said that a member of one group cannot understand and legitimately comment on the circumstances of another group. So, for example, it is said (by some) that men cannot understand and should not presume to comment on the predicaments of women, or that whites are not qualified to offer opinions on the affairs of those who have black skins. An anonymous academic reader of an earlier but similar version of this manuscript took exception to certain parts and particularly to Chapter Twelve on Indigenous People. The main criticism was that I failed to acknowledge points of view and ways of thinking that differ from my own and did not recognize and assess "counter-arguments." The anonymous reader noted that the "voices" I cited lack diversity and are predominantly "white, male, and mainstream authority figures." The chapter is "bookended by white men.", wrote the anonymous reader: "There is no evidence in this manuscript that Mr. Slayton is speaking with indigenous people—just about them." And: "The impression given of the authorial voice is one of a dominant culture man speaking to other dominant culture men."

I take the criticisms of this anonymous reader as urging a moral and intelligent approach to understanding the situation and point of view of others. I have tried to adopt that approach (and I have made some limited revisions based on these comments). The criticisms have some weight, although I think they are exaggerated and vague. But, to the extent the comments of the anonymous reader reject as inappropriate or illegitimate the authenticity and integrity of my own voice and my own point of view—the view of an elderly, white, professionally educated, heterosexual male—I reject them.

RODGER BEEHLER

One day in 1963, when I was a student at the University of Manitoba, I attended a campus conference on a political subject. Someone in the audience tried to shout down a speaker who was expressing unpopular views. Another member of the audience, a student, leapt to his feet and gave an extemporaneous, eloquent, and impassioned defence of freedom of speech. I remember it as if it were yesterday. When the intervener sat down, the audience clapped enthusiastically, the heckler went silent, and the speaker with unpopular views carried on. The student intervener was Rodger Beehler, who became my lifelong friend. In later years, Rodger was a distinguished philosopher, finishing his career as chairman of the philosophy department at the University of Victoria. He died in 2006. I miss Rodger, and his passion for freedom. This book is dedicated to him.

Port Medway, Nova Scotia
October 2019

PART ONE

THE BIG PICTURE

Is Canada free? Not entirely. Does it deserve recent international praise as a bastion of liberal democracy? To a limited extent only. Should Canadians lie smug and superior in their beds at night, confident in their virtue and freedom? No.

Our complacency is unfounded. There are many threats to our freedom. Some are structural. Some are procedural. Some are obvious. Others are insidious, cumulative, hard to spot, easy to ignore. And our natural deference to authority, a particularly Canadian attribute, multiplies the danger many fold.

CHAPTER ONE

IS CANADA FREE?

THE PLACE TO BE

I began this book in the summer of 2016. It was the summer of "sunny ways." Most readers will remember the phrase. Justin Trudeau won the Canadian federal election of October 18, 2015. In a victory speech the day afterwards he promised "Sunny ways, my friends. Sunny ways."[1] Canada was the place to be. It all seems a long time ago.

Trudeau and his cabinet were sworn in on November 4, 2015. Half of his ministers were women. When asked by a reporter why that was important, he replied, "Because it's 2015." "Love U Canada," tweeted British actress Emma Watson, a star of the Harry Potter movies. In the months that followed Trudeau's ways seemed sunny indeed. The country was hailed internationally for welcoming Syrian refugees on a generous scale.[2] In July 2016, an ebullient prime minister marched in Toronto's Gay Pride parade: he wore a pink shirt and white jeans; earlier he had sung Lady Gaga's "Born This Way" at an outdoor church service in the city's gay village. That same month, the *Washington Post* praised Canada's cultural policy: "The arts are part of Canada's effort to

---

1   The expression was first used by Wilfred Laurier in an 1895 speech on the Manitoba Schools Question.

2   See, for example, Jodi Kantor & Catrin Einhorn, "Refugees Encounter a Foreign Word: Welcome," *The New York Times*, 1 July 2016 http://www.nytimes.com/2016/07/01/world/americas/canada-syrian-refugees.html (accessed 12 July 2016).

differentiate itself from a larger Western world move toward nationalism and insularity."[3]

If you were not already in Canada, perhaps you were figuring out how to get here. On July 7, 2016, the BBC reported: "At first it was the Americans. A record number of people in the US searched on Google for how to move to Canada after Donald Trump won seven out of eleven Republican primaries on Super Tuesday in March. More recently, people in the UK have been joining the party. In the days after Britain voted to leave the European Union by 52% to 48%, Google searches for 'move to Canada' hit an all-time high."[4] Canada was now seen as "a haven of stability and hope."[5]

At the end of October 2016, the cover of the *The Economist* magazine had a picture of the Statue of Liberty holding a hockey stick, her normal tiara replaced by a maple leaf. "Liberty moves north," said the headline. "Canada's example to the world." Inside, the magazine's leader said, "Canada has long seemed to outsiders to be a citadel of decency, tolerance and good sense. . . Today, in its lonely defence of liberal values, Canada seems downright heroic. . . The world owes Canada gratitude for reminding it of what many people are in danger of forgetting: that tolerance and openness are wellsprings of security and prosperity, not threats to them."[6] In December 2016, the English newspaper *The Guardian* published a lengthy account of people who had moved to Canada.[7] On the main streets of Canada's cities and

3   Philip Kennicott, "The state of the arts in Canada," 23 July 2016 https://www.washington post.com/entertainment/museums/the-state-of-the-arts-in-canada/2016/07/22/68b7dc98-42e0-11e6-8856-f26de2537a9d_story.html (accessed 15 September 2016).

4   Jasmine Taylor-Coleman, "Keen to move to Canada? Here are some things to consider," 7 July 2016 http://www.bbc.com/news/world-us-canada-36730174 (accessed 13 July 2016).

5   Lawrence Martin, "As the boomers fade, Canada's hopes rise," *Globe and Mail*, 21 July 2016 http://www.theglobeandmail.com/opinion/as-the-boomers-fade-canadas-hopes-rise/article30861271/ (accessed 27 July 2016).

6   http://www.economist.com/news/leaders/21709305-it-uniquely-fortunate-many-waysbut-canada-still-holds-lessons-other-western (accessed 4 November 2016).

7   "'I'm moving to Canada': the cops, pop stars and athletes who made good on the threat," 14 December 2016 https://www.theguardian.com/cities/2016/dec/14/im-moving-to-canada-the-cops-pop-stars-and-athletes-who-made-good-on-the-threat (accessed 15 December 2016).

towns, the citizens of what was now widely acknowledged as world's best country puffed their chests a little, a touch of pride replacing normal Canadian modesty.

It lasted for a while, the good feelings and international acclaim, Canada's enhanced image as an exceptionally free liberal democracy. In February 2019, Nicholas Kristof wrote an opinion piece in *The New York Times* with the headline, "Thank God for Canada! Our boring neighbour is a moral leader of the free world."[8]

SOMETIMES THE THREATS TO FREEDOM ARE BIG

One of the reasons why Canadians and others think Canada is a moral leader, the place to be, is that the country is exceptionally free. That is what we believe. But is it true?

What a question. Of course Canada is free. In 2018 and 2019, Freedom House ranked Canada as one of the freest nations in the world.[9] We elect those who govern us. We have an independent judiciary. We have an unfettered press. Young people have easy access to a competent educational system; this makes them capable of developing economic, social and cultural capital, and permits them to pursue a happy and prosperous life. We have civilian control of the police. We are a tolerant and peaceable people, thoroughly and respectfully multicultural, not given to excess. We acknowledge the worth of the individual. We are socially progressive and right thinking. In some circumstances, for example, assisting a suicide is no longer a crime. Nor, any longer, is the recreational use of cannabis. We have a fine, constitutionally entrenched, bill of rights, the Charter of Rights and Freedoms, which guarantees fundamental freedoms, democratic rights, mobility rights, legal rights and equality rights. What could be better? As our anthem says, *God keep our land glorious and free!*

8   6 February 2019 https://www.nytimes.com/2019/02/06/opinion/canada-trudeau-saudi-arabia.html (accessed 22 February 2019).

9   https://freedomhouse.org/report/freedom-world/2018/canada (accessed 23 February 2019); https://freedomhouse.org/report/freedom-world/2019/canada (accessed 6 August 2019).

But wait a moment. Is our complacency about freedom in Canada well founded?

No, it is not.

We are dangerously deferential to authority. We freely elect those who govern us, true, but the great power we give them can be used in an oppressive manner. Their method of election is democratically flawed because, in particular, little room is given to smaller but important political parties that garner significant percentages of the popular vote. The appointed executive branch of government dominates the elected legislature (and the public service) in the lawmaking process. The country's constitution is lopsided, depriving the cities, where most people live, of the authority and resources to do what their inhabitants want and need and what the cities can do best, look after the basic and daily needs of their inhabitants. Canada's traditional, independent free press, essential to exposing and reining in the excesses of those in authority, is mostly owned by large national corporations and has largely collapsed, replaced by social media commentators for the most part lacking in resources and credibility. The judiciary, made up of appointed bureaucrats wielding the Charter of Rights, increasingly decides issues of fundamental social policy (abortion, assisted suicide, prostitution laws, etc.), which in a democracy should be decided, as a political matter, by those we elect. The cost of education, particularly post-secondary education, has placed it beyond the grasp of many, and has saddled others with vast debt that distorts career choices in unpleasant and antisocial ways. In any event, universities have replaced education with job training and free speech with political correctness. The police can, and have, run rampant. The surveillance society is in place. Economic inequality has increased dramatically and rendered vast parts of the population economically impotent and vulnerable to exploitation by a handful of rich people and corporations. The situation of Canada's Indigenous People remains appalling. Global warming threatens our existence. There is little true political leadership and the concept of citizenry continues to be degraded. Some of these deep structural impediments to freedom have been with us for years. Others are relatively new and growing in importance.

SOMETIMES THE THREATS TO FREEDOM SEEM SMALL

Threats to freedom can be dramatic. Tanks rumble into the public square. Secret police pound on the door in the middle of the night. A dissident journalist is lured into a foreign consulate and is killed and dismembered. These things do not happen in Canada. Except occasionally. In October 1970, during the FLQ crisis, I looked out of the window of my downtown Montreal apartment and saw troops in the streets below.

But it is not just tanks, or secret police, or troops in the streets, that we have to fear. Many of the threats to our freedom are not overt and dramatic but subtle, oblique, indirect, cloaked in apparent legality, and the more dangerous for all of that. Threats to freedom can come, for example, from insistence by officials on compliance with arcane detailed rules promulgated by government committees working in private. The most dangerous agents of repression can be bored government men in suits passing dull resolutions in anonymous and private meeting rooms.

It is difficult to detect and defy the subtle and oblique. Tank Man stared down armoured vehicles in Tiananmen Square. The photograph of his bravely doing so, in a white shirt, holding shopping bags (which made the image unbearably poignant), is famous. But how do you stare down an anonymous bureaucrat who insists that you comply with an incomprehensible regulation of many pages and frequent circumlocutions, a regulation that seems innocuous on the face of it? How do you battle the banality of bureaucracy?

FREEDOM AND FAIRNESS

Freedom and fairness are intertwined. Without fairness there can be little freedom for most citizens. Freedom without fairness is an illusion.

But freedom and fairness compete. Only government has the power to establish fairness. Only government has the power to create social justice and establish equal rights amongst citizens. Only government can eradicate the extreme inequalities of wealth that destabilize society, prevent fairness, and deny freedom. Social democracy requires an interventionist and redistributive state that may, by its very nature, curtail or abridge some freedoms possessed by some people. It may, for example, curtail certain property rights (no one is free to own a slave). And social democracy requires big government. If big government moves in the wrong direction, or is evil, or is simply incompetent, it can be the biggest threat to freedom of them all. This is the central dilemma of democratic government.

Can the fairness/freedom dilemma be resolved? How do we support big government and the far-reaching laws required for fairness while insisting at the same time on maximum possible freedom? One answer is, by constant vigilance. "Let the sentinels on the watch-tower sleep not, and slumber not."[10] A second answer (perhaps a restatement of the first) is to harbour constant skepticism of government. The late David Carr, in *The New York Times*, attributed the success of British journalists in the United States to their suspicious attitude. "The one question all young reporters on Fleet Street are taught to keep foremost in their mind when interviewing public figures can be best paraphrased as, 'Why is this jerk lying to me?'"[11] The citizen of a social democracy should always be suspicious of government.

THE NECESSARY CONDITIONS FOR FREEDOM

There are conditions that are necessary for true freedom to flourish. If these conditions exist but are weak, then freedom will be weak. If they do not exist, there will be no freedom at all. If the conditions disappear, there will be nothing left to lose. Much of this book examines the state in Canada of the following conditions for freedom.

Freedom requires an alert and skeptical citizenry, more inclined to challenge authority than celebrate it. In Canada, as I discuss in the next chapter, there is a long and dangerous tradition of deference to authority, sometimes mistakenly thought of as desirable civility.

10   *The Virginia Free Press and Farmers' Repository*, 2 May 1833, quoted by http://www. thisdayinquotes.com/2011/01/eternal-vigilance-is-price-of-liberty.html (accessed 9 October 2016).
11   "British Invasion Reshuffles U.S. Media," 23 June 2013 http://www.nytimes.com/ 2013/06/24/business/media/britain-as-a-breeding-ground-for-media-leaders.html (accessed 9 September 2016).

Freedom requires a fair electoral system, a strong legislature and legislative process, a balance between the executive and legislative branches, and an appropriate apportionment of power among the different levels of government. As we shall see, these have been compromised in Canada.

Freedom requires a restrained judiciary that understands and reflects the will of the people, an effective justice system accessible to all, one that is not asked to solve problems that are principally political. It also requires an enlightened legal profession. These are all in doubt in Canada.

Freedom requires a vigorous, independent, diverse and disciplined press, with an investigative bent. The traditional fourth estate, embodying these virtues, is almost extinct in our country. It has been replaced by chaotic and untrustworthy social media.

Freedom requires a strong and independent secondary and post-secondary education system, dedicated principally to creating astute citizens who know a good argument from a bad one. The education system in Canada has been undermined by vocationalism and political correctness.

Freedom requires a rejection of heavy-handed political correctness and simplistic ideas of human rights. This has not happened in Canada.

Freedom requires effective civilian control of police, and limits to government surveillance and the citizenry's loss of privacy: these are an issue in our country.

A free country must treat its Indigenous peoples with justice and fairness. Canada has failed to do this.

A free country must have the capacity and will to respond to the greatest threat that we face, the threat of climate change. Canada has not shown this capacity or will.

A free country requires courageous political leadership and a citizenry devoted to the common good.

Do we have these necessary conditions for freedom in Canada? Let us see.

CHAPTER TWO

UNDUE DEFERENCE

POST-TRUTH POLITICS

Modern politicians often appeal to emotions rather than facts, adjusting facts to suit emotions. They are giving people what they want. They are doing what works politically. It is part of that global, populist, majoritarian movement that we constantly hear about. You could say it is a consequence of democracy. You could say we live in a "post-truth age." In 2015, Oxford Dictionaries declared "post-truth" to be its international word of the year.[12] By 2016, the word "post-truth" had become trite. By now, we are all sick of hearing it.[13]

---

12   Alison Flood, "'Post-truth' named word of the year by Oxford Dictionaries," *The Guardian*, 15 November 2016 https://www.theguardian.com/books/2016/nov/15/post-truth-named-word-of-the-year-by-oxford-dictionaries (accessed 18 November 2016).

13   For a fascinating and oblique commentary on post-truth, see Ava Kofman, "Bruno Latour, the Post-Truth Philosopher, Mounts a Defence of Science, *The New York Times,* 25 October 2018 https://www.nytimes.com/2018/10/25/magazine/bruno-latour-post-truth-philosopher-science.html (accessed 25 October 2018). What journalists, scientists and other experts fail to grasp, Latour argues, is that "facts remain robust only when they are supported by a common culture, by institutions that can be trusted, by a more or less decent public life, by more or less reliable media." With the rise of alternative facts, it has become clear that whether or not a statement is believed depends far less on its veracity than on the conditions of its "construction" — that is, who is making it, to whom it's being addressed and from which institutions it emerges and is made visible."

Post-truth politicians repeat talking points they know to be false. Post-truthers and their supporters are fuelled by lack of trust in government and other central institutions, and particularly by a lack of trust in experts, technocrats and bureaucrats, the traditional guardians of facts. It does not matter anymore what experts think or say: they have so often been proven wrong (received wisdom once was that the Sun orbited the Earth), partisan, misguided or corrupt, and, anyhow, they have no understanding of the concerns of the average citizen. They just don't get it. In his 2017 book, *The Death of Expertise*,[14] Tom Nichols writes, "Americans have reached a point where ignorance, especially of anything related to public policy, is an actual virtue. To reject the advice of experts is to assert autonomy, a way for Americans to insulate their increasingly fragile egos from ever being told they're wrong about anything."[15]

Populist post-truth politics were exemplified in 2016 by the disastrous Brexit campaign in the United Kingdom and the appalling presidential campaign in the United States of America. *The New York Times* editorialized in December 2016 that "Donald Trump understood at least one thing better than almost everybody watching the 2016 election: The breakdown of a shared public reality built upon widely accepted facts represented not a hazard, but an opportunity."[16] Mark Thompson, former director-general of the BBC, has written of those campaigning for office: "Once listeners are convinced that you're not trying to deceive them in the manner of a regular politician, they may switch off the critical faculties they usually apply to political speech and forgive you any amount of exaggeration, contradiction, or offensiveness."[17] In the run-up to the 2017 French presidential election, the flamboyant French philosopher Bernard-Henri Levy said the French electorate had lost interest in whether politicians tell the truth. "The

14   *The Death of Expertise: The Campaign against Established Knowledge and Why It Matters*, (New York: Oxford University Press, 2017).
15   p.x.
16   "Truth and Lies in the Age of Trump," http://www.nytimes.com/2016/12/10/ opinion/truth-and-lies-in-the-age-of-trump.html?_r=0 (accessed 11 December 2016).
17   *Enough Said: What's Gone Wrong with the Language of Politics* (New York: St. Martin's Press, 2016), p.22.

people listen less and less to policy and they even seem less concerned about whether the candidates are telling the truth or not. They are more interested in the performance, in the theatrical quality of what is said than whether it is true."[18]

Liberal elites recoil from post-truth politics, mourning the absence of what was once their bread and butter—the clash of complex ideas and endless fact-based debate over complex policies. They condemn post-truth politics, the buffoons who embrace it, the masses that are fooled by it, and its calamitous consequences. They consider that a post-truth world, with government decisions and policy resting on fiction purveyed by ignorant and manipulative leaders (climate change is a Chinese hoax), is perverted and doomed.

CANADA PREFERS DEFERENCE

Canadians have not embraced post-truth politics. They have not lost trust in experts, technocrats and bureaucrats. They prefer a deeply conservative, calm and deliberate deference to order, authority, and expertise. This deference takes many forms and has many benefits. But it also has many drawbacks. The Canadian choice of deference rather than post-truth may seem mature and commonsensical, and in some ways it is, but it carries danger with it.

In 1965, the conservative political philosopher George Grant, published *Lament for a Nation*.[19] Grant confidently predicted that Canada as an independent sovereign state was doomed. Faced with the irresistible global march of modernity, Canada would be unable to resist American cultural and political hegemony. Canada's demise would be accelerated by its liking for liberalism, a political philosophy which, in Grant's view, undermines traditional values and stands in the way of a distinct and unifying national identity. Liberalism allows, indeed

---

18   Quoted by James Rothwell, "Leading French philosopher: Marine Le Pen may win election as people have lost interest in whether politicians tell the truth," *The Telegraph*, 20 November 2016 http://www.telegraph.co.uk/news/2016/11/20/leading-french-philosopher-marine-le-pen-may-win-election-as-peo/ (accessed 20 November 2016).

19   George Grant, *Lament for a Nation* (Montreal: McGill-Queens Press, 1965).

encourages, everyone to pursue his or her personal values so long as that pursuit does not interfere with other people's right to do the same thing. George Grant thought that liberalism was antithetical to a unified value-based society in which everyone agrees on hierarchy, deference, tradition and public morality. Liberalism would flourish. Its opposite, deference, would die. As deference died, so would the state.

Time has proven George Grant utterly wrong. His dichotomy—liberalism versus a unified value-based society—was false. Modern Canada is an independent liberal state that accommodates and celebrates differences, but at the same time, it is also a country wedded to hierarchy and tradition that defers to authority. W.L. Morton, in his 1960 presidential address to the Canadian Historical Association, saw something that George Grant missed. For Morton, allegiance to the monarchy (the concept, not the person) allows disparate groups to gather together, something that a social compact such as that in the United States does not permit. Morton wrote: "Not life, liberty, and the pursuit of happiness, but peace, order, and good government are what the national government of Canada guarantees. Under these, it is assumed, life, liberty, and happiness may be achieved, but by each according to his taste. For the society of allegiance admits of a diversity the society of compact does not, and one of the blessings of Canadian life is that there is not a Canadian way of life, much less two, but a unity under the Crown admitting of a thousand diversities."[20]

Justin Trudeau has on occasion described Canada as the first postnational state, adding, "There is no core identity, no mainstream in Canada."[21] He, like George Grant, is profoundly mistaken. There is a core Canadian identity, one that, paradoxically, shelters a thousand diversities. The core identity depends upon allegiance and deference to institutions, beginning with the monarchy. It remains strong. On Victoria Day 2019, the *Globe and Mail* concluded its lead editorial,

20   "The Relevance of Canadian History," in W.L. Morton, *The Canadian Identity* (Toronto: The University of Toronto Press, 1964), p.111.
21   See Charles Foran, "The Canada experiment: is this the world's first 'postnational' country?" *The Guardian*, 4 January 2017 https://www.theguardian.com/world/2017/jan/04/the-canada-experiment-is-this-the-worlds-first-postnational-country (accessed 24 October 2018).

"Happy and glorious, long to reign over us, God save our distant Queen."[22]

This is unlike the United States where, as George Packer, the American journalist, has observed, one of the narratives is a powerful multicultural story which makes people "less able or less willing to think in terms larger than their own identity group—a kind of intellectual narcissism—which means they can't find common ground or effective arguments that can reach people of different backgrounds and views." This approach values "inclusion, but doesn't answer the question, Included into what? What is the national identity all these subgroups add up into?"[23]

The difference in this respect between Canada and the United States explains their different approach to immigration. The United States, consumed by parochial identity politics, increasingly rejects immigrants and new immigration, unable to accept those who look different and think differently. Canada can be inclusive, allowing everybody to shelter under broad concepts embraced by the country.

All this, driven by deference and rejection of post-truth, seems like a good thing, and by some measure it is. You could argue that it makes Canada a better country than the United States of America. And that is true. But it is not without risk. Serious risk.

CANADIANS LIKE BALLET

In 1980, Edgar Z. Friedenberg, an American teaching at Dalhousie University in Halifax, Nova Scotia (where George Grant also taught for a time), published a book called *Deference to Authority: The Case of Canada*.[24] Canadians, he noted in this strange and prescient volume, "have no tradition identifying government as the source of oppres-

---

22   "The blessings of a faraway monarch," 18 May 2019, p. 10.

23   See David Brooks, "The Four American Narratives," *The New York Times*, 26 May 2017 https://www.nytimes.com/2017/05/26/opinion/the-four-american-narratives. html?_r=0 (accessed 7 January 2018).

24   Edgar Z. Friedenberg, *Deference to Authority: The Case of Canada* (White Plains, New York: M.E. Sharpe, 1980). I am grateful to my friend Patrick Martin for bringing this book to my attention.

sion. They resisted the temptation to join the American revolution; and their loyalty to the Crown was indeed reinforced by the flight of loyalists northward from the revolting colonies."[25] Friedenberg continued: "The enjoyment of conflict is not a part of the Canadian tradition as it is of the American. The Canadian West was won, not by massacre and military conquest . . . but by the Northwest Mounted Police as they were then called, moving ahead of the colonists to inform the native people of their lack of civil rights."[26] The habit of deference is ingrained in Canada, writes Friedenberg, and the dissident "becomes either a victim or a plucky schoolboy, ready, finally, to resolve his dispute with authority by taking six of the best from the prefects."[27] (What a strange, old-fashioned, upper-class English metaphor, coming from an American writing about Canada.) In a curious aside, Friedenberg wrote that Canada particularly excelled in those art forms with the least potential for subversion. He singled out ballet.

Much of the political and institutional analysis in Friedenberg's book is out of date. In particular, he was writing before the 1982 Charter of Rights and Freedoms. His analysis of parliamentary sovereignty, and of the political and lawmaking role of the Supreme Court of Canada no longer applies. But the core of his discussion, on Canadian deference to authority, remains cogent, unlike the analysis of George Grant in *Lament for a Nation*. We remain a country founded, not in revolution, but by a police force. We defer to our elders (whatever their age) and betters (whatever their title). We are polite. Even our cautious embrace of individual rights, particularly since the Charter, has not made much of an impact on our posture of deference.

One day I had lunch with a friend who is a keen observer of the contemporary scene. The conversation strayed to deference. With his usual insight and conviction, my friend said, "We Canadians agree to do and think what we're told to do and think by the people who are supposed to run things. Once we've been given the answer by authority figures, we fall into line. Look at abortion. In 1988 the Supreme Court told us that the Criminal Code provisions about abortion were contrary to the

25 p. 14.
26 pp. 21–2.
27 p. 29.

Charter and struck them down. That was that. The Supreme Court had spoken. They still fight about abortion in the US, but not in Canada." My friend was right. The US Supreme Court decision on abortion, in the 1973 case of *Roe v. Wade*, settled nothing politically. Abortion is still a matter of extreme controversy in the United States, among other things a "litmus test" for judicial nominees. In Canada, the shouting was pretty much over once our Supreme Court had spoken. Canadians fell into line. The matter had been decided. We thought and did what we were told.

Could it be, not that we unquestioningly defer to authority with customary servility, but that our agreement is anterior and our institutions simply reflect a consensus that already exists? Do we place our trust in deeply held shared opinions, rather than in the pronouncements of institutions? The journalist Chantal Hébert wrote in 2016 that in Canada there is a "high level of consensus that transcends party lines."[28] She noted that Canadians agree on free trade (differences were settled twenty-five years ago, in the debate over the North American Free Trade Agreement); public health care (no politician challenges the basic tenets of the public health insurance program); climate change (the arguments are restricted to how best to deal with it); immigration (Canada does not have a serious anti-immigration political party); and social rights (for example, no one argues against same sex marriage). By contrast, as was amply demonstrated in the 2016 election and subsequently, the US political and social scene is roiled by conflict over trade, public health insurance, climate change, immigration, and social rights.

Why does such a diverse people agree on so much? Were we gifted with like-mindedness at our creation? Or is it because we have been told to agree, and it is in our nature to obey?

TWO RUDE LAWYERS

Politeness is an important expression of Canadian deference. It is thought un-Canadian to be rude to fellow citizens, particularly those

---

28   "Canada has consensus U.S. lacks on key issues," *Toronto Star*, 15 October 2016 https://www.thestar.com/news/canada/2016/10/15/canada-has-consensus-us-lacks-on-key-issues.html (accessed 15 October 2016).

with power or status. After all, politeness contributes to the stability of the polity, although there are other reasons to be polite. Yet politeness, like other forms of deference, can be dangerous. The politeness imperative can subvert freedom of expression and undermine political institutions. This is particularly true when politeness is enforced.

Let me give you two examples, drawn from the legal world, a world in which I lived for many years: the Canadian lawyers Joe Groia and Ezra Levant.[29] Groia and Levant were impolite. They were rude to persons of authority. Their profession punished them. What happens within the legal profession—including how and why it polices its members—is important because the justice system is, or should be, an essential part of Canadian democracy (it has failed us to a degree, as I describe in Chapter Four). The justice system, staffed by lawyers, is part of the country's political warp and woof. Its behaviour ripples outward, influencing everything.

Joe Groia is a Toronto lawyer who successfully defended John Felderhof of Bre-X infamy on insider trading charges (the Felderhof case began in 1998 and did not end until 2007).[30] Groia was said to have a "win at all costs" attitude at trial. He was accused of being strident and sarcastic, rude to the lawyer for the Ontario Securities Commission, and prone to "rhetorical excess" and "petulant invective." In 2009, he became the subject of disciplinary proceedings before Ontario's law society. Several of the law society's Rules of Professional Conduct bear on the civility issue. Rule 4.01(6), for example, requires a lawyer to be courteous and civil in the course of litigation; the commentary on the rule says, "A consistent pattern of rude, provocative, or disruptive conduct by the lawyer, even though unpunished as contempt, might well merit discipline." In June 2012, a law society hearing panel found Groia guilty of professional misconduct, delivering an unconvincing fifty-three page pastiche of cut-and-paste reasons.[31] The hearing panel

---

29   I wrote about the Groia and Levant cases in the magazine *Canadian Lawyer* (several times about Groia).

30   *R. v. Felderhof*, 2007 ONCJ 345 (CanLII).

31   *Law Society of Upper Canada v. Joseph Peter Paul Groia*, 2012 ONLSHP 94 (CanLII) http://www.canlii.org/en/on/onlst/#search/type=decision&ccId=onlst&id=groia& origType=decision&origCcId=onlst (accessed 12 November 2016).

pontificated: "Lawyers have a duty to act in good faith, with respect and courtesy to the court, and to all persons with whom they deal in the course of their professional practice." It said, "A pattern of conduct that includes persistent attacks and sarcasm directed at opposing counsel can form the basis of incivility." The panel rejected the argument that a duty of civility can compromise a lawyer's duty to defend a client vigorously. What terrible things did Groia say? Well, for example, he used the word "Government" to refer to the Ontario Securities Commission.

In 2013, another law society panel dismissed Groia's appeal from the earlier finding.[32] The appeal panel said that many of the comments Groia made in the Felderhof case "crossed the line: they included repeated personal attacks on the integrity of the prosecutors and repeated allegations of deliberate prosecutorial wrongdoing that did not have a reasonable basis and were not otherwise justified by the context." Groia's professional misconduct, said the appeal panel, harmed the administration of justice.

Groia appealed again, to the Divisional Court. Once more he lost.[33] Justice Nordheimer gave the judgment for the three-member panel. Nordheimer said that for uncivil conduct to rise to the level of professional misconduct it must be conduct that would "bring the administration of justice into dispute [sic], or would have the tendency to do so. It is conduct that calls into question the integrity of the court process and of the players involved in it." He recognized the need to permit "zealous advocacy," but there was a line that could be crossed and Groia had crossed it. In June 2016, Groia's appeal from the Divisional Court was dismissed by the Ontario Court of Appeal in a split decision.[34]

32   *Law Society of Upper Canada v. Joseph Peter Paul Groia*, 2013 ONLSAP 41 (CanLII) http://www.canlii.org/en/on/onlst/doc/2013/2013onlsap41/2013onlsap41.html?resultIndex=4 (accessed 12 November 2016).

33   *Joseph Groia v. The Law Society of Upper Canada*, 2015 ONSC 686 (CanLII) http://www.canlii.org/en/on/onscdc/doc/2015/2015onsc686/2015onsc686.html?resultIndex=9 (accessed 12 November 2016).

34   *Groia v. The Law Society of Upper Canada*, 2016 ONCA 471 (CanLII) http://www.canlii.org/en/on/onca/doc/2016/2016onca471/2016onca471.html?resultIndex=7 (accessed 12 November 2016).

Groia appealed to the Supreme Court of Canada, and was finally vindicated.[35] The Supreme Court, in a six-three decision, declared the professional misconduct finding to be unreasonable. Mr. Justice Moldaver, writing for five of the six judges in the majority, said, "A lawyer's duty to act with civility does not exist in a vacuum. Rather, it exists in concert with a series of professional obligations that both constrain and compel a lawyer's behaviour. Care must be taken to ensure that free expression, resolute advocacy and the right of an accused to make full answer and defence are not sacrificed at the altar of civility."[36] In a strange footnote to this saga, in 2015 Groia was elected to the governing body of his persecutor, the Law Society (he was re-elected in 2019). He had spent years, and a fortune in legal fees, fighting his case.

The pursuit of Joe Groia by the Law Society of Upper Canada, expending huge resources in the process, was unwise in the extreme. Groia's election as a bencher shows that the law society rank-and-file membership deeply doubted the wisdom of the pursuit. The incident reflects an unsavoury preoccupation of the legal profession's elite establishment, including the judiciary, with politeness, hierarchy and deference to authority (its own), a preoccupation that can subvert the pursuit of justice and betray the profession. Sometimes rough-and-tumble is required to achieve justice.

Ezra Levant is a well-known conservative media commentator. He thrives on controversy and conflict. Until 2016, Levant was a member of the Law Society of Alberta, although he hadn't practised law or lived in Alberta for a long time, earning his living as a Toronto journalist. For years he had wanted to resign from the Alberta bar, but the rules made that difficult.

For almost a decade, a lot of people, including other lawyers, made formal complaints to the Law Society of Alberta about things Levant had said and written, and in particular about his lack of "professional courtesy." Law society rules say that you cannot resign in the face of an unresolved complaint without special permission. Resignation without permission is considered the equivalent of disbarment, which is a

35   *Groia v. Law Society of Upper Canada*, 2018 SCC 27 (CanLII), <http://canlii.ca/t/hsb9d>, (retrieved on 2018-06-20).
36   para. 3.

disgrace. The argument is that to permit unilateral resignation if complaints are outstanding would allow a lawyer to escape the society's disciplinary jurisdiction. The Ontario bar, and the bar of every other province, has similar rules. So, Levant was trapped in the unwanted and clammy embrace of the Law Society of Alberta. Quite reasonably, he said he would only resign if pending complaints against him were dismissed and he could leave the profession unbesmirched.

Levant called the complaints to the law society about his conduct "nuisance complaints." He said they were "free shots" by his political opponents. He pointed out that anyone who objected to his views expressed as a journalist on his website, in newspaper articles, or on television, could tie him up in knots and inflict expense by registering an official complaint. Over the years, twenty-six people did exactly that. Twenty-four of the complaints were dismissed, leaving two outstanding. A number of the complaints were about Levant's criticism of the Alberta Human Rights Commission. He has called the Commission "crazy."

In March 2016, the society finally accepted Levant's resignation, saying that to do so "was in the best interests of the public." It summarily dismissed the two outstanding complaints against him. No doubt law society officials heaved a mighty sigh of relief when Levant left town. Levant thinks he knows why the society decided in his favour. "They want to stop being forced to read my newspaper columns and watch my videos as part of their job."

Levant has argued that at least some of the complaints against him, and the formal process and requirements they triggered, were "a violation of my Charter rights of freedom of expression, freedom of the press and freedom of conscience." He's right. It would be illegal and absurd to allow the demands of courtesy to trump freedom of expression. Courtesy may be a desirable social quality that promotes civility. But freedom of expression is a vital principle on which our free and democratic society depends. It beggars belief that anyone could seriously entertain prizing courtesy over freedom. In particular, it beggars belief that lawyers and the organized legal profession would advance such an idea.

Misplaced emphasis on courtesy, the desire to avoid conflict no matter what, is part of an excessive and dangerous Canadian politeness born of deference to authority. We are too respectful of those who have position and power. Often there is a need for something more robust. Skepticism and suspicion are regarded by many as unpleasant attitudes, but they have their uses. Being obnoxious, like Joe Groia or Ezra Levant, can lead to the truth. Be polite at your country's peril.

As Canadians look around the world, at Brexit and Trump's America for instance, they may with some justification congratulate themselves on a deference and restraint that has helped avoid post-truth politics and other contemporary excesses. But this is not a straightforward calculus. There is a high price to be paid for undue deference and restraint. The consequences can include: pushing underground ideas that have merit and marginalizing their advocates; alienating dissenters from the mainstream political system; limiting participation in public debate and the healthy flow of contrary ideas; engendering mindless acceptance of things that an engaged people should be quarrelling about; betraying our system of democracy; and making a sham of self-government, leaving us vulnerable to those to whom we defer and wherever they would take us.

NINE WISE JUDGES

For another example of Canadian deference to authority, we turn from two rude lawyers to nine wise judges, to the pinnacle of the Canadian justice system, to the Supreme Court of Canada.

No one possesses more authority than Supreme Court justices. Since passage in 1982 of the Canadian Charter of Rights and Freedoms, the Supreme Court has become at least the equal in political power of the other two branches of government, the legislative and executive branches; arguably it has greater power than the legislative branch, which must do the bidding of the executive branch. In Chapter Four I describe the implications for freedom of the Supreme Court's supremacy. Here I will talk only about our unwise deference to that institution.

The Supreme Court is at the centre of the spider web of authority. It is similar in this respect to the Supreme Court of the United States and other final courts of appeal, such as the United Kingdom Supreme Court, the Supreme Court of Israel, and the Constitutional Court of South Africa. Yet the Canadian Court, unlike other supreme courts, particularly the US Supreme Court, seems strangely isolated from public debate and criticism. It is remote, almost unknowable, despite some recent modest attempts from the Court itself to make it more familiar. Individual Canadians understand little about the Court, and would be hard-pressed to find out something about it if they wanted to.

The media follows the Court in a limited and desultory way. The natural reclusiveness, even secrecy, of most of its judges enhances the Court's mystery. All conspires to make the Court a riddle. Few Canadians could name more than one or two Supreme Court judges. Canadians genuflect to a Court they hardly know. Criticism of the Court, by other than a few specialist lawyers and law professors, is almost unthinkable, and even the lawyers and professors, for the most part, tread gently.

This is not true in the United States. One reason is the willingness of US Supreme Court judges to engage widely. For an example, consider the Ruth Bader Ginsburg/Donald Trump contretemps during the 2016 election. In a July 2016 interview with *The New York Times* reporter Adam Liptak, in her Supreme Court chambers, the much-admired Justice Ginsburg unwisely said, "I can't imagine what this place would be–I can't imagine what the country would be–with Donald Trump as our president."[37] A few days after *The New York Times* exchange, in a CNN interview, Ginsburg called Trump a "faker" who "says whatever comes into his head at the moment. He really has an ego." Donald Trump responded that Ginsburg's behaviour was "a disgrace to the court" and Tweeted, "Her mind is shot—resign!"[38] Justice Ginsburg finally apologized in a written statement: "Judges should avoid commenting on a candidate for public office. . . In the future I will be more circumspect."[39]

37　"Ruth Bader Ginsburg, No Fan of Donald Trump, Critiques Latest Term," *The New York Times*, 20 July 2016 http://www.nytimes.com/2016/07/11/us/politics/ruth-bader-ginsburg-no-fan-of-donald-trump-critiques-latest-term.html (accessed 23 November 2016).

38　See Joan Biskupic, "Justice Ruth Bader Ginsburg calls Trump a 'faker,' he says she should resign," *CNN Politics*, 13 July 2016 http://www.cnn.com/2016/07/12/politics/justice-ruth-bader-ginsburg-donald-trump-faker/ (accessed 23 November 2016).

39　See Michael D. Shear, "Ruth Bader Ginsburg Expresses Regret for Criticizing Donald Trump," *The New York Times*, 14 July 2016 http://www.nytimes.com/2016/07/15/us/politics/ruth-bader-ginsburg-donald-trump.html (accessed 23 November 2016).

There's a comic opera written about Justice Ginsburg and her former colleague, the late Justice Antonin "Nino" Scalia. Derrick Wang's *Scalia/Ginsberg* was first performed in 2015. Scalia, who died in February 2016, was famous for being outspoken, blunt, and seeking the public eye. In the decision that legalized same-sex marriage across the United States, Scalia's dissenting judgment, typically pugnacious, said of the majority opinion, "The opinion is couched in a style that is as pretentious as its content is egotistic. It is one thing for separate concurring or dissenting opinions to contain extravagances, even silly extravagances, of thought and expression; it is something else for the official opinion of the Court to do so."[40] It was Scalia who barked "get over it" when challenged by reporter Lesley Stahl about the Court's 2000 decision in *Bush v. Gore* which effectively handed the presidency to George W. Bush. He loved going on television talk shows—Sixty Minutes, Charlie Rose (six times), Piers Morgan.

And American Supreme Court judges write books by the bushel. In 2012, *SCOTUSblog* listed three hundred and fifty-three books written by Supreme Court justices, living and dead.[41] The most prolific justice was William O. Douglas, who "wrote fifty-one books on a wide variety of topics ranging from foreign policy to psychiatry, from corporate reorganization to environmentalism, and from *stare decisis* to manifest destiny." A number of U.S. Supreme Court justices have published books since 2012—a 2013 memoir by Sonia Sotomayor, *My Beloved World*, for example.

The judges of the UK are not far behind. For example, the *Times Literary Supplement* (*TLS*) of November 25, 2016 reviewed *The Safest Shield* by Igor Judge, former Lord Chief Justice of England and Wales; *Let Equity Prevail* by Donald Nicholls, a former Law Lord; *Shaping Tomorrow's Law* by Mary Arden, senior Lady Justice of Appeal; *As In Memory Long* by Peter Millett, a former appeals judge; and *IP and*

---

40   *Obergefell v. Hodges*, 576 US (2015) https://www.supremecourt.gov/opinions/14pdf/14-556_3204.pdf (accessed 24 November 2016).

41   Ronald Collins, "353 books by Supreme Court Justices," *SCOTUSblog* 7 November 2012 http://www.scotusblog.com/2012/03/351-books-by-supreme-court-justices/ (accessed 29 November 2016).

Other Things, by Robin Jacob, also a former judge.[42] The *TLS* reviewer, Michael Beloff, himself a lawyer of distinction, commented, "there is nowadays more to being an appellate judge than simply judging. A modern judge writes, lectures, delivers conference addresses, liaises with foreign judges, sits on or chairs committees or commissions."

So far as I know, not one current sitting judge of the Canadian Supreme Court, or living former judge of that court, has written a book (other than former Chief Justice Beverley McLachlin who has written two, both published after she left the bench: a forgettable mystery novel called *Full Disclosure*, and a memoir entitled *Truth Be Told: My Journey Through Life and the Law*). Whether this is from lack of interest, idleness, excessive reticence, or stems from some deep-seated feeling about some elusive but sacred constitutional principle, I cannot say. In 2013, the *Globe and Mail* even editorialized on this subject: "The late Supreme Court judge John Sopinka said judges don't need to be monks. Heck, even monks write books. So do former prime ministers. So do former governors-general. Even a former king has. As public officials, they have a great deal to contribute to demystifying the court and the law. Whatever the reasons for reticence on the Supreme Court, the silence comes at an enormous cost."[43]

The United States Supreme Court is followed intensely, even obsessively, by the American media. Journalists, many of them legally qualified, report and speculate endlessly on the Court. Sophisticated analysts like Adam Liptak and Linda Greenhouse of *The New York Times*, and Jeffrey Toobin of *The New Yorker*, regularly expose the Court's inner workings, in their newspapers and in books written for a popular audience. This is not true in Canada, where reporting on the Supreme Court is lacklustre and often done by uninformed journalists without legal qualifications. There is only a handful of popular books on the Canadian Court.

Canadians are satisfied with holding their Supreme Court justices in awe from a distance. Contrast the attitude of Americans. For example,

42   "Friends of the People," *Times Literary Supplement*, 25 November 2016, p. 32.
43   "Supreme Court judges would do us a justice if they wrote books," *Globe and Mail*, 27 March 2013 http://www.theglobeandmail.com/opinion/editorials/supreme-court-judges-would-do-us-a-justice-if-they-wrote-books/article9835615/ (accessed 30 November, 2016).

the New York *Daily News* reported, on March 25, 2013: "Hundreds of pro- and anti-gay-marriage activists are camped out in front of the U.S. Supreme Court Building in the hopes of getting inside to witness arguments in two potentially ground-breaking civil rights cases that will be heard Tuesday and Wednesday. Bundled in scarves, parkas and winter hats, people huddled in groups over the weekend as they tried to sleep under tarps coated by 3 inches of slushy snow. They were bracing for temperatures in the 20s Monday night."[44]

DON'T FORGET THE BANKS

Canadians also defer to economic power. Most particularly, Canadians love and respect their banks and those who run them. No people on earth love and respect their banks the way Canadians do. Year after year, the most profitable Canadian companies are banks.[45] A senior Bay Street corporate lawyer once said to me that the chief executive officers of banks were the most powerful people in Canada. They were, he said, with a faraway look in his eyes, "modern colossi who stride the earth."

The so-called Big Five employ almost half-a-million people in Canada. Banks are the staple of every investment portfolio in the country, large and small (there is a lot of cross-ownership, banks owning shares in other banks). Bank stocks, with their unending capital appreciation and steadily increasing dividends, have ensured the satisfactory retirement of many Canadians. Canadian banks, carefully regulated by the federal government, have easily survived international economic difficulties, especially the recession of 2008.

Even in the age of internet banking, bricks and mortar bank branches are prominent on many a Canadian street corner, in small

---

44   Joseph Straw, "Advocates and foes of same-sex marriage line up by the hundreds to witness history as the U.S. Supreme Court prepares to hear two key cases," New York *Daily News*, 25 March 2013 http://www.nydailynews.com/new-york/gay-marriage-cases-draw-long-lines-article-1.1298983 (accessed 30 November 2016).

45   See, e.g., "Canada's Top 15 Most Profitable Companies," *Canadian Business*, 22 June 2016 https://www.canadianbusiness.com/lists-and-rankings/best-stocks/2016-most-profitable-companies/ (accessed 25 October 2018).

towns and big cities, central to local commerce. The job of a bank
branch manager still carries status, prestige, and power, particularly in
a small town. Banks sponsor a huge variety of community events across
the country, from sporting competitions to cultural happenings like the
Giller Prize. Stadiums and concert halls bear their names.

In many countries, democratic and non-democratic alike, from the
United States to Iceland, but not in Canada, the people are skeptical and
suspicious of their financial institutions, generally with good reason. Part
of it is a natural and appropriate wariness of great financial and political
power. Part of it is the poor record of the banking sector—the collapse
of Lehman Brothers in 2008, for example—or the collapse of the entire
Icelandic banking system, also in 2008, or the Wells Fargo 2016 "phony
accounts" scandal. Canada has been spared these banking catastrophes.
In a well-known 2013 segment on The Comedy Channel's *Daily Show*,
Jason Jones asked people on the streets of Toronto and New York
what they thought of bankers. Here is a summary of what they said:
"**Canadians:** trustworthy, considerate, extension of my family, reliable,
transparent, I love Canadian banks. **Americans:** cockroaches, pricks,
sleazy, disrespectful, backstabbing, money-grabbing, pieces of shit."[46]

The Canadian Banking Association periodically conducts a poll
entitled "What Canadians Think About Their Banks." In 2016 the CBA
poll reported that eighty-four percent of Canadians had a favourable
impression of banks in Canada: "Among the companies that consumers
have relationships with, few are more personal and sensitive than the
relationship with their bank. As Canadians have witnessed challenges
in banking in other parts of the world, they appreciate the reliability,
prudence and stability of Canada's banks all the more."[47]

Even the Canadian tax system loves and respects the banks. The
tax rules, and particularly those that allow the establishment of bank
subsidiaries in tax havens that pay tax-free dividends to their parent
companies, have allowed Canadian banks to pay significantly less taxes

46   See "Canada's stable banking regulations fodder for Daily Show," *Canadian Crossing*, 25
     June 2013 http://balanceoffood.typepad.com/canadian_crossing/2013/06/canadas-
     stable-banking-regulations-fodder-for-daily-show.html (accessed 13 December 2016).
47   http://www.cba.ca/Assets/CBA/Files/Article%20Category/PDF/bkg_annualpoll_
     en.pdf (accessed 12 December 2016)

than other types of Canadian corporations, and less taxes than banks in other countries.[48]

ARE WE ADMIRABLE?

Canadians are deferential, polite, unskeptical, and pay largely unquestioning allegiance to their institutions and leaders. Does this make us more free, or safer, or nicer, than those engaged in a vigorous and loud repudiation of experts and traditional authority figures? Are we admirable? Or would we be better off being less deferential, cutting back on allegiance, being tougher, skeptical, more questioning?

Few Canadians would want to abandon kindness and civility—even a little deference—in our affairs. Those things are part of our nature. They promote a gentle life. But a good measure of robust skepticism is required to fully preserve freedom. There is a better balance to be achieved.

---

48   See Marco Chown Oved, Toby A.A. Heaps, Michael Yow, "The High Cost of Low Corporate Taxes," *Toronto Star*, 14 December 2017 http://projects.thestar.com/canadas-corporations-pay-less-tax-than-you-think/ (accessed 21 December 2017).

PART TWO

THE DECLINE OF INSTITUTIONS

Canadian government is failing us. The executive branch rides rough-shod over the legislature. The election system is flawed. Politicians break promises. Anonymous bureaucrats tell us what to do.

The justice system fails us. It puts extraordinary public policy power in the hands of unelected officials. It denies access to justice for most Canadians, saving the justice system for the rich and powerful.

The traditional media, once the dispassionate arbiter of society and government, is almost extinct, replaced by a social media rabble.

The universities have forsaken their traditional and vital role in favour of crass vocationalism larded with political correctness.

CHAPTER THREE

GOVERNMENT

NOBODIES

In 1979 Prime Minister Pierre Trudeau said of members of parliament, "When they are fifty yards from Parliament Hill, they are no longer honourable members, they are just nobodies." You could as easily say that a member of parliament is a nobody even when he is on Parliament Hill, sitting at his seat in the House of Commons—unless, of course, he happens to be something more than just a member of parliament, say, a member of cabinet, and even then it would be easy to exaggerate his importance.

What could be worse than being a backbench MP? In June 2018 the *Globe and Mail* reported on a Samara Centre for Democracy exit poll of fifty-four retired MPs who sat during the Forty-First Parliament that ran from 2011 to 2015.[49] Samara "found many of them questioning the very purpose of being an MP in an era when political power is concentrated in the hands of party leaders."[50]

---

49 Bill Curry, "Party control on Parliament Hill is getting tighter, former MPs warn," 12 June 2018 http://globe2go.newspaperdirect.com/epaper/viewer.aspx?noredirect=true (accessed 19 June 2018).

50 The Samara Centre for Democracy, *Flip the Script: Reclaiming the legislature to reinvigorate democracy*, https://www.samaracanada.com/docs/default-source/reports/

In a parliamentary democracy, the legislative branch is subservient to the executive branch, and the executive branch is run by the prime minister as he or she sees fit. (Things are a little more complicated in the case of a minority government, or if constitutional chaos prevails, as it did during the United Kingdom's endless Brexit debate, and we must remember the enhanced role of the judiciary in Canada since the 1982 Charter of Rights and Freedoms.) In a parliamentary democracy, a member of cabinet serves at the prime minister's pleasure and must do what the prime minister says. The supreme power of the Canadian prime minister is widely recognized. Ralph Heintzman, a long-time Ottawa senior public servant, has written, "The Canadian prime minister is probably the most powerful political executive in the world because there is nothing, once he has a majority in Parliament, to restrain him or her."[51] The political journalist Doug Saunders has said, "The Prime Minister and his staff are not just an important part of the government; for all intents and purposes, they are the government."[52] Saunders, writing during the SNC-Lavalin crisis of early 2019, thinks that it should be easier for MPs to vote out the prime minister. "Our governments would work far better if, as in other parliamentary democracies, the Prime Minister's staff lived in constant fear of censure by MPs–the opposite of the current situation."

There is one moment when a Canadian MP is enormously important to the leader of his party, and that is election day. The leader desperately wants each of his party's candidates to win. He needs at least one hundred and seventy constituency victories, a majority of the three hundred and thirty-eight seats in Parliament, to reach the pinnacle of power. He becomes a somebody on the backs of one hundred and seventy nobodies. How the election system works, how MPs get elected is, then, the most important thing about MPs and the legislative branch.

flip-the-script---by-the-samara-centre-for-democracy.pdf?sfvrsn=2d09002f_2 (accessed 19 June 2018).

51   See Frances Russell, "Senate 'reform' dangerous," *Winnipeg Free Press*, 1 June 2011 https://www.winnipegfreepress.com/opinion/columnists/senate-reform-dangerous-122926813.html (accessed 3 January 2018).

52   "The overpowering PM: It's time to give authority back to Canadian MPs," *Globe and Mail*, 9 March 2019, P.O11.

A BROKEN PROMISE

Canada has a first-past-the-post (FPTP) federal voting system. This simple system, used by many countries, invites a voter to pick a candidate, and whichever candidate gets the most votes—not necessarily a majority—wins the election. The first-past-the post system typically produces majority governments elected by less than fifty percent of those voting, and gives short shrift to small parties. The alternative system is, broadly speaking, proportional representation, in which parties gain seats according to the number of votes cast for them; many countries employ this system (e.g., Belgium, Denmark, Finland, Norway, and Sweden). There are many varieties of proportional representation, and the details can be complex. Proportional representation tends to favour smaller parties, and makes it difficult to achieve majority governments, often leading to coalitions of several parties.

In the 2015 federal election campaign, Justin Trudeau criticized FPTP and promised electoral reform. He appeared to prefer a ranked ballot to simple proportional representation.[53] The Liberal Party campaign platform stated, "We will make every vote count. We are committed to ensuring that 2015 will be the last federal election conducted under the first-past-the-post voting system. We will convene an all-party Parliamentary committee to review a wide variety of reforms, such as ranked ballots, proportional representation, mandatory voting, and online voting. This committee will deliver its recommendations to Parliament. Within 18 months of forming government, we will introduce legislation to enact electoral reform."[54] What could be clearer than that?

For fifteen months following the 2015 election, the Trudeau government repeated this promise. An all-party Commons committee, the

53 "Under a ranked ballot, voters mark their first, second and subsequent choices. If no candidate wins more than 50 per cent of the vote, the contender with the fewest votes is dropped from the ballot and his or her supporters' second choices are counted. That continues until one candidate emerges with a majority." See "The pros and cons of ranked ballots," *Maclean's*, 15 August 2016 http://www.macleans.ca/politics/the-pros-and-cons-of-ranked-ballots/ (accessed 3 January 2018).
54 https://www.liberal.ca/realchange/electoral-reform/ (accessed 3 January 2018).

Special Committee on Electoral Reform, was convened in the spring of 2016, and reported in December. It proposed a proportional system of representation and recommended a national referendum on the question. But at the beginning of 2017, Trudeau announced he was abandoning the idea. He said it might lead to "an augmentation of extremist voices in the House." He suggested it could lead to the rise of small, regional parties that might end up holding the balance of power in Parliament. He argued it might stimulate excessive partisanship. Nor, according to him, did electoral reform have broad support from the Canadian people. Most Canadians were not interested in the issue. As for a referendum, Trudeau, perhaps remembering the Quebec referendums on independence, was wary of such a thing. National unity, said Trudeau, was more important than electoral reform. All these insights apparently came to Trudeau after 2015. And that was that. Cynics, and members of the National Democratic Party and the Green Party, said it was simple: the Liberals just wanted to give themselves the best chance of retaining a House of Commons majority and staying in power.[55]

REFERENDUMS

Justin Trudeau was right not to want a referendum on Canada's voting system (this does not excuse his promise-breaking on FPTP). Referendums are not the road to freedom and democracy—quite the opposite. They lead to chaotic populism. They are "messy and dangerous."[56] When I took an introductory political science class at the University of Manitoba in 1962, Professor Bill Hull taught us that

---

55   Some analysts have concluded that a ranked ballot, apparently favoured by Trudeau, would have ensured a Liberal government forever. Note that there has been some movement by municipalities and provinces towards electoral methods other than first past the post. In October 2018, London, Ontario used a ranked ballot in its municipal elections. British Columbia held a mail referendum in November 2018 on whether to accept some form of proportional representation. 61.3% of ballots were cast in favour of FPTP.

56   Amanda Taub and Max Fisher, "Why Referendums Aren't as Democratic as They Seem," *The New York Times*, 4 October 2016 https://www.nytimes.com/2016/10/05/world/americas/colombia-brexit-referendum-farc-cameron-santos.html?module=inline (accessed 3 March 2019).

there was no place for referendums in a parliamentary system of government. We studied Edmund Burke's 1774 *Speech to the Electors of Bristol*. (Burke was a British member of parliament.) In his famous oration, he said in part:

> Your representative owes you, not his industry only, but his judgment; and he betrays, instead of serving you, if he sacrifices it to your opinion. . . . If government were a matter of will upon any side, yours, without question, ought to be superior. But government and legislation are matters of reason and judgment, and not of inclination. . . To deliver an opinion, is the right of all men; that of constituents is a weighty and respectable opinion, which a representative ought always to rejoice to hear; and which he ought always most seriously to consider. But *authoritative* instructions; *mandates* issued, which the member is bound blindly and implicitly to obey, to vote, and to argue for, though contrary to the clearest conviction of his judgment and conscience; these are things utterly unknown to the laws of this land, and which arise from a fundamental mistake of the whole order and tenor of our constitution.[57]

In a proper representative democracy, electors choose the best people to govern them, and those chosen then decide what to do. The people trust their elected representatives. The system depends on it. Going directly to the people for a vote proclaimed or believed to be binding on government is a very bad idea. Referenda undermine a central precept of democracy, the one expressed by Edmund Burke. In a parliamentary system, they can easily create a direct, unresolvable and untenable conflict between the alleged "will of the people" and parliament itself. There is no better example of this than the disastrous United Kingdom Brexit constitutional crisis.

Referendums sow instability. Decisions on complicated issues can be based on little understanding and less knowledge. They are used by political leaders who lack convictions and courage and are eager to move

---

57   Philip P. Kurland and Ralph Lerner (eds.), *The Founders' Constitution* (web edition) http://press-pubs.uchicago.edu/founders/documents/v1ch13s7.html (accessed 23 October 2016).

the most difficult and controversial decisions away from themselves and to "the people." It is widely believed that British voters in the 2016 Brexit referendum had little or no understanding of the issues and facts underlying the question they were asked. An Ipsos poll shortly before the referendum demonstrated that the public had huge misperceptions about the EU and how it affected life in the UK, particularly when it came to immigration and Britain's contribution to the EU budget (two key issues). So, for example, voters "massively overestimate how many EU-born people now live in the UK. On average we think EU citizens make up 15% of the total UK population (which would be around 10.5m people), when in reality it's 5% (around 3.5m people)."[58]

Traditional referendums may now be discredited, to some extent. That is part of the bitter Brexit harvest. But traditional referendums have been replaced by a new and worse form of popular vote, the unfettered and influential expression of uninformed opinion on social media by a self-selecting electorate. There are no constraints, no discipline, and no order, in these new social media referendums. Crowd protest is a first cousin of social media agitation. Politics moves out of government institutions and onto the street. Marching, shouting and shoving take the place of measured debate and deliberation. Crowds replace the professional political class. Formal and careful participation in the political process becomes less important. The will of the people must be expressed directly and loudly. The mob shall rule.

MAKING LIFE EASIER

Once a government is elected and a prime minister assumes power, the legislative branch is of little interest (assuming there is a majority government). Much of what government wants to do does not even require legislation; it can be accomplished by orders-in-council made under previous statutory authority, approved by cabinet on the direction of the prime minister. If legislative action is necessary, then the legislature's

---

58   Ipsos MORI, *The Perils of Perception and the EU*, 8 June 2016 https://www.ipsos.com/ipsos-mori/en-uk/perils-perception-and-eu (accessed 3 November 2018).

job is to do what it is told. But lack of interest in the legislature does not mean lack of tinkering by the executive with the way the legislature functions, generally with a view to further enhancing the power of the executive branch which is never great enough for those who have it. As the *Toronto Star* put it, "For those in power trying to push through an agenda, robust democratic institutions—a working Parliament, for instance, or watchdogs with teeth—are too often seen as a nuisance."[59] This has been as true of Justin Trudeau as it was of his predecessor, Stephen Harper, notwithstanding Trudeau's 2015 election promises of a post-Harper post-partisan open government and his specific rejection of the use of omnibus legislation.

In the spring of 2017, in accordance with its 2015 promises, the Liberal government proposed "parliamentary reform" in the interests of "efficiency," such reform to be accomplished by amending the Standing Orders of the House of Commons, the written rules under which the Commons regulates its proceedings. So, for example, under the efficiency proposals it would be more difficult for the opposition to delay legislation using procedural tactics, and debate on a bill would be limited to a fixed number of days and in other ways including by limiting filibustering. Some of the proposed rules, said the *Globe and Mail* in a powerful editorial, were "clearly designed to make life easier for a majority government. And that is unacceptable."[60]

The proposed changes to the Standing Orders met with almost universal criticism and the opposition parties threatened to use all possible means to thwart them. This led the government to scale back its changes dramatically. But despite this retreat and the negative emotions evoked by the proposed reforms, the Liberal government retained a cynical liking for omnibus bills that stuff a wide variety of measures into one huge piece of legislation, often with a controversial measure deeply buried inside. (Stephen Harper was very fond of this technique,

59 "A blow to democracy," 29 March 2017 https://www.thestar.com/opinion/editorials/ 2017/03/28/potential-parliamentary-reforms-would-strike-a-blow-to-democracy- editorial.html (accessed 5 January 2018).

60 "A Liberal fixing of the rules," 1 April 2017 https://www.theglobeandmail.com/opinion/ editorials/globe-editorial-the-dangers-in-a-liberal-plan-to-fix-parliament/article 34527814/ (accessed 5 January 2018).

despite having attacked it eloquently in 1994 when he was a Reform member of parliament). An example is Bill C-74, introduced in the House of Commons in March 2018. This was part one of a "routine" budget implementation bill, over five hundred pages long that had hidden within it, among other things, controversial new carbon-pricing legislation and an amendment to the Criminal Code providing for deferred prosecution agreements in lieu of criminal prosecution, an amendment that proved highly controversial in the 2019 SNC-Lavalin scandal. The Finance Minister, Bill Morneau, claimed Bill C-74 was not really an omnibus bill. The *Toronto Star* commented, "whether or not the bill is truly an omnibus, it seems clearly to violate the spirit of the Liberals' campaign promise not to table bills that 'prevent Parliament from properly reviewing and debating' their proposals."[61]

Another 2018 example was Bill C-75, the so-called justice reform legislation introduced in April 2018 by then Justice Minister Jodi Wilson-Raybould. It was described in a *Globe and Mail* editorial as "a crazy quilt of proposals, with a range of motivations and without a common theme or goal."[62] In October 2018, the government buried the controversial Pay Equity Act inside part two of the budget implementation bill, this part being eight hundred and fifty-four pages long, virtually guaranteeing that the Pay Equity Act would not receive careful consideration by parliament or committee.

THE MAN IN SHORT PANTS

There is a giant flaw in Canada's constitution, largely hidden and unaccountably ignored, a flaw that hobbles most voters on issues that they

---

61   "Trudeau government continues cycle of criticism with overlong budget bills," 4 April 2018 https://www.thestar.com/opinion/editorials/2018/04/03/trudeau-government-continues-cycle-of-cynicism-with-overlong-budget-bills.html (accessed 4 April 2018). The *Globe and Mail* was similarly critical: Campbell Clark, "The same-old, same-old way of pushing bills through Parliament," 6 April 2018 https://www.theglobeandmail.com/opinion/article-liberals-are-using-the-same-old-same-old-way-of-pushing-bills-through/ (accessed 6 April 2018).

62   "There's no justice in an omnibus bill," 7 April 2018 https://www.theglobeandmail.com/opinion/editorials/article-globe-editorial-ottawas-omnibus-justice-bill-needs-to-be-broken-up/ (accessed 7 April 2018).

care about a lot. More than eighty percent of Canada's population lives in urban areas and depends on municipal governments for essential daily services, such as education, police protection, and public transportation. But cities have no place in our national Constitution. They are entirely creatures of their provinces. They are in thrall to their provincial governments. They depend for their powers on provincial legislation, which can be changed, or not, at the whim of the provincial government. They do not have the political powers and fiscal tools they desperately need. As the parliament of Canada is to the prime minister, so city government is to the premier of the province. As a result, Canada's cities are in a state of precipitous decline, in stark contrast to many cities elsewhere, particularly those of Western Europe.[63]

There is only one mention of municipalities in Canada's Constitution Act 1867. Section 92(8) says, "In each Province the Legislature may exclusively make Laws in relation to . . . Municipal Institutions in the Province." Using this empowerment, every province and territory has a general municipal act that grants enumerated powers to its cities. Some major cities, so-called "charter cities," do not rely on the province's general municipal act but have their own individual legislation, their "charter," supposedly tailor made. A charter, of course, is nothing more than another provincial statute, which can be amended by the legislature at any time without consulting the city in question.

Cities need powerful and independent revenue streams, completely within their control, to fund the projects they should undertake and the services they should provide. Inevitably, this means a city income tax, or a city sales tax, or both, however unpopular such taxes may be. As it is now, cities rely on property and development taxes, user and license fees, and transfers and grants from the provincial and federal governments, all inadequate and uncertain. Property taxes are the biggest source of revenue, generally accounting for about half of a Canadian city's budget (the percentage is far lower in most other countries). Reliance on property and development taxes turns cities into reckless promoters of real estate development, sacrificing sound growth for tax revenue. And,

---

63   For a full analysis of this issue, and a proposed solution, see Philip Slayton, "Devo-Max for the Cities of Canada," *Public Sector Digest*, Winter 2015, p. 68, and also Slayton, *Mayors Gone Bad*, (Toronto: Viking 2015).

as almost everyone agrees, property taxation is a highly undesirable tax—inelastic, regressive, and inequitable.

Not surprisingly, provincial governments turn a deaf ear when asked by city leaders for financial help. Premiers enjoy the frequent visits by servile mayors who go on bended knee begging for money. They respond grudgingly and modestly, if at all. An excellent example was Toronto mayor John Tory's 2017 plan to toll two major Toronto roads, both used by daily commuters into Toronto, and use the revenue for road upkeep and public transportation. A great idea. But the City of Toronto Act requires provincial approval of city road tolling. When Mayor Tory asked for such approval, expecting it to be routine, it was denied. Speculation had it that Premier Wynne, with the 2018 provincial election in mind, did not want to upset voters in suburbs outside Toronto who commuted into the city by imposing new costs on them. The Mayor of Toronto was not amused. "It is time that we stop being treated, and I stop being treated, as a little boy going up to Queen's Park in short pants to say, 'Please, could you help me out with something that I thought was in the City of Toronto Act that I could do,' and to be told, 'No, I'm terribly sorry, go away and come back some other day.'"[64]

The short pants problem must be fixed in the interests of freedom and democracy. What is needed, ideally, is an amendment to the constitution recognizing the practical pre-eminence of cities as a unit of government and giving them corresponding constitutional status and the ability to run and finance their affairs without interference and control. This will properly enfranchise those who vote in city elections.

Many careful thinkers about municipal affairs have raised the idea of major cities becoming "city-provinces." But this kind of constitutional change is not going to happen. The political forces and technical difficulties arrayed against it are too great. Amending Canada's constitution requires the approval of the Senate and the House of Commons, and of the legislative assemblies of at least two-thirds of the provinces

64   Quoted by David Rider and Jennifer Pagliaro, "Tory challenges Wynne's leadership after she rejects road tolls, but 905 leaders celebrate," *Toronto Star*, 27 January 2017 https://www.thestar.com/news/city_hall/2017/01/27/councillors-blast-short-sighted-decision-to-block-tolls-on-gardiner-dvp.html (accessed 5 January 2018).

with at least fifty percent of the population of all provinces. It is easy
for a few provinces to block constitutional changes giving cities more
independence and power. And they would. The battle will have to
be purely political. The mayors of Canada's great cities must make
clear to their provincial premiers that the price of provincial political
pre-eminence is to grant the cities more and greater powers.

GOVERNMENT MEN IN SUITS

I wrote in Chapter One that serious threats to freedom may sometimes
seem small. Let me give you a detailed example. In recent times, free
speech was threatened by government tax policy towards some registered charities. The issue and what happened may, at first glance, seem
dull, perhaps inconsequential, the outcome anticlimactic, the threat to
freedom minor, but events as they unfolded offered an archetype of
insidious institutional threats to freedom. Things worked out in the
end, but it was a close-run thing, and the costs of battle were high.

From 2013 to 2015, I was president of PEN Canada, the Canadian
branch of an international organization devoted to protecting and promoting freedom of expression. PEN is one of about eighty-five thousand
registered charities in Canada. Individual contributions to a registered
charity reduce personal income tax and have other tax advantages: as
a result, for most charities, registration is essential to their continued
existence. While I was president of PEN Canada, a dispute with the
Canada Revenue Agency showed how freedom of expression can be sur-
reptitiously attacked by politicians and their public service foot soldiers
if they don't like what you say and write.

On July 23, 2012 Dick Benner, editor and publisher of *Canadian
Mennonite* magazine, received a letter from Canada Revenue Agency
saying that the magazine's publisher, Canadian Mennonite Publishing
Service, was in danger of having its charitable status revoked because six
articles it had published were considered by the CRA to be "partisan."[65]

---

65   Part of this account of PEN Canada's involvement with the Canadian Revenue agency
     relies on a timeline constructed by PEN Canada. See "How hard is it to get information
     on political activity from the CRA?" http://pencanada.ca/political-activity-atip-request/

(A registered charity is forbidden to engage in any partisan activity, and at the time was strictly limited when it came to "political" activity.) The six articles dealt with the importance of international peacemaking by Canada; alleged overspending on military hardware, particularly aircraft; the need for young people to vote in elections; and the importance of rehabilitating criminal offenders. PEN Canada got interested in this story for freedom of expression reasons and in November 2012 published a blog that said, in part, "In effect, CRA prohibits charitable organizations from discussing any politics whatsoever. This definition is entirely too broad, and stifles any political dissent, which is a necessary condition for the existence of a healthy democracy."

Curious about why CRA sent the Brenner letter, and about who else might have received such a letter, PEN filed several Freedom of Information requests with the federal government beginning in January 2013. A bureaucratic ballet began. In May, the government sent PEN some redacted documents of limited significance but, in general, we were ignored. In July 2013, we submitted a complaint to the Information Commissioner of Canada, followed by further complaints to the same office later in the year. In response to PEN's first complaint, the Information Commissioner found that when the CRA did not respond by the deadline its officials were "in a state of deemed refusal and failed in their duty to assist."

The other shoe dropped on April 9, 2014. The CRA called PEN Canada to tell us we ourselves were going to be audited, and the audit would include a review of our own "political activity." The audit proceeded through the summer. Our small staff responded to detailed questions from the two CRA staff assigned to our case, putting their normal freedom-of-speech work aside. As PEN Canada president, I spoke and wrote at every opportunity about what I saw as a government

(accessed 14 June 2016). Here is a sample paragraph from one of the six articles in *Canadian Mennonite*: "Unfortunately, the political voices with a background in our core beliefs—such as Vic Toews, Canada's Public Security Minister who was born in Paraguay to a Mennonite refugee family—have succumbed to the fear-mongering of the present government by postponing Bill C-49, which would provide a safe haven for refugees and not return them to their country of origin. Instead, Toews has called the Tamils who came to our shores last year, 'terrorists.'" Dick Benner, "Vote Your Core Beliefs," *Canadian Mennonite*, 18 April 2011, p. 2.

attempt to intimidate freedom-of-expression organizations critical of some government policies and practices by characterizing that criticism as political activity. My central argument was that freedom of expression was a fundamental freedom constitutionally guaranteed by the Charter of Rights and Freedoms and that any advocacy in favour of such a fundamental freedom was above politics.

The CRA's audit findings were laid out in a letter to PEN in January 2015. A so-called "compliance agreement" was signed by PEN in May of that year. As part of the process, PEN signalled that in its view upholding human rights was not political activity. The CRA responded that actively communicating to the public that the law, policies or decisions of the government should be changed or defeated was political rather than charitable activity. We agreed (for the time being) to disagree. It was a stalemate.

PEN Canada's travails were only part of a gathering storm threatening free speech by Canadian charities. In March 2015, the Environmental Law Centre (ELC) of the University of Victoria published a detailed study of the tax treatment of environmental law groups.[66] The ELC study began:

> At the same time as the Federal Government slashed its overall 2012 budget, it set aside a special allocation of $13.4 million dollars to audit "political activities" of Canada's charitable groups. Since then, the Canada Revenue Agency (CRA) has undertaken audits of more than 52 charities for the purpose of investigating whether these organizations have exceeded their allowable limits of political activities. CRA has audited groups such as Amnesty International Canada, Pen Canada, and the Canadian Centre on Policy Alternatives – as well as seven of Canada's most prominent environmental charities, including the David Suzuki Foundation, Tides Canada, West Coast Environmental Law, the Pembina Foundation, Environmental Defence, Equiterre and the Ecology Action Centre. Since several of these organizations had previously criticized government policies,

---

66 *Tax Audits of Environmental Groups: The Pressing Need for Law Reform,* http://www. elc.uvic.ca/wordpress/wp-content/uploads/2015/03/Tax-Audits-of-Environmental-Groups_2015Mar25.pdf (accessed 23 September 2016).

many observers accused government of using audits to intimidate
and silence opposing political views.

. . .

Even if the audits do not lead to de-registration of charitable
groups, the auditing process by itself has had a profound effect across
all Canadian charities. Although most groups audited so far have been
found without fault, an audit is an intimidating, time-consuming, costly
and resource-intensive process that all want to avoid. Responding to
an audit uses up scarce resources and diverts the charity from doing
its regular charitable work, sometimes for several years.

Or, as the *Toronto Star* put it in a November 2017 editorial:

> Back in 2012 the Conservatives sicced the Canada Revenue Agency on
> at least 60 organizations, ranging from the David Suzuki Foundation
> to Environment Defence to PEN Canada. By an astounding coinci-
> dence, the vast majority of the targeted groups spent time advocating
> for positions that the government of the day found antithetical – on
> the environment, social justice, human rights and more. It was, to
> be blunt, a thinly disguised attempt to limit public debate. The CRA
> launched audits of the charities, tying them up in red tape and putting
> a chill on their efforts to speak out on public issues.[67]

Did anything change when the Liberals were elected to office in the
autumn of 2015? Not to begin with; there was little interest in the issue.
Then a judge forced the Liberal government's hand.

In September 2016, the Minister of National Revenue, Diane
Lebouthillier, appointed the Consultation Panel on the Political
Activities of Charities. PEN Canada made written and oral representa-
tions to this panel. The panel reported at the end of March 2017,[68] and

---

67   "It's time to finish the job on charities," https://www.thestar.com/opinion/editorials/
      2017/11/17/ottawa-should-finish-the-job-on-advocacy-work-by-charities-editorial.
      html (accessed 14 December 2017).
68   Canada Revenue Agency, *Report of the Consultation Panel on the Political Activities
      of Charities*, March 31, 2017 http://www.cra-arc.gc.ca/chrts-gvng/chrts/cmmnctn/
      pltcl-ctvts/pnlrprt-eng.html (accessed 5 April 2017).

made several recommendations. It proposed that the government, (1) revise the CRA's administrative position and policy to enable charities to fully engage in public-policy dialogue and development; (2) amend the Income Tax Act by deleting any reference to non-partisan «political activities» to explicitly allow charities to fully engage, without limitation, in non-partisan public policy dialogue and development, provided that it is subordinate to and furthers their charitable purposes; and (3) modernize the legislative framework governing the charitable sector to ensure a focus on charitable purposes rather than activities, and adopt an inclusive list of acceptable charitable purposes to reflect current social and environmental issues and approaches.

The government suspended ongoing tax audits of charities for political activities while it considered the panel's recommendations. But by April 2018, more than a year after those recommendations had been made, nothing had been done. Dean Beeby of the CBC reported, following a meeting between fourteen environmental charities and Finance Minister Bill Morneau, "Some Canadian charities are feeling a new degree of chill, as a Liberal government election promise to ease restrictions on their political activities appears to be on ice more than two years later."[69]

But then, in the summer of 2018, a judicial bombshell burst. Canada Without Poverty, a small charity committed to public advocacy for policy and attitudinal change as its primary means of achieving an end to poverty, had launched a court challenge of the constitutionality of CRA's distinction between charitable and political activity. In January 2015, a CRA audit report concluded that virtually all of Canada Without Poverty's activities involved political engagement, namely communicating with the public to advocate policy changes. The charity argued that public advocacy for policy change was fundamental to its charitable purpose of poverty relief. In a judgment handed down in July 2018, Mr. Justice E.M. Morgan, of the Ontario Superior Court, agreed.[70]

---

69   "Charities 'worried' after meeting with Morneau on 'political activity' law," 19 April 2018 http://www.cbc.ca/news/politics/liberal-charity-income-tax-1.4624600 (accessed 20 April 2018).

70   *Canada Without Poverty v. AG Canada*, 2018 ONSC 4147 (CanLII), http://canlii. ca/t/ht153 (accessed 26 July 2018).

Justice Morgan's disposition of the case was sweeping: "The interpretation and enforcement by CRA of the 'substantially all' requirement in s. 149.1(6.2) of the *ITA* [the Income Tax Act] by limiting to 10% a charitable organization's use of its resources for political activities, as set out in the CRA Policy Statement, violates s.2 (b) of the Charter and is not saved by s.1. There shall be a Declaration to that effect and an Order that CRA cease interpreting and enforcing s. 149.1(6.2) in that way. There shall be a further Order that the phrase 'charitable activities' used in s. 149.1(6.2) be read to include political activities, without quantum limitation, in furtherance of the organization's charitable purposes."[71]

The government appealed this decision, but at the same time announced it would introduce legislation to change the Income Tax Act in exactly the way Justice Morgan wanted. (Apparently, the Ministers of Finance and National Revenue disagreed with the technical reasoning of Justice Morgan—hence the appeal.) In September 2018, the Finance Department released draft legislation and explanatory notes for discussion. Said the press release: "Under these draft legislative proposals, charities would still be required to be constituted and operated for exclusively charitable purposes, meaning they cannot have a political purpose, and restrictions against partisan political activities would remain."[72]

On December 13, 2018, Bill C-86, the second 2018 omnibus budget implementation act, received royal assent. It included new rules in the Income Tax Act to permit charities to carry on unlimited public policy dialogue and development activities (PPDDAs) in furtherance of a stated charitable purpose. PPDDAs generally involve seeking to

71 Section 149.1(6.2) of the Income Tax Act read: "For the purposes of the definition 'charitable organization' in subsection (1), where an organization devotes substantially all of its resources to charitable activities carried on by it and (a) it devotes part of its resources to political activities, (b) those political activities are ancillary and incidental to its charitable activities, and (c) those political activities do not include the direct or indirect support of, or opposition to, any political party or candidate for public office, the organization shall be considered to be devoting that part of its resources to charitable activities carried on by it."

72 Department of Finance, *Consulting Canadians on Draft Legislative Proposals Regarding Political Activities of Charities*, https://www.fin.gc.ca/n18/18-083-eng.asp (accessed 22 October 2018).

influence the law, policies or decisions of a government. In January 2019, the government dropped the appeal of Justice Morgan's decision. The dispute seemed over, for once and for all. There had been considerable government foot-dragging. The Liberal government had been obliged by a judge to do the right thing. The charities had got what they wanted. But not without a difficult and debilitating fight with an unsympathetic government.

THE WAR ON SCIENCE

Another example of oblique government-inspired bureaucratic interference with freedom is the widely documented silencing by the Stephen Harper government of publicly funded scientists who wished to report on scientific findings incompatible with that government's policies. This became known as the "War on Science."[73]

Starting in 2006, the Harper government required journalists who wanted to speak to a government scientist to first seek permission from a government communications officer. Permission was not always granted. Scientists had to get pre-approval from the relevant minister's office before speaking on their own initiative to members of media. Approval was not always forthcoming. A 2013 survey conducted on behalf of the Professional Institute of the Public Service of Canada found that hundreds of federal scientists "had been asked to exclude or alter technical information in government documents for non-scientific reasons, and thousands said they had been prevented from responding to the media or the public."[74]

In late 2015, newspapers reported that the newly-elected government of Justin Trudeau "had removed the muzzle" on government scientists, although many formal internal communications policies

---

73 The fullest account, although now somewhat outdated, is Chris Turner, *The War on Science: Muzzled Scientists and Wilful Blindness in Stephen Harper's Canada*, (Vancouver: Greystone Books, 2013).

74 See Emily Chung, "Muzzling of federal scientists widespread, survey suggests," CBC News, 21 October 2013 http://www.cbc.ca/news/technology/muzzling-of-federal-scientists-widespread-survey-suggests-1.2128859 (accessed 4 October 2016).

remained unchanged and it still remained unclear how free government scientists were to report their findings. In September 2017, the government of Canada appointed Mona Nemer as Chief Science Advisor, a position that had been eliminated by Stephen Harper in 2008. A press release commented, "She will . . . make recommendations to help ensure that government science is fully available and accessible to the public, and that federal scientists remain free to speak about their work."[75] The press release said nothing about how these recommendations, once made, would be treated.

The War on Science was not just a Canadian phenomenon. In January 2017, Canadian scientists offered support for their US counterparts, increasingly under siege from the Trump administration. *The Guardian* reported: "Recent days have seen the Trump administration reportedly considering scrubbing all mentions of climate change from the Environmental Protection Agency website, while the Associated Press reported that EPA scientists could be subject to a 'temporary hold, pending review by political appointees'."[76] In April 2017, a March for Science was held in Washington DC. Over a hundred thousand people attended, protesting that politicians were rejecting science-based policies. In September 2018, it was reported that the US Environmental Protection Agency was dissolving its Office of the Science Advisor, a senior post that was created to counsel the EPA administrator on the scientific research underpinning health and environmental regulations.[77] In October 2019, a non-partisan taskforce of former US government officials warned: "The treatment of science by the Trump administration has hit a 'crisis point' where research findings are manipulated for

75   "Prime Minister introduces Canada's new top scientist," 26 September 2017 https://pm.gc. ca/eng/news/2017/09/26/prime-minister-introduces-canadas-new-top-scientist (accessed 23 October 2018).

76   Ashifa Kassam, "Canadian scientists offer support to muzzled US counterparts," *The Guardian*, 27 January 2017 https://www.theguardian.com/science/2017/jan/27/ canadian-scientists-lend-support-to-muzzled-us-counterparts (accessed 27 February 2017).

77   See Coral Davenport, "E.P.A. to Eliminate Office That Advises Agency Chief on Science," *The New York Times*, 27 September 2018 https://www.nytimes.com/2018/09/27/ climate/epa-science-adviser.html?emc=edit_clim_20181003&nl=climate-fwd&nlid= 8765915820181003&te=1 (accessed 3 September 2018).

political gain, special interests are given improper influence and scientists are targeted for ideological reasons."[78]

Meanwhile, in February 2018, the Professional Institute of the Public Service of Canada released the surprising results of a June 2017 survey of federal scientists.[79] CBC News reported: "When asked if they agree with the statement 'I am allowed to speak freely and without constraints to the media about work I do at my Department/Agency,' 53 percent of 3,025 respondents answered 'No.'" The results of the survey were better than those of 2013, but were still of concern to many people. Mona Nemer commented, "After more than two years, the signal from political leadership that scientists are free to speak with journalists and the public about their work has yet to penetrate across government."[80]

On August 30, 2018, the federal government released a new "model policy" intended to apply to all federal researchers and scientists.[81] Among other things, it gives researchers and scientists the right, subject to certain limits, to speak freely about their research results. It seemed like a step in the right direction. Meanwhile, Premier Doug Ford of Ontario, in July 2018, shortly after taking office, fired the province's chief scientist, Molly Shoichet.

DEMOCRACY

Nobodies scurrying around Parliament Hill, taking their orders from the prime minister if they are members of the governing party, powerless and irrelevant if they are not. An electoral system that effectively

78   Oliver Milman, "Trump administration's war on science has hit 'crisis point', experts warn," *The Guardian*, 3 October 2019 https://www.theguardian.com/science/2019/oct/03/science-trump-administration-crisis-point-report?CMP=Share_iOSApp_Other (accessed 8 October 2019).

79   *Defrosting Public Science*, http://www.pipsc.ca/news-issues/scientific-integrity/defrosting-public-science (accessed 3 March 2018).

80   "Federal scientists feel they are still being muzzled, survey finds," *Globe and Mail*, 22 February 2018 https://www.theglobeandmail.com/news/national/survey-reveals-federal-departments-still-blocking-access-to-scientists/article38052629/ (accessed 3 March 2018).

81   "Model policy on scientific integrity," https://www.ic.gc.ca/eic/site/052.nsf/eng/00010.html (accessed 31 July 2018).

excludes a substantial number of voters and gives a lock on power to two dominant parties. Parliamentary procedures that emasculate parliamentary debate. A constitutional flaw that renders cities—the level of government that most citizens care about the most—impotent. Repressive behind-the-scenes work of anonymous government men. These are some important characteristics of Canadian governance. How free are we?

CHAPTER FOUR

JUSTICE

THE SYSTEM FAILS US

An independent and fair justice system, accessible to all, is an essential part of a free democracy. One job of the justice system is to protect citizens from government and each other. Protection from government, especially the defence of minority rights, is important in Canada, a country with few effective checks on the executive branch. Since the 1982 Charter of Rights and Freedoms, the courts have from time-to-time quite appropriately held government at bay. But on other occasions, using the Charter, they have inappropriately decided public policy matters that properly belong to elected politicians. Meanwhile, for economic reasons, few individual Canadians have access to the justice system and are therefore unable to assert or defend their rights against government or each other.

RISE OF THE JUDGES

In a true democracy, laws are made by a legislative branch composed of persons elected by the people in a fair process. There is an executive branch to administer and apply those laws in an organized and effective way. In a true democracy, the executive branch is drawn from members of the legislative branch and is answerable to it. Judges, in an ancillary role, interpret laws when necessary and ensure their impartial application, as well as resolve private disputes.

All of this seems elementary and self-evident, and yet it does not describe today's governance of Canada. We have already seen that Canada's first-past-the-post electoral system is considered unfair by many (including, at one time, Justin Trudeau). We know that the executive branch normally dominates and controls the legislative branch, rather than answering to it. Finally, particularly since passage in 1982 of the constitutionally entrenched Charter of Rights and Freedoms, unelected officials—judges—increasingly make laws, determine public policy, and control our destiny. Matters previously considered political issues, to be dealt with by application of generally-accepted public policy legislated into law, have been enthusiastically re-characterized as legal questions to be answered by judges, not least by gun-shy politicians trying to sidestep controversial debates.

In a 2007 New Zealand law review article, three legal scholars described Canada's judges as "by most accounts, the most judicially activist in the common law world—the most willing to second-guess the decisions of the elected legislatures."[82] The former chief justice of Canada, Beverley McLachlin has said, "If existing laws did not comply with the rights in the *Charter*, then those laws had to change. If government action did not comply with the *Charter*, then government had to change the way it acted."[83] I have written elsewhere, "Those who want to change the law move away from the political arena, where moral and social policy arguments can be considered head on, and where due weight can be given to public opinion. They go to court, and make complex and technical constitutional arguments that obscure the real issues. This shift is a basic change in Canada's constitutional arrangements."[84]

82   James Allan, Grant Huscroft, and Nessa Lynch, "The Citation of Overseas Authority in Rights Litigation in New Zealand: How Much Bark? How Much Bite?" *Otago Law Review*, Vol. 11, No. 3, 2007.

83   "Human Rights Protection in Canada," Fourth Annual Human Rights Lecture, Law Society of Ireland, Dublin, Ireland, 7 May 2008, p. 10 http://digitalcommons.osgoode.yorku.ca/cgi/viewcontent.cgi?article=1001&context=ohrlp (accessed 19 January 2018).

84   Philip Slayton, *Mighty Judgment: How the Supreme Court of Canada Runs Your Life* (Toronto: Allen Lane, 2011), p.12. Some of this chapter has been drawn from parts of *Mighty Judgment*.

Much has been written about this phenomenon by scholars, lawyers, and journalists. There is general recognition and acceptance of
the vast post-1982 power of the judiciary, although there is a difference of opinion about whether it is a good thing or a bad thing. Some
Canadians, particularly those on the political right, think the Supreme
Court has dramatically and dangerously usurped the power of other
branches of government. For example, in 2003, more than twenty years
after the Charter became part of the Constitution, a retired law professor, Robert Martin, wrote an incendiary book called *The Most Dangerous
Branch: How the Supreme Court of Canada Has Undermined Our Law
and Our Democracy*.[85] Martin argued that the Supreme Court, in hot
pursuit of a left-wing agenda, had derailed the legislative process in
an egregious way. Nigel Hannaford of the *Calgary Herald* referred
in 2009 to "the subtle replacement of the will of Parliament . . . by the
will of the Supreme Court of Canada."[86]

Others, mostly on the left, believe that the will of the majority can
easily become the tyranny of the majority, and that only the courts,
defining and enforcing minority rights, stand in the way of that tyranny.
These commentators insist that respect for minority rights is an essential
attribute of democracy, and if that requires a shift of power from the
legislative branch to the judiciary, then so be it. Professor Kent Roach,
of the University of Toronto, has advanced a cogent middle-of-the-
road view. In his 2001 book *The Supreme Court on Trial*, Roach writes,
"Canadians are losing sight of the genius of the *Charter*, which gives
both judges and legislatures robust roles in determining the way rights
are treated in our free and democratic society."[87]

Judicially decided changes have been paramount in the making of
recent Canadian public policy. Here are some examples (there are many

85 Robert Martin, *The Most Dangerous Branch: How the Supreme Court of Canada Has
    Undermined Our Law and Our Democracy* (Montreal: McGill-Queen's University Press,
    2003).
86 Nigel Hannaford, "Will the real radical please stand up?" *Calgary Herald,* 4 July 2009,
    www.calgaryherald.com/news/Will+real+radical+please+stand/1759640/story.html
    (accessed 5 July 2009).
87 Kent Roach, *The Supreme Court on Trial: Judicial Activism or Democratic Dialogue*
    (Toronto: Irwin Law, 2001), pp. 7–8.

more). In 1988, the *Morgentaler*[88] decision invalidated Canada's abortion laws. *Delgamuukw*,[89] in 1997, determined the extent of Aboriginal title. The 2004 *Amselem*[90] case decided that the state cannot regulate personal religious belief, however eccentric. The *Same-Sex Marriage Reference*,[91] also 2004, determined that the federal government could change the definition of marriage and give gays and lesbians the legal right to marry. *Chaoulli*,[92] in 2005, struck down a Quebec law banning private medical insurance. In 2005, *Labaye*[93] decided that group sex at a commercial club was not indecent. In 2013, *Bedford*[94] decided that provisions of the Criminal Code criminalizing various activities associated with prostitution were unconstitutional. In the 2015 *Carter* case,[95] the Supreme Court struck down provisions of the Criminal Code that prohibit the provision of assistance in dying in Canada.

An outside observer, someone who had not followed the recent evolution of Canadian law and governance, might look at a list of cases like this and be astonished at how so much policy-making power had been assumed by non-elected officials in an allegedly democratic country. I have written before, "In a democracy, we might expect such questions to be settled by political means, by elected representatives sitting in Parliament, and only after vigorous public debate. Yet in Canada they have often been answered by Supreme Court judges: nine men and women appointed by the prime minister who are little known to the average citizen, serve in the shadows for decades, and carefully guard their remoteness."

THE REAR-VIEW MIRROR

Queen Elizabeth II and Prime Minister Pierre Elliot Trudeau signed the Proclamation of the Constitution Act, which included the Charter of

---

88   *R. v. Morgentaler*, 1988 CanLII 90.
89   *Delgamuukw v. British Columbia*, 1997 CanLII 302.
90   *Syndicat Northcrest v. Amselem*, 2004 SCC 47 (CanLII).
91   *Reference re Same-Sex Marriage*, 2004 SCC 79 (CanLII).
92   *Chaoulli v. Quebec (Attorney General)*, 2005 SCC 35 (CanLII).
93   *R. v. Labaye*, 2005 SCC 80 (CanLII).
94   *Canada (Attorney General) v. Bedford*, 2013 SCC 72 (CanLII).
95   *Carter v. Canada (Attorney General)*, 2015 SCC 5 (CanLII).

Rights and Freedoms, on April 17, 1982 in the rain on Parliament Hill. At the time, I was dean of law at the University of Western Ontario (now rebranded as Western University). Generally (but not unanimously), legal academe welcomed the Charter. It was an interesting addition to constitutional law, and something new to teach. Many Canadian law professors had done graduate studies in the United States, typically a Masters of Law degree at a better American university, and were comfortable with and attracted to the idea of a constitutionally-embedded bill of rights. Practising lawyers, I think, were more skeptical. For the most part, they hadn't much of an idea what it was all about, and weren't minded to find out—it seemed irrelevant to who they were and what they did. The general public hardly noticed, although a Royal visit to Canada, with its pomp and ceremony, turned out the crowds.

As for myself, I was not a Charter fan in 1982, on the grounds that it derogated from parliamentary sovereignty, which then seemed to me to be all-important in a democratic country. I believed that our system of government required significant matters to be decided by elected representatives. That's the whole point, isn't it? People had died in wars to assert and protect that principle.

The Charter handed huge power to the judiciary. What were judges but unelected, well-fed, upper-middle-class bureaucrats, drawn from a narrow and elite sector of society, with similar backgrounds, education, and world view, safe in their jobs, immune from criticism? It was fine for them to resolve private disputes and to interpret and apply the law routinely. But it wasn't right that they decide important matters of policy and politics. It wasn't democratic. It impinged on freedom.

In 1983, I left the academic life to become a business lawyer on Bay Street. As I mentioned, practising lawyers of what was now my ilk were not interested in the Charter. Criminal defense lawyers and constitutional litigators got something out of it, but the rest of us couldn't have cared less as we set about the important work of making the rich a little richer.

I retired from the practice of law in 2000. Using my new leisure, I thought some more about the Charter. The cases decided since the Charter came into effect in 1982 demonstrated the great power that judges, and particularly the Supreme Court of Canada, had acquired. This was a source of concern. But what about the overweening power of the modern executive branch and the governance implications of that power? The executive branch was in your face, particularly in the years of the authoritarian and abrupt Stephen Harper administration (2006-2015). Who, if not a powerful judiciary, would guarantee the protection of minorities and prevent the abuse of executive power? And you had to be impressed by the honest and intelligent attempt of judges to understand and resolve complex issues. There's something to be said for a disciplined decision-making process, free from simplistic political rhetoric, which, following careful argument from opposing sides, delivers to the public a detailed written explanation of why a decision was made. Maybe Jean Chrétien, then minister of justice, was right in 1981 when he gave testimony to a parliamentary committee considering the Charter. Said Chrétien: "I think we are rendering a great service to Canadians by taking some of these problems away from the political debate and allowing the matter to be debated, argued, coolly before the courts."[96]

Is it possible to have the good without the bad? Can judges protect our rights, particularly if we belong to a minority, and stop abuse of executive power, without being serial policy makers who cannot be called to account? Can we rely on judicial restraint? It's a delicate balance, a fluid situation, and a continuing debate. There is no easy answer. Maybe Kent Roach was right when he wrote that the genius of the *Charter* is that it "gives *both* judges and legislatures robust roles in determining the way rights are treated in our free and democratic society."

THE MAN IN THE STREET

Just as the average person will never be a senior politician or an appeals court judge who has to decide great policy matters of the day, so they are unlikely to be a participant in Charter litigation that helps frame and decide those matters. This sort of litigation is mostly the province

96 See Philip Slayton, "Judicial activism protects us from the tyranny of the majority," *Globe and Mail*, 15 September 2018 https://www.theglobeandmail.com/opinion/article-judicial-activism-protects-us-from-the-tyranny-of-the-majority/?cmpid=rss

of human rights activists, criminal defence lawyers, and the occasional provocateur.

That does not mean that access to and participation in the legal system is not essential for protection of the average person's democratic rights. In particular, the ordinary citizen may desperately need the protection of the courts if they are the target of the awesome legal power and unmatched financial resources of the government, the monstrous adversary of everyone's nightmares. There are many non-criminal ways one can run afoul of the government—for example, by getting into a tax dispute with the Canada Revenue Agency, or by building a house that the municipality demands you tear down because of alleged infringement of city by-laws. If it's not the government that's after you, it could be a mighty corporation pursuing your pocketbook—a telecom inexplicably demanding thousands of dollars in cell phone roaming fees, for example, or a rich man alleging he was defamed in a column you wrote for the local newspaper and seeking punitive damages. The point is, to live in freedom and democracy means to live with and rely on laws, and that means to live with and rely on lawyers and courts.

But, in Canada, if you're an ordinary person, you cannot do it. The courts are closed to you. For all practical purposes, the ordinary Canadian is denied access to justice.[97] According to Statistics Canada, in 2015 the median after-tax income for Canadian families of two or more was $70,366. This is a median. There are a large number of Canadians who earn less. With this kind of income, you won't get legal aid (available only to those who are really poor, and of very limited scope anyway), and you will almost certainly be denied the *pro bono* legal services that a handful of socially concerned lawyers occasionally offer. If you need a lawyer, you'll have to dig into your own pocket.

In the cities, where most Canadians live, even a junior lawyer charges three hundred dollars or more for an hour's work (senior lawyers may charge more than a thousand dollars an hour). A relatively straightforward trial can easily cost a hundred thousand dollars or more in legal fees. Amounts like these are beyond almost everybody's ability to pay.

---

97 Some of this discussion draws from my book *How To Be Good: The Struggle Between Law and Ethics* (Toronto: Oblonsky Editions, 2017).

The result is that the legal profession has become the handmaiden of the powerful—government, corporations and wealthy individuals—who can afford to foot the bill. In a book published in 2007, I asked, "How much justice can the average Canadian afford?" I answered, "None. For financial reasons, he or she is denied use of the legal system and courts, key institutions of government and democracy. It is as if the right to vote in a general election were given only to those with an income above a certain level."[98] The situation has not changed since 2007.

The former chief justice of Canada, Beverley McLachlin, has frequently spoken about the problem of access to justice. David Johnston, the former governor general and a lawyer himself, gave a hard-hitting speech at the 2011 annual meeting of the Canadian Bar Association in Halifax. He said, "For many today, the law is not accessible, save for large corporations and desperate people at the low end of the income scale charged with serious criminal offences. We must engage our most innovative thinking to redefine professionalism and regain our focus on serving the public." But this has not happened. For some reason, the lack of access to justice, a profound problem of our democracy and for the freedom of citizens, has little or no political or social traction, despite the admonitions of chief justices and governors-general.

Do not look to lawyers to fix the acute and profound problem of access to justice. It is not in their culture, or interests, to do so. Sometimes the right things are said by leaders of the bar. Sometimes token *pro bono* initiatives of a sort are taken, particularly by the largest firms who can afford to do so. Sometimes the rules are fiddled with by governments or regulators in the name of access to justice, to make it easier, for example, to charge contingency fees, or proceed with a class-action lawsuit. It doesn't add up to much. We must look elsewhere for relief. Lawyers won't help.

98   Philip Slayton, *Lawyers Gone Bad: Money, Sex and Madness in Canada's Legal Profession* (Toronto: Viking Canada, 2007), p. 234.

TWO TASKS AHEAD

There are two great tasks ahead. Neither will be easy. First, the balance between democratically-elected government and appointed judiciary must be recalibrated. When judges decide great questions of social policy, citizens are deprived of their entitlement. We cannot rely on judicial restraint: sometimes restraint is there, sometimes it is not. But the recalibration must provide for the judicial protection of minority rights. Second, access to the justice system must be dramatically and immediately improved (there are ways of doing this). While the system remains the playground of the powerful—governments, corporations and a handful of wealthy people—the freedom that requires access to justice for everyone is in jeopardy.

CHAPTER FIVE

THE FOURTH ESTATE

DEATH OF THE NEWSPAPER

When I was a boy in the 1950s I delivered the *Winnipeg Tribune* in Winnipeg's south end every afternoon after school. In the 1950s, newspapers were a big deal: at the beginning of that decade, one hundred and two newspapers were sold for every hundred households.[99] I still remember the headline in the *Tribune's* April 1, 1958 edition announcing John Diefenbaker's stunning triumph in the federal election of the day before. That headline was not an April Fool's Day joke, although I expect many readers, for a moment or two, thought that it was. Diefenbaker won two hundred and eight of the two hundred and sixty-five seats in parliament. I read the story of his astonishing victory paragraph-by-paragraph as I tossed newspapers one-by-one onto the front porches of my customers.

I think the *Winnipeg Tribune* was a pretty good newspaper. In those days it competed heavily with the *Winnipeg Free Press*. The *Tribune* was conservative; the *Free Press*, liberal. The two of them fought a lively editorial fight to the benefit of everyone. The *Tribune* closed up shop in 1980. The *Free Press* still publishes, one of the very few independently-owned major Canadian newspapers. The *Free Press* newsroom

99   Public Policy Forum, *The Shattered Mirror: News, Democracy and Trust in the Digital Age* (2017), p. 15.

went from a hundred employees in the summer of 2010 to sixty-seven in July 2017.

Later, in the 1970s, when I lived in Montreal, I wrote the occasional op-ed piece for the *Montreal Star*. The *Star* was founded in 1869 and was once Canada's largest daily newspaper. For a long time it competed vigorously with the *Montreal Gazette*. Montreal's English community was well served by two good English-language newspapers that often took opposing views on the controversial issues of the day (there were lots of controversial issues). In 1979, the *Montreal Star* closed after an eight-month pressmen's strike. The *Gazette*, owned today by Postmedia, still publishes, but is a faint shadow of what it once was.

Postmedia owns major city newspapers across Canada, including the *National Post*, the *Ottawa Citizen*, the *Province* in Vancouver, the *Edmonton Journal*, and the *Calgary Herald*. Controlled by US hedge funds which hold massive amounts of secured Postmedia debt paying high interest rates, the company has been in slow-motion collapse for years. In May 2016, Paul Godfrey, then CEO of Postmedia Network (he resigned as CEO in January 2019 but remains as the company's executive chairman), told the House of Commons Standing Committee on Heritage, "The newspaper industry in Canada is in peril and urgently needs some form of government help."[100] In 2017, Postmedia had a plan to reduce its workforce by twenty percent on top of the three thousand jobs it had cut in the previous six years. In November 2017, Postmedia and Torstar Corporation swapped forty-one local and community papers, and then shut down most of them. In June 2018, Postmedia announced that it was closing newspapers in Ontario and Alberta and ending print production at three others and announced another round of layoffs and buyouts aimed at cutting staff by a further ten percent. In a note to employees, Postmedia said, "The traditional revenue balloon continues to deflate at a much faster rate than we can inflate the digital revenue balloon." In July 2018, Postmedia reported a $15.5-million net loss in its third quarter ended May 31. In another three months, the company reported declining revenues and a net loss

---

100 David Akin, "Postmedia CEO warns MPs newspaper industry 'ugly and getting uglier'," *Toronto Sun*, 12 May 2016 http://www.torontosun.com/2016/05/12/postmedia-ceo-warns-mps-newspaper-industry-ugly-and-getting-uglier (accessed 5 May 2017).

of $22.8 million in its fourth quarter. Losses lessened somewhat in 2019, mitigated by growth in digital revenue.

The story is the same across the country. In September 2016, John Honderich, the chairman of Torstar Corporation, publisher of the *Toronto Star*, told the Standing Committee on Heritage, "There is a crisis of declining good journalism across Canada."[101] He said that by the end of 2016 the Star's newsroom would have one hundred and seventy journalists, down from four hundred and seventy about ten years before. In 2018, Honderich was quoted as saying, "we're very, very close to the end."[102] In November of that year, Torstar announced that earnings for the third quarter of 2018 were $1.4 million, down $9.8 million from the third quarter of 2017.[103] The company later announced that, in the fourth quarter of 2018 it had lost $3.1 million, for a total loss in 2018 of $31.5 million.[104] Torstar went on to report that it had lost $17.4 million in its second quarter of 2019 and that revenue had dropped eleven percent from the same time last year.[105] And in the summer of 2018, Power Corp of Canada threw in the towel, handing ownership of Montreal's *La Presse*, an all-digital newspaper since 2017, to a "social utility trust," La Fiducie de soutien à La Presse, able to ask private citizens for donations and the Québec and federal governments for public aid. *La Presse* nevertheless cut thirty-seven jobs in November 2018.

101 Bruce Campion-Smith, "Canadian media 'crisis' puts democracy at risk, says Torstar chair John Honderich," *Toronto Star*, 29 September 2016 https://www.thestar.com/news/canada/2016/09/29/canadian-media-crisis-puts-democracy-at-risk-says-torstar-chair-john-honderich.html (accessed 4 March 2017).

102 Quoted by Brent Popplewell, "Inside the Toronto Star's Bold Plan to Save Itself," *The Walrus*, 10 May 2018 https://thewalrus.ca/inside-the-toronto-stars-bold-plan-to-save-itself/#.WzzjpOBxyFU.email (accessed 7 July 2017).

103 See David Olive, "Torstar sees digital transformation progress in third quarter," *Toronto Star*, 1 November 2018, p. B2.

104 See David Paddon, "Torstar reports fourth-quarter loss of $3.1 million," *Globe and Mail*, 28 February 2019 https://www.thestar.com/business/2019/02/27/media-company-torstar-reports-31-million-q4-loss-revenue-down-from-year-ago.html (accessed 28 February 2019).

105 See David Paddon, "Torstar reports loss as revenue falls and restructuring costs rise from last year," *Globe and Mail*, 31 July 2019 https://www.theglobeandmail.com/business/article-torstar-reports-loss-as-revenue-drops-and-restructuring-costs-rise/ (accessed 11 August 2019).

Other countries are no different. In Australia, in April 2017, Fairfax Media, publisher of the *Sydney Morning Herald*, announced the elimination of up to one hundred and twenty editorial positions and News Corporation sacked most of its Australian photographers and editorial production staff. In Australia, more than three thousand journalists lost their jobs between 2008 and 2013.[106] Germany's giant Axel Springer corporation has sold newspapers and magazines in recent years and made digital acquisitions to replace these assets. Jill Lepore reported in the *New Yorker*, "Between 1970 and 2016, the year the American Society of News Editors quit counting, five hundred or so dailies went out of business; the rest cut news coverage, or shrank the paper's size, or stopped producing a print edition, or did all of that, and it still wasn't enough."[107] Mark Thompson, former director general of the BBC and now president and CEO of The New York Times Company, has called traditional journalistic organizations "failing cultural institutions."[108]

The principal reasons for this dramatic world-wide decline are the replacement of immensely profitable newspaper classified advertisements by eBay, Kijiji, Craig's List, and the like, the replacement of expensive display advertisements by targeted feeds on Google, YouTube, and Facebook, and a substantial drop in paid subscriptions. There is no longer enough revenue to sustain a traditional newspaper. Other mass media, notably television, have experienced similar declines, particularly in local markets. The disappearance of the traditional Fourth Estate is inevitable and will happen soon.

The thing about newspapers in the good old days was that they were imbued with rigour and discipline. Senior editors assigned stories carefully. Facts were checked. Sources were verified. Opinions were considered and tempered if necessary. Grammar and spelling were scrutinized. There were standards. There was a hierarchy. If you were a

---

106 See Margaret Simons, "Journalism faces a crisis worldwide – we might be entering a new dark age," *The Guardian*, 15 April 2017 https://www.theguardian.com/media/2017/apr/15/journalism-faces-a-crisis-worldwide-we-might-be-entering-a-new-dark-age (accessed 5 May 2017).

107 "Hard News," 28 January 2019 https://www.newyorker.com/magazine/2019/01/28/does-journalism-have-a-future (accessed 1 March 2019).

108 *Enough Said: What's gone wrong with the language of politics?* (New York: St. Martin's Press, 2016), p. 287.

journalist, you had a boss. You had an editor. Someone was in charge. Someone could, and did, tell you, "It's not good enough. Fix it." The reader could rely on what he read.[109]

Now we live in cyberspace. Tom Friedman of *The New York Times* wrote, "we're all connected but no one's in charge."[110] The internet, says Friedman, is "an open sewer of untreated, unfiltered information." Information is fragmented, with each person relying on social media, Facebook and Twitter in particular, individually configured to conform with their preferences and prejudices, propped up by algorithms designed to give them what they want, to provide the untreated and unfiltered "news" and "information" that suits. There is no Norman DePoe or Walter Cronkite, beloved news anchors believed by everyone, offering the same news at the same time to everyone, to be discussed by everyone. There is no longer a common pool of information. We are "sucked into a maelstrom of pettiness, scandal and outrage."[111]

Some argue that social media-inspired "democratization of justice" has empowered the people. Now there is a way for anyone to express any idea and that idea might gain wide currency—go "viral" to use internet argot. Governments and entrenched ways of thinking can be seriously challenged using Twitter, Facebook, Instagram, WeChat and other platforms. Opposition groups can be created. Mass protests can be organized in an instant. The 2011 Arab Spring could not have happened without social media. The 2019 (and earlier) protests in Hong Kong relied on Facebook and Twitter. In Canada, might social media offer a way out of the excessive deference to authority that I have deplored, a path to a greater and more sophisticated form of freedom?

---

109 A friend who read this chapter in draft, and who had a long and distinguished career as a journalist, commented: "As one who toiled in those vineyards, I think you overestimate the rigour with which newspapers went about their work. [Some] editors were bigots and ignoramuses, and the standards were often not very high. An ideal, yes, but seldom lived up to. . ."

110 "Online and Scared," *The New York Times*, 11 January 2017 https://www.nytimes.com/2017/01/11/opinion/online-and-scared.html?_r=0 (accessed 5 March 2017).

111 "Do social media threaten democracy?" *The Economist*, 4 November 2017 https://www.economist.com/news/leaders/21730871-facebook-google-and-twitter-were-supposed-save-politics-good-information-drove-out (accessed 22 December 2017).

I don't think so. There is nothing in recent Canadian history to suggest this possibility. Chaos is not a viable alternative to deference.

The family no longer gathers together to watch the ten o'clock news on television. There is no longer the rustle of the broadsheet over morning coffee; it has been replaced by the glow of the iPad in the darkened night-time bedroom. Except, perhaps, at least a little bit, in Paris, where newspaper kiosks built one hundred and fifty years ago are still everywhere, and where the law requires them to carry *all* newspaper titles. "As a member of society, when you go to your local kiosk, you'll see all the headlines, whether they're from the left or right of political opinion – which is something we're desperately lacking on the internet. In other words, by law, a Parisian kiosk cannot make the decision to only sell radical news, clickbait and cat videos, for example."[112] But Paris newspaper kiosks are a strange anomaly: otherwise and elsewhere, McLuhan-like nihilism prevails. Marshall McLuhan wrote more than fifty years ago: "Once we have surrendered our senses and nervous systems to the private manipulation of those who would try to benefit by taking a lease on our eyes and ears and nerves, we don't really have any rights left."[113]

Once an energetic Fourth Estate was a stalwart protector of our freedoms. Thomas Carlyle wrote, "Burke said there were Three Estates in Parliament; but, in the Reporters' Gallery yonder, there sat a Fourth Estate more important far than they all." (The first Three Estates are monarch, lords and commoners.) Alan Rusbridger, former editor of *The Guardian* newspaper and now head of an Oxford college, wrote in 2011: "It's not the job of journalists to run things: they are literally without responsibility. They don't have to respond to a party whip, make the compromises necessary in politics or answer to shareholders. They are not bound by the confidentiality agreements that bind others. They are careless of causing inconvenience or embarrassment. They

---

112 Messynessy, "Why the Newspaper Kiosks in Paris are so important," 7 March 2017 https://www.messynessychic.com/2017/03/07/why-the-newspaper-kiosks-in-paris-are-so-important/ (accessed 8 March 2017).

113 Marshall McLuhan, *Understanding Media* (New York: New American Library,1964). See Nick Carr, "McLuhan would blow hot and cool about today's internet," *The Guardian*, 1 November 2007 https://www.theguardian.com/technology/2007/nov/01/comment. internet (accessed 10 April 2017).

don't have to win votes. They can write things – about the economy, say, or the environment – which may need saying but which are unsayable by politicians."[114] Everyone, from the Organization for Economic and Cultural Development, to the US Congress, to the UK House of Commons, agrees that a vigorous and free media is essential to democracy: you could fill a book with their platitudes on the subject.

Ironically, the role of the traditional press as protector of our freedoms was never more apparent, albeit for a brief time, than in the early post-truth, alternative facts, days of the Trump administration, when the media were correctly branded as the "opposition party" and obscenely (by President Trump) as "enemies of the people." (Interestingly, the same fraught phrase, "enemies of the people," was used by Britain's *Daily Mail* in 2016 to describe judges who had ruled that the assent of the British parliament was necessary to trigger the Brexit process.[115]) In those dark hours, some newspapers enjoyed a fleeting resurgence of interest and popularity. Circulation went up. The truth had to be told. Fact checkers had a new spring in their step. But all soon sank beneath the ineluctable weight of the internet and its economics.

The role of the traditional newspaper, and to a lesser extent that of radio and television, once was an essential pillar of our freedom and democracy. Now that role is played out. As social media supplants traditional journalism, freedom is increasingly in jeopardy. The Public Policy Forum, in *The Shattered Mirror*, its important and gloomy 2017 report studying Canadian mass media, commissioned by the Government of Canada and written by journalist Ed Greenspon, concluded, "The odd blend of content fragmentation, revenue consolidation and indifference to truth has overtaken simple concentration of ownership as the main

114 "The importance of a free press," 6 October 2011, https://www.theguardian.com/media/2011/oct/06/importance-free-press-alan-rusbridger (accessed 5 May 2017).

115 The then-editor of the *Daily Mail*, Paul Dacre, later claimed his decision to use that headline "helped push the issue of judicial involvement in politics on to the national agenda – and that his critics missed the fact that the headline was a reference to a play by the Norwegian playwright Henrik Ibsen." This has become known in some circles as "playing the Ibsen Card." See Jim Waterson, "Departing Daily Mail editor Paul Dacre lashes out for final time," *The Guardian*, 4 November 2018 https://www.theguardian.com/media/2018/nov/04/paul-dacre-ex-daily-mail-liberal-brexit-hating-media-speech?CMP=Share_iOSApp_Other (accessed 5 November 2018).

threat to holding public officials to account and reflecting Canadian society back to its citizens. The internet, whose fresh and diverse tributaries of information made it a historic force for openness, now has been polluted by the runoff of lies, hate and the manipulations of foreign powers. The 'truth neutrality' of the dominant digital platforms is incompatible with democracy."[116]

The Canadian government has been repeatedly and desperately asked to help and has been cautious and oblique in its response. In June 2017 the House of Commons Standing Committee on Canadian Heritage released a report that documented the dramatic decline of Canadian print journalism and broadcasting across the board and suggested ways Canadian journalism could be assisted.[117] It suggested a smorgasbord of tax measures, controls on media consolidation, and government financial support. None of these recommendations seemed to attract much interest or support from the Trudeau government. The idea of imposing a tax on the internet to support Canadian content was met with particular hostility. A letter responding to the report, signed by then-Canadian Heritage Minister Mélanie Joly, Innovation Minister Navdeep Bains, and Finance Minister Bill Morneau, either ignored or rejected the Standing Committee's various recommendations. But later there was something of a change of heart. In November 2018, as part of a Fall economic statement, the government proposed a $595 million five-year package to help the media sector, including a refundable tax credit to support "labour costs associated with producing original news content." Provision was also made for tax deduction for individual contributions to non-profit organizations such as La Fiducie de soutien à La Presse (now owner of *La Presse*). The overall package was to be developed and administered by an "independent panel" comprised mostly of journalists. Many welcomed this initiative, but some were skeptical. Was this an indirect way of the government exerting influence, if not control, over the media? Was the game worth the candle? Andrew Coyne wrote in the *National Post*, "The effect will be to inevitably and irrevocably

---

116 *The Shattered Mirror*, p.3.

117 "Disruption: Change and Churning in Canada's Media Landscape," https://www.our-commons.ca/DocumentViewer/en/42-1/CHPC/report-6 (accessed 24 December 2017).

politicize the press. . . . The money the government is giving us is not going to solve our problems. It is only going to ensure we put off confronting them. Before long we will be back for more—after the same mutual dance of veiled threat and implicit promise."[118] The government package was seen by some as inadequate and by others as a poisoned chalice. It was refined and largely implemented by the federal budget introduced in March 2019, with most of the money to be spent in the fiscal year beginning April 1, 2020.

Traditional newspapers have almost given up on reporting strict news. How can they compete with the internet and social media? By the time you read the "news" in the morning newspaper, it is stale. You know all about it already. So, newspapers have turned themselves into mini-magazines, full of a mish-mash of often second-rate opinion and features, frequently borrowed from each other, heavily reliant on ludicrously underpaid freelancers, no longer central to the world's affairs but operating on the periphery, despairingly trying and failing to keep up with their jazzy digital competition.

THE AGE OF ACCUSATION

Madelaine Drohan, Canadian correspondent for *The Economist*, argued in 2017 that, although traditional media firms are suffering in the digital age, it does not follow that the public is being harmed. "Is the public really not as informed as it was in the recent past?" she asks. "Or could people be getting information from sources other than journalists? The Internet has allowed governments, advocacy groups, businesses, universities and individuals to get their messages out without going through media outlets, which used to be the only game in town. Might they be helping to fill the gap?"[119] In the digital age, says Drohan, "any causal

---

118 "Liberals' $600 million aid package for news media will irrevocably politicize the press," 23 November 2018 https://nationalpost.com/opinion/andrew-coyne-liberals-600m-aid-package-for-news-media-will-irrevocably-politicize-the-press (accessed 1 March 2019).

119 "Don't touch that chequebook! A second look at The Shattered Mirror," *JSource*, 8 February 2017 (http://www.j-source.ca/article/don%E2%80%99t-touch-chequebook-second-look-shattered-mirror (accessed 10 April 2017).

link between a free press and a well-functioning democracy should be tested anew before it can be affirmed with confidence."

Drohan's analysis is completely wrong. Social media has not just taken away the Fourth Estate. It has replaced it with a new institution that threatens us at every turn; that undermines the rule of law and the justice system; that denies due process; that does not protect, but imperils, our freedom; that offers no credible alternative to undue deference. The lynch mob, fuelled by emotion rather than evidence, no longer rampages down the city street or country lane, but rages down the digital highway. The amplification and validation effects of the internet allow isolated individuals to join together electronically in hate and become a threatening and cocksure worldwide community. Social media is used by malevolent powers to interfere in free elections and damage important institutions.

Twitter, Facebook, and other social media, allow and encourage the instant gathering of a chaotic group whose members come together self-righteously to condemn and destroy someone who has offended or upset them. Members of the group typically are vague on the facts and have not thought seriously about the issues. This phenomenon has been called approvingly "the democratization of justice." Democratization perhaps, but justice, no. The chilling effect of this development is enormous. It is dangerous to resist the social media mob. It is better to keep quiet. Many have found this out.

The first victim of digital "public shaming" seems to have been a thirty-year old woman called Justine Sacco. Her December 2013 Tweet (to one hundred and seventy followers) from Heathrow Airport, sent before she boarded a flight to Cape Town, was an inept attempt at irony and humour ("Going to Africa. Hope I don't get AIDS. Just kidding. I'm white!"). It was instantly and understandably interpreted as racist. As Sacco's plane flew south through the night, her message was re-Tweeted over and over again, often with extreme (and sometimes obscene) commentary attached. By the time Sacco's flight landed, she was infamous (she was the #1 trending topic on Twitter worldwide), her reputation was in tatters, and she had been fired by her employer.

Then there is the case of Minnesota dentist Dr. Walter Palmer, briefly the most famous dentist in the world. In 2015 he used a bow and arrow to shoot Cecil the Lion in Zimbabwe, apparently contrary to local law. News and photos about Dr. Palmer killing Cecil somehow got onto Twitter, and Dr. Palmer's world went mad. On just one day, there were close to a million Tweets about the incident, almost all of them hideously critical of Palmer and many calling for his blood in the most vivid terms. As several journalists put it, "The hunter became the hunted." Palmer's home was vandalized. His was expelled from his dentistry practice. He went into hiding. He feared for his life.

Christopher Filardi is a biologist. In September 2015, while on a mountain in the Solomon Islands as a member of an American Museum of Natural History research team, Filardi captured a rare mustached kingfisher for the museum's research collection. When the news broke, social media swung into action. He was called a murderer. "While Dr. Filardi was still on the mountain, almost entirely off the grid, the rage spread. Tens of thousands of people signed petitions that condemned his actions, and thousands more signed a petition calling for him to be fired, or even jailed. . . . His wife began receiving phone calls with death threats, at all hours of the night. A petition that stated, 'Chris Filardi is a disgrace and frankly does not deserve to breathe another breath,' was signed by 3,798 people. He descended from the mountaintop into an inferno of hate."[120]

Which brings me to Jian Ghomeshi, a case now mercifully fading from collective memory. You may recall that in October 2014 allegations surfaced that Ghomeshi, an important CBC radio personality, had sexually assaulted several women. Twitter exploded. Initially there were expressions of support for Ghomeshi and doubt about the allegations, but the tide quickly turned. After the first few hours, almost all those who tweeted about Ghomeshi assumed the allegations were true and reviled him in extravagant terms. Within a few days, he was fired from his talk show job. His public relations firm dumped him. His friends turned their backs. His publisher cancelled a book contract. His agent dropped him. He went to California to hide out. All this took place *before* criminal charges were laid—that happened about a month later. In March 2016, in the first of two scheduled trials, Ghomeshi was found

---

120 Kirk Wallace Johnson, "The Ornithologist the Internet Called a Murderer," *New York Times*, 15 June 2018 https://www.nytimes.com/2018/06/15/opinion/sunday/moustached-kingfisher-internet-harassment.html (accessed 18 June 2018).

not guilty of all charges. He avoided the second trial, on additional charges, by signing a peace bond. Too late: he had been convicted of nothing, but his life and career were wrecked.

There was a bizarre and ironic epilogue to the Jian Ghomeshi affair. In September 2018, Ian Buruma, editor of the prestigious *New York Review of Books*, was forced to resign after publishing an essay by Ghomeshi online. The essay ("Reflections of a Hashtag") "caused immediate furor, with some criticizing what they saw as a self-pitying tone, and soft pedaling of the accusations."[121] Buruma commented, "I made a themed issue about #MeToo perpetrators who were not convicted by the judiciary but by social media. And now I am on the pillory myself." It was reported that part of the problem was that university presses (Columbia University Press for one), alarmed about possible reaction on campus to the Ghomeshi article, threatened to pull financially critical advertising from the review. Conor Friedesdorf asked in the *Atlantic* magazine: "What if essays that express popular or uncontroversial perspectives from well-liked authors are held to one factual standard while those expressing dissenting opinions from widely disliked authors are held to a different standard?"[122]

The Ghomeshi case now seems like a trial run for the #MeToo movement that began in the fall of 2017 when numerous serious allegations of sexual misbehaviour were made against Hollywood producer Harvey Weinstein. The Weinstein allegations triggered an avalanche of accusations of sexual misbehaviour levelled against prominent people. For the most part, these accusations were made on social media. Traditional publications, such as *The New York Times* and the *New Yorker*, mitigated the chaos of accusations by careful reporting and fact checking in certain cases. But the most prominent characteristic of the accusations is that

---

121 Cara Buckley, "New York Review of Books Editor Is Out Amid Uproar Over #MeToo Essay," *The New York Times,* 19 September 2018 https://www.nytimes.com/2018/09/19/arts/ian-buruma-out-jian-ghomeshi.html (accessed 1 October 2018).

122 "The Journalistic Implications of Ian Buruma's Resignation," 25 September 2018 https://www.theatlantic.com/ideas/archive/2018/09/resignation-new-york-review-books/563069/?utm_content=edit-promo&utm_medium=social&utm_term=2018-09-25T19%3A36%3A14&utm_source=twitter&utm_campaign=the-atlantic (accessed 1 October 2018). Friedesdorf gives a comprehensive and balanced account of the various reactions to publication of the Ghomeshi essay.

they were automatically accepted as the truth once made. Anyone who questioned their truth was in danger of becoming a target.

Canada's post-Ghomeshi Weinstein moment came at the beginning of 2018 when allegations of sexual misbehaviour were levelled at Albert Schultz, one of the founders and the artistic director of Soulpepper, an important and highly successful Toronto-based non-profit theatre company. Four Soulpepper actresses launched civil lawsuits against Schultz and the theatre company alleging a long history of sexual harassment and degradation by Schultz that had been tolerated by the company. Support for the actresses was considerable, including from members of Soulpepper, and Schultz was quickly forced to resign. By choosing civil litigation, rather than pursuing criminal charges, the four actresses retained control over the narrative and did not subject their allegations to the requirements of proof in criminal proceedings, although they made it likely, if matters proceeded, that they would have to pay substantial legal fees and endure the usual litigation delays. Nor did they, as civil litigation plaintiffs, run as severe a risk of being discredited in court the way the Ghomeshi complainants were. However, by eschewing the criminal process in favour of civil litigation based on the law of tort, the plaintiffs framed the matter as a personal grievance rather than an offence against state-sanctioned norms, which some thought less than satisfactory.

Predictably, the staying power and commitment of the plaintiffs in the Schultz case, as they were faced with the arduous and expensive civil litigation process, proved feeble. Leah McLaren reported in *Toronto Life* that a settlement was reached in May 2018. "Alexi Wood [one of the plaintiffs' lawyers] asked all four claimants to write down the lowest possible dollar figure they would settle for. They were exhausted and desperate for the whole saga to be over. All sides signed non-disclosure agreements forbidding them from discussing the case publicly, but according to a source close to the case, the settlement covered their legal fees and a small payout 'in the low thousands' for each woman." Presumably, the plaintiffs thought themselves victorious nonetheless. They had, after all, inflicted huge personal damage on Albert Schulz.[123]

---

123 "Downfall," 13 July 2018 https://torontolife.com/city/dramatic-fall-albert-schultz/ (accessed 24 July 2018).

Julius Grey is a distinguished Montreal lawyer with a long history of pursuing human rights issues. Shortly after the Schultz affair began, Grey published an important article in the *Montreal Gazette* discussing what he described as "the new reign of terror against alleged sexual delinquents and the termination of careers on the basis of bare allegations."[124] He put forward several cogent arguments against ending careers in this manner. First, "The rule of law is not compatible with punishment before trial." Second, "the wave of accusations seems to conflate very serious matters like rapes, physical assaults and systematic blackmail with ones of a very different character, like 'lewd looks' or 'sexually charged conversations'." Third, "the denunciations ignore history. . . It is unfair to turn remarks or gestures that were normal and not criminal at the time they occurred into a career-ending catastrophe."

Note that a Twitter mob can chase down things as well as people. Online pre-publication "reviews" of books can destroy their prospects, or require that those books be censored or rewritten before they are published. *The New York Times* has described "today's hair-trigger, hyper-reactive social media landscape, where a tweet can set off a cascade of outrage and prompt calls for a book's cancellation."[125] Many publishers, reported the newspaper, "are turning to sensitivity readers, who provide feedback on issues like race, religion, gender, sexuality, chronic illness and physical disabilities."

Anyone can be unjustly accused of anything. For starters, you can be accused of not being a nice person (e.g., "Hey buddy, I think you're a racist!") There are laws and codes of behaviour that offer some protection against this kind of accusation although they're largely ineffectual as anyone knows who has been the object of unfounded rumour or gossip. Much more seriously, like Jian Ghomeshi, you can be accused of criminal behaviour. There are traditional systems and rules to ensure, so far as possible, that in the case of crimes guilt is clearly established

---

124 "Denunciations, dismissals and the excesses of revolutions," 3 January 2018 http://montrealgazette.com/opinion/opinion-denunciations-dismissals-and-the-excesses-of-revolutions (accessed 8 January 2018).

125 Alexandra Alter, "In an Era of Online Outrage, Do Sensitivity Readers Result in Better Books, or Censorship?" 24 December 2017 https://www.nytimes.com/2017/12/24/books/in-an-era-of-online-outrage-do-sensitivity-readers-result-in-better-books-or-censorship.html?ref=todayspaper&_r=0 (accessed 24 December 2017).

according to a high standard before punishment is imposed. When the vehicle for accusation was a newspaper, or television or radio, charges and claims were carefully assessed by editors and lawyers who looked for credibility and were anxious to avoid being sued. If a mistake was made, there was a proprietor with deep pockets who might have to compensate the wrongfully accused. But the Ghomeshi and other cases dramatically illustrate that these systems and rules don't apply to a social media gathering, which pronounces guilt and imposes punishment in the twinkling of an eye. The criminal justice system, or even civil law concepts like the tort of defamation, is never engaged. The accusation simply hangs there. In this way, social media subverts and undermines a critical part of the legal system that many people, lawyers and legislators, laboured mightily for many years to put in place and develop appropriately. It erodes an important aspect of our freedom.

Daphne Merkin is an American literary critic, essayist and novelist. In early January 2018, she published an op-ed article in *The New York Times* that raised important issues about the #MeToo movement and similar social media phenomena.[126] Many feminists, she wrote, have "had it with the reflexive and unnuanced sense of outrage that has accompanied this cause from its inception, turning a bona fide moment of moral accountability into a series of ad hoc and sometimes unproven accusations. For many weeks now, the conversation that has been going on in private about this reckoning is radically different from the public one. This is not a good sign, suggesting the sort of social intimidation that is the underside of a culture of political correctness, such as we are increasingly living in . . . we seem to be returning to a victimology paradigm for young women, in particular, in which they are perceived to be—and perceive themselves to be—as frail as Victorian housewives. . . I don't believe that scattershot, life-destroying denunciations are the way to upend it. In our current climate, to be accused is to be convicted. Due process is nowhere to be found. . . There is a disturbing lack of clarity about the terms being thrown around and a lack of distinction regarding what the spectrum of objectionable behavior really is."

---

126 "Publicly, We Say #MeToo. Privately, We Have Misgivings." 5 January 2018 https://www.nytimes.com/2018/01/05/opinion/golden-globes-metoo.html (accessed 5 January 2018).

How do you mesh the demands of the complex traditional legal system, developed carefully over centuries to deal with a huge variety of human behaviour, with the new world of social media, a chaotic, simplistic behemoth barely a decade old? Part of the tension is between the right to free expression and other individual rights that can be threatened by freedom of expression. How to resolve that tension is an enduring and delicate political and ethical conundrum. Most would agree on one thing: free expression does not trump everything. But when should it give way?

DAYS OF PAIN

Traditional journalists are on the verge of extinction. Their last days are filled with pain. As their power and influence ebbs, indignities are heaped upon them.

On Thursday October 15, 2015, during a federal election campaign, Justin Trudeau held a news conference in Montreal. CTV reporter Omar Sachedina asked a tricky question and was booed by Trudeau supporters standing behind the Liberal leader. Trudeau whirled around and shouted: "Hey! Hey! We have respect for journalists in this country. They ask tough questions and they're supposed to. OK?"[127] On January 19, 2016, now prime minister, Trudeau tweeted: "Journalists are vital to our democracy. I'm saddened to hear of the cuts at #Postmedia today and my thoughts are with those affected." There are other examples of Justin Trudeau's (presumably sincere) appreciation of the traditional role of the press in a democracy. But in that he is unusual, and as I shall note in a moment, his appreciation of the press waned as his political life waxed. But there is still a stark contrast with President Trump's well-known attitude to the press. On his first day as president, Trump called journalists "among the most dishonest human beings on Earth," and that was just the beginning.

---

127 The incident was widely reported. See, for example, "'Hey! Hey!' Trudeau berates his own supporters who tried to shout down reporter's question," *National Post*, 15 October 2015 http://news.nationalpost.com/news/canada/canadian-politics/hey-hey-trudeau-berates-his-own-supporters-who-tried-to-shout-down-reporters-question (accessed 11 March 2017).

Trudeau is an exception, not just internationally, but in the recent history of Canada as well. It was all very different when Stephen Harper was prime minister. Jennifer Ditchburn wrote:

At the 2009 Summit of the Americas in Trinidad and Tobago, I recall a strong feeling of shame as I waited for then-prime minister Stephen Harper and then-president Barack Obama to emerge from a meeting. I was the designated pool reporter with The Canadian Press, killing time with my Associated Press counterpart. I sheepishly admitted that reporters were forbidden from asking the prime minister an unscheduled question at an official event — on pain of being barred from future events.

"Why the hell would you put up with that?" was the general reaction from my American colleague, suggesting that the Washington press corps would never accept such restrictions on speech. . . It's not an overstatement to say the first few months of the Harper administration in 2006 were traumatic for the parliamentary press gallery. In Ottawa, journalists went from weekly access to cabinet ministers, unfettered "scrums" of leading parliamentarians and frequent background briefings to nearly nothing. The flow of information was throttled. On one trip to Vietnam, we turned to Chinese officials for information about a meeting between their president and our own prime minister.

Harper's people also thwarted the "first-come-first-served" tradition for reporters posing questions, instead requiring journalists to submit names in advance. This allowed Harper's office to pick who addressed him. And there was the odious ban on questions at photo ops. Reporters were threatened with being banned from future events if they dared to shoot a question at the prime minister during activities designated as "photo opportunities."[128]

Under the Harper administration things did not get better for the press as time went by. Just before the October 2015 election, Reporters

128 "Lessons from the Harper years for U.S. journalists covering Trump," *Ottawa Citizen*, 23 January 2017 http://ottawacitizen.com/opinion/columnists/ditchburn-lessons-from-the-harper-years-for-u-s-journalists-covering-trump (accessed 11 April 2017).

Without Borders noted, "Systematic curtailment of photographers' freedom of movement and limited access to the Prime Minister for interviews or even during press events seem to be the tenets of the Conservatives' philosophy on the media."[129]

Reporters Without Borders 2017 World Press Freedom Index ranked Canada twenty-second in the world, down four places from the year before, behind Surinam and Samoa, and just ahead of the Czech Republic and Namibia. "Press Freedom on Decline," trumpeted Reporters Without Borders in discussing Canada:

> Prime Minister Trudeau has strongly advocated for a "free media" but the past year has shown this to be dead letter. While Canada guarantees freedom of the press under its 1982 constitution, circumstances faced by journalists say otherwise. Several members of the press have been under police surveillance in Quebec in an attempt to uncover internal leaks. A VICE News reporter is currently fighting a court order compelling him to hand over communications with his source to the Royal Canadian Mounted Police, while another journalist for *The Independent* is facing up to 10 years in prison for his coverage of protests against a hydroelectric project in Labrador. Journalists in the country are not currently protected by any "shield law" and legislation like controversial Bill C-51 uses national security as an excuse to chill free speech and expression online.

In 2018 Canada moved up four places in the Reporters Without Borders world rankings, to number eighteen.[130] It retained the number eighteen spot in 2019 (the United States was ranked number forty-eight, behind Romania).[131]

---

129 See, for example, "The Harper Years: Tough Times For Reporters In Canada," *Reporters Without Borders*, 16 October 2015 https://rsf.org/en/news/harper-years-tough-times-reporters-canada (accessed 11 April 2017).

130 See https://rsf.org/en/ranking (accessed 27 October 2018).

131 See https://rsf.org/en/ranking (accessed 11 August 2019).

DIGITAL NEWS

As traditional journalism collapses, the void is filled by the Internet and social media, with the bad consequences I have described. But not all is gloom and doom. New and promising models of journalism are emerging. Two Nova Scotia digital news outlets, for example, build on the tradition of printed "alt weeklies" such as *The Coast* (Halifax), *NOW* (Toronto) and *Georgia Straight* (Vancouver). Tim Bousquet's daily *Halifax Examiner* and Mary Campbell's weekly *Cape Breton Spectator* are both advertising free and rely on subscribers. They exhibit a high standard of journalism, including deeply researched investigative journalism, mordant humour, and a feisty independence, and emphasize local reporting. Independent digital newspapers have become important outside Canada, particularly in Latin America, and particularly when it comes to challenging oppressive government—for example, Venezuela's *Efecto Cocuya*, Cuba's *El Estornudo* and *Periodismo de Barrio*, and Mexico's *Aristegui Noticias*.[132]

The importance of independent local digital newspapers has been dramatically highlighted by two developments. In April 2017, all of Transcontinental's twenty-eight local newspapers in Nova Scotia, New Brunswick, PEI, and Newfoundland and Labrador were sold to SaltWire Network Inc., a newly-created media group established by the owners of the Halifax *Chronicle Herald*. In May and July 2018, SaltWire announced a number of mergers among these newspapers, and some dailies became weeklies. In November 2017, Postmedia and Torstar executed their swap of forty-one local newspapers with the intention of together closing down all but four of them (so-called "consolidation"). Said Paul Godfrey, then Postmedia's CEO: "The continuing costs of producing dozens of small community newspapers in these regions in the face of significantly declining advertising revenues means that most of these operations no longer have viable business models." The newspapers that were closed were in communities where Postmedia or Torstar, as a result of the swap, own two newspapers that hitherto have competed with each other. Some of these local community newspapers

132 See "Yes to a free online press," *The Economist*, 14 July 2018, p. 29.

were more than a hundred years old. The new digital newspapers help fill the ever-expanding void.

THE COP HAS LEFT THE BEAT

In 2008, commenting on the shrinking and closure of news bureaus in Washington DC, Andy Alexander, at the time the Washington bureau chief for Cox News, himself about to retire as the Cox Washington bureau closed its doors for good, said, "I think the cop is leaving the beat here, and I think it's a terrible loss for citizens."[133]

The traditional Fourth Estate protected our freedom in essential ways. Its replacement, the internet and social media, does not. Chaos has replaced discipline. "News" is now fragmented, targeted to special interest groups, often unreliable, often untrue. Rumour and gossip have replaced facts and serious analysis. Citizens have suffered a terrible loss. We have lost an essential component of our freedom. The cop has left the beat.

---

133 See Richard Pérez-Peña, "Big News in Washington, but Far Fewer Cover It," *New York Times*, 17 December 2008 https://www.nytimes.com/2008/12/18/business/media/18bureaus.html (accessed 27 October 2018).

CHAPTER SIX

COLLEGELAND

A WISE WORD FROM JIM GIBSON

Many years ago, I went to England to study at university. I travelled from my parents' home in Victoria, British Columbia to Montreal to board the RMS Carinthia, a Cunard passenger liner bound for Liverpool. On the way to Montreal, at the suggestion of Bill Hull, a former professor of mine at the University of Manitoba, I stopped in St. Catharines, Ontario, to meet James Gibson, the founding president of Brock University, who as a young man had studied at the English university that was my destination. Gibson had pursued a distinguished career in the public service, including time as private secretary to Prime Minister Mackenzie King. He was hospitable and gracious. As we talked, he said to me, "You are going to a good university. A good university teaches you only one thing, but it is a very important thing. It teaches you how to know a good argument from a bad argument."

What could be better preparation for life as a responsible citizen in a free democracy than learning to distinguish a good argument from a bad argument? So many bad arguments are made every day, often by our leaders, to try and persuade us to believe and do foolish things to our detriment and the detriment of society.

Jim Gibson, of course, was making a particular point and sought to do it in a precise fashion. He knew better than most that universities teach much more than just one thing. A good university education teaches us to understand life in all its complexity and enjoy it more.

It gives us insight into the sciences and their context, into history, music, philosophy, and literature. It teaches us languages, and how to speak and write and converse well. It teaches us many things.

Acquiring the knowledge, understanding, and insight that makes you a better citizen may or may not help you gain suitable employment. That hardly matters and is beside the point, although it was once thought, in Britain and its empire, that being able to read Thucydides in Greek made you a better public servant.

THE UNIVERSITY AS THEME PARK

Universities today are engulfed by vocationalism. They enthusiastically seek to train students in specific and technical skills, promising jobs that often fail to materialize upon graduation. They are seduced by the idea that "the content of the curriculum should be governed by its occupational or industrial utility, and marketability as human capital."[134] They think, not of students, but of "clients" or "consumers." Vocationalism crowds out real learning and turns everyone into a journeyman. "When students become valued clients instead of learners," writes Tom Nichols, "they gain a great deal of self-esteem, but precious little knowledge; worse, they do not develop the habits of critical thinking that would allow them to continue to learn and to evaluate the kinds of complex issues on which they will have to deliberate and vote as citizens."[135]

And then there is extreme vocationalism, not just offering job training as a practical stratagem, but glorifying it. Professional schools, and particularly law and business schools, are prime examples. The most famous case is the Harvard Business School. In his book *The Golden Passport*,[136] Duff McDonald argues that "the marriage of Harvard's

134 A definition of "vocationalism." <u>Dictionary of Sociology</u>. *Encyclopedia.com*, http://www. encyclopedia.com/social-sciences/dictionaries-thesauruses-pictures-and-press-releases/ vocationalism (accessed 7 May 2017).

135 *The Death of Expertise: The Campaign against Established Knowledge and Why It Matters* (New York: Oxford University Press, 2017), p. 9.

136 Duff McDonald, *The Golden Passport: Harvard Business School, the Limits of Capitalism, and the Moral Failure of the MBA Elite* (New York: HarperCollins, 2017).

prestige and intellectual pedigree to overtly moneymaking pursuits has yielded an institution that not only teaches the fundamentals of business education but also provides its soon-to-be-wealthy graduates with 'unrivaled opportunity,' and has become a 'money machine unto itself'."[137]

Ideological criticism of this phenomenon has come from within business schools themselves. Professor Martin Parker of the University of Bristol business school, for example, has described B-schools as "places that teach people how to get money out of the pockets of ordinary people and keep it for themselves."[138] A pernicious offshoot of the university's desire to make money (a desire encouraged, of course, by government, which wants to allocate less funds to post-secondary education) is the university regarding itself as a business. Money is to be made from post-secondary education. Fees can be hiked, saddling graduates with huge and life-distorting debt. Profitable foreign students can be cynically welcomed and courted, even if their limited foreign language and other skills make it doubtful that they can benefit from a university education.[139] Every service provided by the university can have a price tag. As Tegan Bennett Daylight wrote about Australian universities:

> Universities are businesses. Students are customers. The more customers, the better the business does. . . Asking universities to stop making it easy for students to gain entrance, and making it easy for them to pass, is like asking Coca-Cola to slow down its sales. The logic of capitalism overrides everything. . . Every academic is caught between their principles and the rewards that come from abandoning them, between the demands of capitalism and their old

---

137 James B. Stewart, "How Harvard Business School Has Reshaped American Capitalism," *The New York Times*, 24 April 2017 https://www.nytimes.com/2017/04/24/books/review/golden-passport-duff-mcdonald.html (accessed 31 May 2017).

138 "Why we should bulldoze the business school," *The Guardian*, 27 April 2018 https://www.theguardian.com/news/2018/apr/27/bulldoze-the-business-school?CMP=Share_iOSApp_Other (accessed 12 May 2018).

139 It was reported in October 2019 that two-thirds of the students at Cape Breton University were foreign students. The number of international students in Canada has tripled in the past decade. See Joe Friesen, "In Cape Breton, international students transform a campus," *Globe and Mail*, 7 October 2017, p. A1.

role as guardians of higher learning. Teaching is valued less and less; our new god is management. And all corrupt systems must have their collaborators.[140]

Francine Prose, the American writer, argues that post-secondary education has been reduced to "a corporate consumer-driven model, providing services to the student-client." Describing recent developments at one American university, the State University of New York at Stony Brook, she observed in 2017: "SUNY Stony Brook is spending millions on a multi-year program entitled 'Far Beyond' that is intended to 'rebrand' the college's image: a redesigned logo and website, new signs, banners and flags throughout the campus. Do colleges now care more about how a school looks and markets itself than about what it teaches? Has the university become a theme park: Collegeland, churning out workers trained to fill particular niches?"

In Collegeland, the humanities are marginalized. Francine Prose laments what has been lost:

> Those of us who teach and study are aware of what these areas of learning provide: the ability to think critically and independently; to tolerate ambiguity; to see both sides of an issue; to look beneath the surface of what we are being told; to appreciate the ways in which language can help us understand one another more clearly and profoundly – or, alternately, how language can conceal and misrepresent. They help us learn how to think, and they equip us to live in – to sustain – a democracy.[141]

There are similar appalling branding developments in Canada. Canadian newspapers are routinely and bizarrely cluttered with large corporate-style newspaper advertisements by universities, purveying meaningless

---

140 "'The difficulty is the point': teaching spoon-fed students how to really read," *The Guardian*, 23 December 2017 https://www.theguardian.com/books/2017/dec/24/the-difficulty-is-the-point-teaching-spoon-fed-students-how-to-really-read?CMP=share_btn_fb (accessed 26 December 2017).

141 "Humanities teach students to think. Where would we be without them?" *The Guardian*, 12 May 2017 https://www.theguardian.com/commentisfree/2017/may/12/humanities-students-budget-cuts-university-suny (accessed 15 May 2017).

slogans and messages, as if they are selling soap or cars. In one Saturday edition of the *Globe and Mail*,[142] for example, in the front news section, Western University urged us to "Be Extraordinary," Ryerson University touted its development of "innovative techniques," and the University of Windsor told the reader it was a "place of promise." In April 2018, the University of Regina, in a risible half-page advertisement in the *Globe*, demonstrating a cavalier approach to language and grammar, touted its "impactful research" and asked, "Not bad for the little university on the prairie, huh?" What is the point of these jejune appeals? I received an email in May 2019 from an official of my alma mater, the University of Manitoba, which began, "I am pleased to share an update with you about our brand initiative." It announced a new university logo and talked about "the brand experience and the relationship people have with our brand."

Stefan Collini, Professor Emeritus of Intellectual History and English Literature at the University of Cambridge, has argued, "Universities have to be partly-protected spaces in which the extension and deepening of human understanding has priority over any more immediate practical purpose."[143] Universities, writes Collini, must not be subordinated to economic or other utilitarian purposes. But that subordination, he says, particularly to economic purposes, is precisely what is happening, and as a result the modern university is an institution in ruins. "If 'prosperity' is the only overriding value which politicians in market democracies can assume commands general support, then universities have to be repurposed as 'engines of growth'. The value of research has then to be understood in terms of its contribution to economic innovation, and the value of teaching in terms of preparing people for particular forms of employment."[144] Universities, Collini continues, are victims of "the great mudslide that increasingly sees the vocabulary of exchange-value sweep aside the vocabulary of use-value. . . It is becoming increasingly difficult to find a language in which to characterize the human worth of

142 13 May 2017 (chosen at random).

143 *Speaking of Universities*, (London: Verso, 2017), pp. 58-9. For a somewhat different perspective on U.K. universities, see David Willetts, *A University Education* (Oxford: Oxford University Press, 2018).

144 Collini, p. 156.

various activities, and almost impossible to make such assessments tell in public debate. Instead, contribution to 'growth' monopolizes the field."[145] This, Collini notes later, is treating something that may be an indirect by-product of intellectual activity as its principal direct purpose.

As for thinking of students as "clients" or "consumers," Collini writes, "the fundamental model of the student as consumer is inimical to the purposes of education. The paradox of real learning is that you don't get what you 'want' – and you certainly can't buy it. . . The really vital aspects of the experience of studying something (a condition very different from 'the student experience') are bafflement and effort."[146]

Jim Gibson died in 2003, "clear-headed to the end," according to his obituary in the *Ottawa Citizen*. He managed to avoid the worst of the great mudslide. He did not live to see freedom put in jeopardy by the inability of citizens to tell a good argument from a bad argument because no one taught them how to do it. Rest in peace, Jim Gibson.

POLITICAL CORRECTNESS

The university as a place of disinterested reasoning and clear thinking is under attack by political extremists.

In October 2015, Candis McLean, a Canadian investigative journalist of some standing, published a book called *When Police Become Prey*.[147] It argued that two Saskatoon police officers blamed for the 1990 freezing death of an Indigenous man, Neil Stonechild, had been falsely implicated (the police officers were never criminally charged, but were dismissed from the police force following an inquiry). McLean had a variety of speaking events to promote her book scheduled for Regina in 2016 and 2017. A University of Regina associate professor in the Department of Justice Studies, Michelle Stewart, who described McLean's book as "racist garbage," launched a sustained social media campaign that led to the cancellation of these engagements. McLean

---

145 Collini, p. 157.
146 Collini, p. 107.
147 Candis McLean, *When Police Become Prey: The Cold, Hard Facts of Neil Stonechild's Freezing Death* (Audacious Books, 2015).

complained to the president of the University of Regina who replied
that there was nothing she could do, ironically noting and endorsing
"the right of one of the university faculty members to impede your right
to free speech and assembly."

Jordan Peterson, now famous, is a psychology professor at the
University of Toronto. In October 2016 he posted a video on his
YouTube channel attacking proposed federal legislation (Bill C-16)
that would make "gender identity" and "gender expression" protected
categories under the Canadian Human Rights Act and the Criminal
Code. The video made clear Peterson's refusal in his teaching to apply
so-called "preferred" pronouns—e.g., "ze," "vis," "hir," and the singu-
lar use of "they"—to people who apparently do not fit into traditional
gender categories. In a subsequent newspaper article, Peterson took the
position that "the government, advised by radical leftist social justice
warriors, has decided what we must say, instead of what we can't say.
I believe this is extremely ill-advised. I believe it constitutes a serious
restriction of free speech."[148]

Peterson was accused of being a bigot, biased against transgender
and non-binary people, and a racist to boot. The University of Toronto
sent Peterson two letters, he reported, "warning me about the potential
illegality of my actions, and reminding me of my obligations to students
as detailed in its own recent equity-based policies." Public appearances by
Peterson, including at other universities, were disrupted. After a March
2017 incident at McMaster University in Hamilton, where Peterson was
met by cowbells and air horns, and shouted down, a statement was
released by a coalition of student groups, faculty, and staff that opposed
Peterson but claimed that they were not against free speech. The statement said in part: "The concept of freedom of speech has most often
been mobilized to protect specifically counter-hegemonic ideas, ideas
that actually challenge, rather than reiterate, the status quo. There is
nothing rebellious or revolutionary about insisting on the naturalness
of the (now long-debunked) gender binary."[149] This incoherent state-

148 "Why I won't use 'preferred' pronouns – and why you shouldn't either," *Toronto Sun,*
    3 November 2016 http://www.torontosun.com/2016/11/03/why-i-wont-use-pre-
    ferred-pronouns--and-why-you-shouldnt-either# (accessed 8 May 2017).
149 Quoted by Dave Beatty, "McMaster debate with controversial professor Jordan Peterson

ment dramatically illustrated one of the intellectual consequences of poor education, the inability to formulate a clear idea and express it simply.

In an ironic twist, Peterson's supporters took to social media in their thousands to attack, harass and vilify his critics.[150] By January 2018, *The New York Times* was reporting that Jordan Peterson, whose YouTube videos had been viewed over forty million times, might be the most influential public intellectual in the world.[151] On April 1, 2018, Ross Douthat, on the opinion page of *The New York Times*, described Peterson as a "moral-philosophical guru for a large and grateful cohort of young men . . . a tacitly religious figure, a would-be prophet for lost boys."[152] Or, as Jesse Brown wrote in the same newspaper, Peterson is "something of a national archetype, the default setting of the Canadian male: a dull but stern dad, who, under a facade of apparent normalcy and common sense, conceals a reserve of barely contained hostility toward anyone who might rock the boat."[153]

disrupted by activists," *CBC News*, 19 March 2017 http://www.cbc.ca/news/canada/hamilton/mcmaster-debate-with-controversial-professor-jordan-peterson-disrupted-by-activists-1.4031843 (accessed 8 May 2017).

150 See Simona Chiose, "The trolls in the ivory tower," *Globe and Mail*, 3 June 2017 https://www.theglobeandmail.com/news/national/education/jordan-peterson-crowdfunding/article35174379/ (accessed 4 June 2017). Chiose reports that Peterson has thousands of patrons on a crowd-funded subscription site where he earns more than $30,000 a month. Later reports said Peterson was making $50,000 a month from the subscription site, and that his goal was to make $100,000. See Alex McKeen, "Controversial U of T professor making nearly $50,000 a month through crowdfunding," *thestar.com*, 4 July 2017 https://www.thestar.com/news/gta/2017/07/04/controversial-u-of-t-professor-making-nearly-50000-a-month-through-crowdfunding.html (accessed 5 July 2017).

151 David Brooks, "The Jordan Peterson Moment," *The New York Times*, 25 January 2018 https://www.nytimes.com/2018/01/25/opinion/jordan-peterson-moment.html (accessed 26 January 2018).

152 "God and Men and Jordan Peterson," https://www.nytimes.com/2018/03/31/opinion/god-jordan-peterson.html (accessed 1 April 2018).

153 "Only a Country Like Canada Could Produce a Guy Like Jordan Peterson," 6 April 2018 https://www.nytimes.com/2018/04/06/opinion/jordan-peterson-canadian-deference.html (accessed 6 April 2018). For a devastating critique of Peterson and his ideas, see Bernard Schiff, "I was Jordan Peterson's strongest supporter. Now I think he's dangerous," *Toronto Star*, 26 May 2018 https://www.thestar.com/opinion/2018/05/25/i-was-jordan-petersons-strongest-supporter-now-i-think-hes-dangerous.html (accessed 26 May 2018).

Andrew Potter, former editor of the *Ottawa Journal* and director of McGill University's Institute for the Study of Canada, wrote
a 2017 column in *Maclean's* magazine which argued, "Quebec is an
almost pathologically alienated and low-trust society, deficient in many
of the most basic forms of social capital that other Canadians take for
granted."[154] Two days after publication of this article, Potter resigned
his Institute directorship citing "the ongoing negative reaction within
the university community and the broader public to my column." Word
had it that McGill, under pressure from outraged politicians and bene-
factors, gave him the choice of resigning his directorship or being fired.
In the *National Post,* Andrew Coyne described the affair as "a calamity for the university, and for the principles of academic freedom and
intellectual inquiry for which it supposedly stands."[155]

There is nothing new under the sun. Some will remember the 1958
Harry Crowe Affair. Crowe, a tenured history professor at United
College in Winnipeg (now the University of Winnipeg), was fired
because of a private letter he wrote expressing concern with the religious and academic environment at United College and the prospect of
a Conservative victory in the upcoming federal election. Thus ensued a
national controversy about academic freedom that reverberates to this
day.[156]

In the fall of 2017, Wilfred Laurier University (WLU) teaching
assistant and Master's student Lindsay Shepherd showed some students
in a communications tutorial a television clip in which Jordan Peterson
questioned the need to use special pronouns for those not identifying
as male or female. She was summoned before a panel of three WLU

154 "How a snowstorm exposed Quebec's real problem: social malaise," *Maclean's,* 20 March
2017 http://www.macleans.ca/news/canada/how-a-snowstorm-exposed-quebecs-
real-problem-social-malaise/ (accessed 9 May 2017).

155 "This is not how a liberal society responds to criticism," 24 March 2017 http://news.
nationalpost.com/full-comment/andrew-coyne-quebecs-reaction-to-potters-critiques-
shows-it-is-no-liberal-society (accessed 9 May 2017).

156 See "Report of the Investigation by the Committee of the Canadian Association of
University Teachers into the Dismissal of Professor H.S. Crowe by United College,
Winnipeg, Manitoba" [Published as a special issue of the CAUT Bulletin 7 (3), January
1959], http://www.crowefoundation.ca/documents/CroweReport.pdf (accessed 17
May 2017).

academics who berated her for not condemning Peterson's views and accused her of creating a toxic climate in the classroom and breaking the law. One professor said that showing the video without denouncing Peterson was like "neutrally playing a speech by Hitler." Shepherd recorded this meeting on her computer, and made the recording public. A scandal ensued. A *Globe and Mail* editorial commented, "this university's message is that there are lines of inquiry that are no longer open for study, in particular ones that have been politicized in left-right terms. The only options are agree, or be silenced. This is not scholarship—it's ideology. It views education as indoctrination, where those doing the teaching must be monitored to make sure their views are acceptable to self-imposed gatekeepers."[157]

What is extraordinary about the stories of Candis McLean, Jordon Peterson, Andrew Potter, and Lindsay Shepherd—and they are only examples, there are many other such stories—is how they reveal the attitude of some university professors and administrations to freedom of expression. Rather than defend this fundamental and constitutionally guaranteed freedom, they stand aside when it is denied or actively encourage its repression. The freedom-seeking liberal arts universities that democracy requires for its continued sustenance have been replaced by vocational schools frightened of freedom.

IT'S THE SAME EVERYWHERE ELSE

The tyranny of the politically extreme, primarily but not exclusively the left, is an international phenomenon. Here are some non-Canadian examples. In March 2017, at Middlebury College in Vermont, Dr. Charles Murray, who believes that intelligence is partly genetic, was prevented from speaking by a student mob. Middlebury College apologized and disciplined a number of the students who participated, but the students involved (and others who supported them, including some professors) were unrepentant. A non-protesting professor of political

---

157 "Globe editorial: Why are we killing critical thinking on campus?" 16 November 2017 https://www.theglobeandmail.com/opinion/editorials/globe-editorial-why-are-we-killing-critical-thinking-on-campus/article37008714/ (accessed 22 December 2017).

science at Middlebury said the episode reflected an institutional failure in the way students are taught at the college. "They don't understand the value of free speech at a college and what free speech really means," said Professor Matthew Dickinson.[158] Murray subsequently spoke at Harvard and Columbia without incident.

Interestingly, Charles Murray has been influenced by the writings of Canadian Philippe Rushton. In the 1980s, Rushton was a psychology professor at the University of Western Ontario (this before it was rebranded as "Western"). He published a series of papers claiming that whites, blacks, and Asians could be grouped according to intelligence, and claiming that blacks were generally less intelligent that whites. He was accused of racism including by the then-premier of Ontario, David Peterson, and was regularly shouted down at lectures. When Rushton died in 2012, the journalist John Allemang wrote in the *Globe and Mail* that Rushton's motivation for ranking racial groups "came from the purer intentions of science: to take the evidence of research to its most logical and unavoidable conclusion. . . Rushton saw himself as a lonely empiricist in a world of mental make-believe."[159]

The notorious right-wing commentator Anne Coulter, prompted by threats of violence, cancelled a scheduled speech at Berkeley in April, 2017. This was reminiscent of an earlier incident in Canada involving Coulter. In 2010, she cancelled a scheduled speech at the University of Ottawa citing security concerns. In a pompous and condescending letter sent to her before her planned visit, University of Ottawa academic vice-president François Houle wrote, "I hereby encourage you to educate yourself, if need be, as to what is acceptable in Canada and to do so before your planned visit here."[160] The cancellation of Coulter's Berkeley speech followed the last-minute cancellation of another speech

158 See Stephanie Saul, "Dozens of Middlebury Students Are Disciplined for Charles Murray Protest," *The New York Times*, 24 May 2017 https://www.nytimes.com/2017/05/24/us/middlebury-college-charles-murray-bell-curve.html (accessed 25 May 2017).
159 "Philippe Rushton, professor who pushed limits with race studies, dead at 68," 2 November 2012 https://www.theglobeandmail.com/news/national/philippe-rushton-professor-who-pushed-limits-with-race-studies-dead-at-68/article4901806/?page=all (accessed 29 May 2017).
160 See Steven Chase, "Ann Coulter's speech in Ottawa cancelled," *Globe and Mail*, 23 March 2010 http://www.theglobeandmail.com/news/politics/ann-coulters-speech-in-ottawa-cancelled/article4352616/ (accessed 17 May 2017).

scheduled at Berkeley, this one by Milo Yiannopoulos, a right-wing commentator associated with Breitbart News. The Yiannopoulos cancellation came after masked protestors caused considerable damage on campus. CNN reported, "Black-clad protesters wearing masks threw commercial-grade fireworks and rocks at police. Some even hurled Molotov cocktails that ignited fires. They also smashed windows of the student union center on the Berkeley campus where the Yiannopoulos event was to be held."[161]

In August 2017, Professor Amy Wax of the University of Pennsylvania law faculty co-authored an op-ed in the *Philadelphia Inquirer* which argued, in part, that some cultures, e.g. that of the Plains Indians, are less suited to preparing people to be productive citizens in a modern technological society.[162] Wax received an outpouring of criticism, including from many of her law school colleagues. The dean of the law school asked her to take a one-year leave of absence, explaining that he was being pressured because of her unpopular views.[163]

Nor is the fear confined to North American campuses. Here is an international example, from an African university where I taught in the early 2000s. The University of Cape Town Vice Chancellor, Max Price "disinvited" the Danish journalist Flemming Rose from giving an annual talk on academic and human freedom in July, 2016. Rose is foreign affairs editor of the Danish magazine that in 2005 published a notorious set of cartoons considered blasphemous by many Muslims. In a letter to the university's academic freedom committee,[164] Price wrote in part:

161 Madison Park and Kyung Lah, "Berkeley protests of Yiannopoulos caused $100,000 in damage," *CNN*, 2 February 2017 http://www.cnn.com/2017/02/01/us/milo-yiannopoulos-berkeley/ (accessed 17 May 2017).

162 "Paying the price for breakdown of the country's bourgeois culture," 9 August 2017 http://www.philly.com/philly/opinion/commentary/paying-the-price-for-break-down-of-the-countrys-bourgeois-culture-20170809.html (accessed 3 March 2018).

163 See Amy Wax, "The Closing of the Academic Mind," *Wall Street Journal*, 17 February 2018, page C1.

164 For the complete letter, see "Why UCT has decided to disinvite Flemming Rose – Max Price," *politicsweb*, 22 July 2016 http://www.politicsweb.co.za/documents/why-uct-has-decided-to-disinvite-flemming-rose--ma (accessed 6 June 2017).

Public order on many campuses is in a fragile state and in some cases volatile. It would be ill-advised to add a highly contentious speaker to the mix at this time. . . . The rise of Islamophobia, the undeniable turmoil in the Middle East in general, the Palestinian question, the rise in extremist terrorist groups, and the violent consequences of these factors in the world (including West and East Africa) is the context in which one must consider the consequences of hosting Mr. Rose.

The risks are to the security and bodily integrity of Mr. Rose himself; to those who will host him, and those who will attend the lecture; to the ability to hold a public lecture without total disruption; to the fragile but uneasy calm which currently exists on campus; and to the positive interfaith relations which currently mark public life in the Western Cape.

In summary, in considering the predictable polarisation such an invitation will very likely bring to our campus and our wider community, the current climate on campus in which challenging conflicts have already left people feeling uneasy or silenced in regard to certain kinds of conversations, coupled most importantly with very serious security considerations, we have decided that we should not host the address by Mr. Flemming Rose at the University of Cape Town at this time.

The Index on Censorship condemned this craven decision by the University of Cape Town as "a decision that makes a mockery of the university's supposed defence of free speech and academic freedom."[165]

FEES

Given despair over the current state of university education in Canada and elsewhere, and university emphasis on attracting "customers," it

165 See "Index on Censorship condemns decision to axe Flemming Rose as speaker on academic freedom," 22 July 2016 https://www.indexoncensorship.org/2016/07/index-censorship-condemns-decision-axe-flemming-rose-speaker-academic-freedom/ (accessed 6 June 2017).

may seem odd that another criticism of post-secondary institutions is the increasing difficulty of gaining access to the education they offer. Access to university education, like access to justice, is limited mostly for financial reasons. Gone are the days when a year's university fees were a few hundred dollars. The past several decades have seen a dramatic increase in tuition fees, with many tripling or more over the past twenty years. Additionally, a variety of compulsory non-tuition fees, such as library fees, have been introduced.

Universities have become increasingly dependent on fee revenue and other non-government sources of income (particularly "research grants" from large corporations which have particular research that benefits them in mind) as the government share of their funding has decreased. It is another expression of the university as a business. The Canadian Centre for Policy Alternatives reported in September 2015: "Average tuition and other fees for Canadian undergraduates have tripled between 1993–94 and 2015–16, ranging from an increase of 35% in Newfoundland and Labrador to 248% in Ontario. Over roughly the same period (1992–2012), government funding for university operating revenue declined from 77% to 55%, while tuition fees as a share of university operating revenue increased from 20% to over 37%."[166] The result, concluded the CCPA, is an ongoing erosion of the principle of universality across the higher education sector.

Many students borrow money to pay their fees; they graduate with huge debts. These debts distort career choices in ways that harm society and, it has been suggested, can cause stress and other mental health issues. A few years ago, I was taken to lunch by a group of third-year law students at an Ontario university. I asked what they intended to do when they graduated. Almost all said they wanted to practice business law with one of the huge, downtown Toronto corporate law firms. I asked if anyone wanted to open a storefront law office serving the needs of ordinary people, or practise the law of civil liberties, or work for Indigenous People. I was told I didn't get it. Debts had to be paid. The

---

166 Erika Shaker and David Macdonald, *What's the Difference? Taking Stock of Provincial Tuition Fee Policies* https://www.policyalternatives.ca/sites/default/files/uploads/publications/National%20Office/2015/09/Whats_the_Difference.pdf (accessed 31 May 2017).

students had to go where the salaries were big. Today the University of Toronto Faculty of Law charges forty thousand dollars a year in tuition fees (the highest law school fees in Canada). That means that only students from wealthy families, or those prepared to take on crippling debt and then seek work on Bay Street, can afford to attend.

In 2012, the system of funding universities in the UK changed radically. Direct public funding of universities was dramatically cut. Universities were permitted to charge up to nine thousand pounds a year for their courses. Almost all universities quickly started charging the maximum, creating one of the world's most expensive university tuition systems. Students were required to pay much more of the cost of their education themselves, with access to long-term publicly funded loans to help them do so (some commentators suggested the scheme amounted to a "quasi-tax" on university education). The Education Maintenance Allowance that helped students from lower-income households was abolished. There were unprecedented student riots when these changes were first proposed.[167]

Astute and eloquent on the business of tuition fees, Stefan Collini argues that the new system in the UK has a fatal, conceptual error:

> It treats the fee as payment by an individual customer to a single institutional provider for a specific service in the present. By contrast, the proper basis for funding education is a form of social contract whereby each generation contributes to the education of future generations. . . What we call a 'fee' is not really the price of a product: it is an undertaking to contribute to the costs of the system. In this respect it is more like a tax: just as a tax is the tithe which the citizen, as a member of society, pays towards the upkeep of that society, so a university fee is . . . a recognition of human solidarity in facing the common perils and opportunities of life.[168]

The UK tuition scheme, close to collapse, has become "a toxic mess of soaring debt and graduate grievances."[169] The average debt of graduates

---

167 See Matt Myers, *Student Revolt*, (London: Pluto Press, 2017).
168 Collini, pp. 238-9.
169 Andrew Rawnsley, "You don't need a double first to see university funding is in chaos,"

from English universities is more than fifty thousand pounds. Many will never pay it off, but "still have the psychological burden of carrying that debt and dealing with the impact it has on life prospects, such as the chance of securing a mortgage."[170] Now many believe that fees should be abolished entirely. In February 2018, the government announced a review of education funding for over-eighteens. The then education secretary, Damian Hinds, hinted at forthcoming selective reductions in university fees. By the end of 2018, nothing had happened. The government had other things on its mind.

LAW SCHOOL BLUNDERS[171]

In February 2018, an all-white jury in Saskatchewan acquitted a white man, Gerald Stanley, of murdering an Indigenous youth, Colten Boushie. The acquittal attracted a huge amount of attention. Many felt that justice had not been done, including Prime Minister Trudeau and the then-Minister of Justice, Jody Wilson-Raybould, both of whom misguidedly tweeted about the case. Many felt that racism lurked behind the jury's verdict. Some law schools joined the chorus of indignation. At the forefront was the University of Windsor Law Faculty. It quickly issued a statement, which said in part: "What happened to Colten Boushie and law's response to his murder are tragic, unnecessary and unacceptable. We stand with Colten Boushie's family. We stand with Red Pheasant First Nation. We stand with Indigenous Peoples. We stand with Indigenous scholars, students, activists and families who remind all of us of our moral responsibilities as guests in the Territories of the Three Fires Confederacy to generate change."[172] Several other law

---

The Guardian, 8 July 2017 https://www.theguardian.com/commentisfree/2017/jul/08/dont-need-double-first-to-see-university-funding-in-chaos (accessed 26 Deceember 2017).

170 Rawnsley, note 166.

171 This section is based on my article in *Canadian Lawyer*, "Politicized law schools," 16 July 2018 https://www.canadianlawyermag.com/author/philip-slayton/politicized-law-schools-15846/ (accessed 29 October 2018).

172 "Windsor Law's Statement on Stanley Trial Verdict," http://www.uwindsor.ca/law/2018-02-16/windsor-laws-statement-stanley-trial-verdict (accessed 22 April 2018).

schools, deans of law, and law professors, across the country, expressed similar sentiments in a less formal and portentous way. Some of these professors and institutions have since been described as "social justice warriors," a dubious compliment given the history of that descriptor.

Not everyone was convinced that law schools should get involved. Writing in the *National Post*, Bruce Pardy, a law professor at Queen's University in Kingston, said, "Legal education has lost its way. One could be forgiven for thinking that the purpose of law schools was to train lawyers to understand legal principles and to think logically and critically. Instead, some law schools portray themselves as political actors working for a cause."[173] Two of Professor Pardy's Queen's law school colleagues, Professors Lisa Kerr and Lisa Kelly, fired back in the *Globe and Mail*. "Calls for a return to legal formalism–a legal education free of politics–are themselves deeply political. Stripping law of context allows supporters of the status quo to portray legal rules as neutral or apolitical."[174]

No one who has thought about it for more than a minute will deny that law exists in a broad political, cultural, historical, ethical, and social context. Law reflects and influences society. We all know that. The proper study of law recognizes and explores this complex relationship. In law schools, the relationship is dealt with, for better or worse, in courses that specifically address the issue (e.g., legal history, law and economics, legal philosophy), and interstitially in other subjects (e.g., how tax law works to redistribute wealth). But, apparently, some law schools want to go further and promote explicit political agendas.

Many law students will not be too keen on this development (some, of course, will embrace it with fervour). Almost all law students intend to practise law and are in law school to learn how to do it. To them, anything else is peripheral, if not irrelevant and unwelcome. The irony is that most law professors are theoreticians with little or no experience practising law. As a result, they often don't give the students what they

---

173 "The social justice revolution has taken the law schools. This won't end well," 27 February 2018 http://nationalpost.com/opinion/the-social-justice-revolution-has-taken-the-law-schools-this-wont-end-well (accessed 22 April 2018).

174 "Yes, law schools must be political," 17 March 2018 https://www.theglobeandmail.com/opinion/article-yes-law-schools-must-be-political/ (accessed 22 April 2018).

want. That's true in spades if, perhaps to fill the gap, professors pursue a political agenda in the classroom and law schools try to become political actors in their own right. It's a recipe for frustration, trouble, and—ultimately—irrelevance. For one thing, a law school that promotes a specific political agenda disrespects the political autonomy of its students. Some students will agree with the agenda, others will not, yet they will all be lumped together. Those who don't agree may feel pressured to conform. Christie Blatchford in the *National Post* reported the comments of a law student whose dean, in an email message to students, condemned the Boushie decision. This particular student had a somewhat different and complicated view of the case. "The dean's message made clear, these kinds of ideas are not acceptable. All twelve of the jurors were bigots. As students of the faculty, we had our marching orders. The decision was racist and so is our legal system."[175]

There is also the danger of dubious trading on limited expertise. A statement by a law faculty on a legal matter carries weight. Presumably the professors in a law school know a lot about the law and the legal system. We should pay attention to what they have to say. But expertise has its limits. Does a law school's collective legal knowledge make its view on racism particularly compelling? As I have written before, "If you win the Nobel Prize for, say, chemistry, suddenly everyone wants your views on, I don't know what, maybe world peace. Why being a whiz at infrared chemiluminescence makes you an expert on nuclear disarmament is not clear."[176]

Some might argue that law schools have a positive obligation to sensitize students to political and social issues, to get them fully involved in the big controversies of the day, to insist that they commit to particular and progressive points of view. Not to do so—to produce politically neutral, indeed neutered, graduates—would be to abdicate responsibility and fail in the mission. It would also ignore the inherent political nature of some legal rules. But this line of thinking misses the

---

175 Christie Blatchford, "The wrong kind of justice warriors at Canada's law schools," 13 March 2018 http://nationalpost.com/opinion/christie-blatchford-the-wrong-kind-of-justice-warriors-at-canadas-law-schools (accessed 22 April 2018).

176 Philip Slayton, *How To Be Good: The Struggle Between Law and Ethics* (Toronto: Oblonsky Editions, 2017), p.11.

mark. Education should teach us how to tell a good argument from a bad argument, not promote a particular argument. Adopting particular arguments can wait for later, once our knowledge is greater and our sensibilities refined.

There's a lot of law. The Great Library at Osgoode Hall in Toronto holds about one hundred and twenty thousand volumes. The Bodleian Law Library at Oxford has four hundred and fifty thousand volumes. To know and understand even a little of all this takes a big effort. The task is made easier if it is guided by those who are wise, knowledgeable, and objective. The law school and its professors are there to teach the law as it is: the learning comes first, the ideology can come later.

THE UNIVERSITY AND FREEDOM

A curious and well-informed mind is a free mind. A person with a free mind is a free person. To create this free person is the job of education, particularly post-secondary education. To do this job, universities need to reject a corporate consumer-driven model and emphasize the development of critical thinking, eschewing misguided and misleading vocationalism. They need a fee structure that makes post-secondary education available to all without career distorting long-term debt. And universities need to welcome the expression of all views, even extreme views, rejecting attempts to suppress them whether they come from the political right or the political left, and relying on critical thinking and good judgment—not suppression—to repudiate those that are wrong and dangerous.

PART THREE

PUBLIC DISCOURSE

Expansive notions of human rights, and an energetic human rights bureaucracy enforcing these notions, can easily chill the free expression of unpopular ideas and opinions. Be wary of "human rights" newly invented by special interest groups. Some may have a legitimate place in the permanent list of human rights that must be protected. Others are repressive ideas dressed up in misleading costume intended to deceive.

The "CanLit" concept, with its attendant rivalries and controversies, demands and constraints, has become a cultural straitjacket. It does not promote, protect, and celebrate Canadian writers and their work. Instead, it interferes with their freedom to write what they want, and consumes their time in pointless and destructive arguments.

CHAPTER SEVEN

HUMAN RIGHTS

A PARADOX

Some argue that there are human rights that must be enforced even if that incidentally restrains freedom of speech and other freedoms. Some things, after all, should not be said or done. Should we not deny expression of anti-Muslim sentiments, or the voicing of extreme white nationalism, or promotion of misogyny? Freedoms can be the playground of the rich and powerful who use them against the poor and weak. That is why we need human rights law and its attendant bureaucracy, to act as a counter balance and protect the fragile from the strong. There is merit in this idea. But a good idea can be used for a contrary purpose.

Political correctness and the modern Canadian concept of human rights overlap in unexpected ways, creating a paradox. Sometimes it seems as if the main purpose of human rights laws and principles, capaciously defined and aggressively promoted by bureaucrats, ideologues, and opportunists, is to enforce what is politically correct, rather than— as one might expect—to protect freedom of speech and action by those who think differently. In this way, something supposed to protect and promote freedom can become its enemy.

The human rights idea is vague, expansive, and accommodating. It is the easy resting place of disparate causes and complaints. It gives bureaucrats staffing powerful federal and provincial governmental human rights agencies political and cultural power. It gives non-elected officials intrusive and arbitrary jurisdiction over important areas of life. To some extent, Canadians, wisely, have pushed back against this development over the last decade or so. Sometimes the power of human rights agencies seems to have retreated to a more defensible place. Yet problematic thinking and the powerful human rights infrastructure are still with us.

SOME HISTORY

The modern era of human rights in the western world began following World War Two.[177] One of its principal architects was a Canadian, John Humphrey, once a colleague of mine at McGill's Faculty of Law. In 1946, Humphrey interrupted his career as a law professor to become the first director of the United Nations Division of Human Rights. He was the principal drafter, along with Frenchman René Cassin, and working with Eleanor Roosevelt, of the 1948 United Nations Universal Declaration of Human Rights. Initially the human rights movement in Canada, inspired in part by the Universal Declaration, was slow to start, although the general idea of human rights was in the post-war air and gained strength steadily. Saskatchewan passed a provincial Bill of Rights in 1947, the first province to do so. Discussion about a national bill of rights began shortly afterwards. A federal Bill of Rights, promoted by Prime Minister John Diefenbaker, passed in 1960 but this was just an ordinary statute like any other without the force and status of a constitutional amendment and did not apply to areas of provincial jurisdiction. Two years later Ontario passed a Human Rights Code that incorporated existing anti-discrimination laws into a single statute to be enforced by a powerful Human Rights Commission with full-time human rights investigators. The new Ontario Code provided for a conciliation process, formal inquiries, and the enforcement of settlements. The Canadian Civil Liberties Association, a private organization, was created in 1964. The CCLA went on to become an important human

---

177 The intellectual foundations had been laid long before. See, for example, Philippe Sands, *East West Street: On the Origins of "Genocide" and "Crimes Against Humanity"* (London: Weidenfeld & Nicholson, 2016).

rights institution, particularly under its long-time (1968-2009) general counsel Alan Borovoy.[178] A new federal Human Rights Act was enacted in 1977, creating an independent human rights commission. Today, every province and territory of Canada, in addition to Canada as a whole, has a fully functioning human rights commission funded by the government.

Separately, as part of major constitutional reform in 1982, the Charter of Rights and Freedoms became part of the constitution of Canada. The Charter guarantees a variety of rights and freedoms. Its effect has been profound. Let me mention just one Charter case, to give an example of its reach. In 1991 Delwin Vriend, a laboratory coordinator, was fired from King's College in Edmonton, a private fundamentalist Christian institution, because he was gay. He complained to the Alberta Human Rights Commission but was told that he could not make a complaint under the Alberta Individual's Rights Protection Act (IRPA) because the Act did not include sexual orientation as a protected ground. This was a deliberate omission by the Alberta legislature. The case ended up at the Supreme Court of Canada which ruled in 1998 that IRPA's omission of sexual orientation violated the Charter. The Supreme Court ordered the government of Alberta to interpret the statute as if it included sexual orientation.[179] In doing so, the Court overrode the clearly expressed wishes of the Alberta legislature and rewrote legislation passed by elected provincial lawmakers. This striking example of the post-Charter judicial role in lawmaking was highly controversial at the time. Today, twenty years later, I doubt whether the decision would raise many eyebrows, positions on these matters having evolved dramatically.[180]

178 See Marian Botsford Fraser, *Acting for Freedom: Fifty Years of Civil Liberties in Canada* (Toronto: Second Story Press, 2014).

179 *Vriend v. Alberta,* 1998 CanLII 816 (S.C.C.).

180 For a full discussion of the *Vriend* case, see Philip Slayton, *Mighty Judgment: How the Supreme Court of Canada Runs Your Life* (Toronto: Allen Lane, 2011), pp. 58-62.

HUMAN RIGHTS AS LANGUAGE

There is hardly an issue that has not been characterized as a human rights issue by somebody. Dominique Clément, a professor of sociology at the University of Alberta, writes, "Human rights is the language we use to frame the most profound–and the most commonplace— grievances."[181] Human rights, says Clément, has become "Canadians' primary language for social change," or "the dominant language people use to express their claims against the state and society."[182] He writes of the "malleability" of human rights discourse. His argument is that "rights are always changing and that rights have a 'social life' in that they are a product of our society."[183]

Some issues quickly and rightly gained human rights legitimacy— discrimination based on sex or sexual orientation, for example, or on the basis of race, colour, or disability. The human rights status of other issues, such as environmental rights, mineral rights, access to clean water, a safe learning environment, housing, and internet connectivity, has been controversial. Are these really human rights? And some assertions of human rights have been ridiculous—for instance, the alleged right of a woman worker in a restaurant not to wash her hands regularly because of a medical condition. For a time "human rights" was a bucket into which were dumped holus-bolus the desires and grievances of many unhappy individuals and groups.

Prominent and respectable civil libertarians, such as the late Alan Borovoy, and David Matas, a Winnipeg human rights activist, sounded early alarms about the rapid encroachment of human rights into areas of political and social concern and disagreement. Later, more controversial persons joined the attack. The most vociferous critic of human rights encroachment has been Ezra Levant (I discuss his battle with the Alberta Law Society in Chapter Two). In a powerful, often humorous, frequently intemperate, always exaggerated book published in 2009, Levant wrote, "Human rights commissions now monitor political

181 *Human Rights in Canada: A History* (Waterloo: Wilfred Laurier University Press, 2016), p.1.
182 p. 5.
183 p. 3.

opinions, fine people for expressing politically incorrect viewpoints, censor websites, and even ban people, permanently, from saying certain things."[184] Levant talks about the "grievance industry" of government bureaucrats fuelled by "crackpot narcissists, angry loners, and professional grievance collectors." His book chronicles some of the most egregious cases that have been before Canada's human rights tribunals. He writes: "The phrase *human rights* in Canada has come to mean any desire, entitlement, or grievance dressed up as a right."[185]

Of course, this type of criticism is exaggerated and does not sit well with certain groups. Mark Freiman, a lawyer and former president of the Canadian Jewish Congress, has described such criticism of the Canadian human rights system this way:

In its most strident manifestation, it attacks the human rights system as an embodiment of the worst excesses of the nanny state, bent on micromanaging our social interactions in aid of enforced conformity to laughably abstract and unreasonable standards of 'political correctness.' The stated goal of this campaign of attack has been to 'denormalize' the concept of human rights codes and of the machinery by which they are enforced, to take them off the pedestal onto which high school civics curricula have placed them and to make them controversial.[186]

In his 2009 book, Levant argued that human rights commissions have become an obsolete industry. "Two generations ago, racism, sexism, and homophobia were still harboured–and sometimes openly espoused–in mainstream Canadian society. But those days are over. Canadians now bend over backwards to demonstrate our respect for others".[187] What was true in 2009 is doubly true today, more than a decade later. Canada

184 *Shakedown: How Our Government Is Undermining Democracy in the Name of Human Rights* (Toronto: McCLelland & Stewart, 2009), p. 3.
185 p. 99.
186 Mark J. Freiman, "Analysis vs. Polemic: A scholarly defence of Canada's human rights regime," (a review of *Speaking Out on Human Rights: Debating Canada's Human Rights System* by Pearl Eliadis), *Literary Review of Canada*, December 2014 http://review-canada.ca/magazine/2014/12/analysis-vs-polemic/ (accessed 12 June 2017).
187 *Shakedown*, p.185.

has become a remarkably tolerant society quite independently of clumsy bureaucratic attempts to make it so. Next to the sweep of social and cultural change the role of human rights commissions has been, and is, miniscule. So, for example, in 2017 the Canadian Human Rights Commission received one thousand and eighty-three complaints (down about four hundred from the previous year) and accepted seven hundred and ninety-five. In 2016-17, the British Columbia Human Rights Tribunal received one thousand four hundred and thirty-three complaints and accepted one thousand three hundred and forty. The Alberta Human Rights Commission received one thousand five hundred and eighty-eight complaints and accepted nine hundred and twenty-three. The Nova Scotia Human Rights Commission received two thousand five hundred and sixty-seven complaints and only accepted one hundred and ten. Very few Canadians are choosing these institutions to pursue grievances. Of course, numbers are not everything. One tribunal decision can have a profound effect. In recent years, I have seen no such decision. My review of recent cases shows them to be almost uniformly of the bread-and-butter variety.

Despite their being shoved to the sidelines by the Canadian people, human rights commissions themselves seem to envisage no limits to their mandate. Consider the message of Marie-Claude Landry, Canadian Human Rights Chief Commissioner, in the Commission's 2016 Annual Report:

> As I reflected upon this message, I could not ignore the events of the past year. We have read hate-filled words directed towards various communities; we have learned of threats aimed at religious and ethnic groups; we have been exposed to political messaging that capitalizes on exclusion and discrimination; and we have seen misogyny aimed at women who dare to speak out against the status quo—all of which were eclipsed by the horror of witnessing a violent shooting in a mosque.
>
> . . .
>
> While these forms of hate and intolerance are taking center stage, this year was also marked by human rights violations that may be far less worthy of headlines, but that have no less of a devastating impact—people living on reserves who don't have clean water or safe homes; children who are held in detention because of

the ambiguous immigration status of their families; children who choose to take their own lives because they can't get the support they need in their communities.

The Chief Commissioner characterizes lack of clean water on reserves, or youth suicide, as human rights issues, rather than what they obviously are—profound social policy concerns to be addressed urgently by the regular institutions of democratic government on the demand of the citizenry. Only government has the power and the tools to address such issues comprehensively and effectively. The annual reports of other commissions typically contain similar grandiose statements. In particular, in recent years, concern about Indigenous People has been a central theme. And yet actual recent decisions by commissions and tribunals have been, for the most part, routine and prosaic, dealing quite appropriately with issues like alleged discrimination based on colour or race, sexual harassment in the workplace, and discrimination because of physical disability, considering specific instances, and often rejecting allegations that human rights have been breached.

THE MARRIAGE IS OVER

The watershed moment was the controversy over, and subsequent repeal, of section 13(1) of the original 1977 Canadian Human Rights Act. This section (amended several times since 1977) read:

It is a discriminatory practice for a person or a group of persons acting in concert to communicate telephonically or to cause to be so communicated, repeatedly, in whole or in part by means of the facilities of a telecommunication undertaking within the legislative authority of Parliament, any matter that is likely to expose a person or persons to hatred or contempt by reason of the fact that that person or those persons are identifiable on the basis of a prohibited ground of discrimination.

This provision, the so-called "hate speech provision," became the subject of intense controversy in the early 2000s when it started to be applied to the developing internet. It was the basis for several Canadian Human Rights Tribunal cases that attracted widespread criticism, particularly from Ezra Levant, Jonathan Kay, and other right-wing commentators. They were joined by Alan Borovoy, David Matas, and Noam Chomsky—improbable bed fellows. At about the same time, a handful of notorious cases before provincial tribunals soured popular perception of these institutions and the human rights juggernaut in general, notably the 2007 complaint to the BC Human Rights Tribunal, the Ontario Human Rights Tribunal, and the Canadian Human Rights Tribunal, alleging that *Maclean's* magazine had published Islamophobic articles (the complainants lost in all three places after lengthy and expensive proceedings). In 2009, the Canadian Human Rights Tribunal found that s.13 violated freedom of expression. In 2013 a private member's bill repealing section 13(1) was passed by Parliament, to take effect in 2014. The section was repealed despite a finding by the Federal Court of Appeal shortly before that, contrary to the 2009 Tribunal decision, it did not violate freedom of expression and was not contrary to the Charter of Rights and Freedoms.[188]

Repeal of section 13(1) marked the turning point. The marriage between political correctness and human rights was in trouble and unlikely to survive. Alberta Conservative MP Brian Storseth who proposed the repeal said his bill repealed a "flawed piece of legislation" and called Canada's Human Rights Tribunal "a quasi-judicial, secretive body that takes away your natural rights as a Canadian." The Canadian Civil Liberties Association applauded the death of s. 13(1).

The story of section13(1) may not be over quite yet. Hate, sometimes leading to violence, blossoms on the internet. We search for an appropriate response. What legal rules, if any, can address this issue? Lately it has been suggested by some, including members of the Trudeau government, that a more limited version of 13(1) might be appropriate. The section may yet be reborn.

---

188 *Lemire v. Canada (Human Rights Commission)*, 2014 FCA 18 (CanLII) https:// www.canlii.org/en/ca/fca/doc/2014/2014fca18/2014fca18.html?resultIndex=26 (accessed 29 December 2017).

NOT ALL HUMAN RIGHTS ARE HUMAN RIGHTS

Expansive notions of human rights, and a human rights bureaucracy that enforces them, can easily chill the expression of unpopular ideas and opinion. Free expression of unpopular ideas and opinion is an essential component of freedom. We should be wary of "human rights" newly invented by special interest groups. Some may rightfully claim a place in the permanent list of human rights that must be protected. Others are repressive ideas dressed up in misleading costume; all the more dangerous for their deceptive appearance.

CHAPTER EIGHT

THE CANLIT DUMPSTER FIRE

A CULTURAL STRAIGHTJACKET

Why should literature, or any artistic expression, be defined and limited by geography or a particular culture? Don't the best writers and their books transcend where they live and where they're written, often finding inspiration in other ways of life and thought? In Canada, the CanLit concept, and its attendant rivalries and controversies, demands and constraints, has become a cultural straitjacket. It does not promote, protect, and celebrate Canadian writers and their work. Instead, it interferes with their freedom to write what they want and consumes their time in pointless and destructive arguments.

ONCE THE CUTTING EDGE OF BLANDNESS

In 2006 writer and artist Douglas Coupland wrote an article in *The New York Times* explaining "CanLit" to American readers.[189]

---

189 "What is CanLit?" 22 August 2006 https://coupland.blogs.nytimes.com/2006/08/22/what-is-canlit/ (accessed 19 July 2017).

I'm often asked by writers from other lands, "Doug, what, exactly, *is* CanLit?" Basically, but not always, CanLit is when the Canadian government pays you money to write about life in small towns and/or the immigration experience. If the book is written in French, urban life is permitted, but only from a nonbourgeois viewpoint. . . There is also a grimness around CanLit—the same sort of grimness that occurs when beautiful young adults are forbidden to leave home and are forced to tend to aging and dying family members, when they are forbidden to lead their own lives.

Written more than a decade ago, Coupland's explanation is mean but witty. It had the ring of truth at the time (and perhaps today). He is particularly nasty about watching the Giller Prize dinner on television: "It was as if I'd tuned into the Monster Mash—not a soul under 60, and I could practically smell the mummy dust in the room."

Doug Coupland has not been alone in criticizing traditional CanLit. In 2007, the writer Stephen Marche moved from Brooklyn to Toronto. He didn't like what he found, and, in the style of Coupland, was mean but witty.[190]

It's not just that young people write in Brooklyn; writing itself is considered a youthful activity. It's the kind of thing that 32-year-old men who go to work by skateboard do. Literature in Toronto is something your smartest aunt does once she's cozied up in her favourite sweater. And the work therefore is less exciting. The popular novels here are generally ponderous, draped in sanctimony over suffering and history, melodramas in exotic settings. One thing you are not going to get out of a novel on the Giller list or indeed the best-seller list is a good laugh. . . Brooklyn's books are like toys, meant to excite and give pleasure and challenge a little bit. In Canada, we are the oatmeal of world literature. We are on the cutting edge of blandness.

190 "Raging against the tyranny of CanLit," *thestar.com*, 20 October 2007, https://www.thestar.com/news/insight/2007/10/20/raging_against_the_tyranny_of_canlit.html (accessed 19 July 2017).

Marche was still ranting about CanLit in 2015, this time with a somewhat different, almost elegiac, slant: "The sense of writing as a national
project is stuttering to its final end. . . Canadian writers are happy to
say they're from Canada; they just don't want to write about what it
might mean. Canadian literature, in the sense of a literature shaped by
the Canadian nation and shaping the nation, is over."[191]

Until recently, CanLit was unjustifiably considered by its more
extravagant critics as stereotypical and boring, predictable, unimagina-
tive, the product of an entrenched, privileged, and dull establishment. Its
great and venerated living representatives and leaders were the famous
and fabulously successful trio of Alice Munro, Margaret Atwood, and
Michael Ondaatje. Many of those who railed against CanLit were unsuc-
cessful and envious outsiders who seemed personally aggrieved. With
haggard gaze, wearing literary rags, they looked in through the window
of the manor house at an unreachable and sumptuously set banquet
table where Munro, Atwood, and Ondaatje dined. In the CanLit manor
house, all was good and comfortable. The critics were easily fended
off or dismissed. Although, Nick Mount's 2017 book *Arrival*, full of
anecdotes and gossip about CanLit in the 1960s and 1970s, tells a
somewhat different tale, a breezy one of rivalry and intrigue, insecurity,
and sex.[192]

But things have changed dramatically. All hell has broken loose.
Most observers and critics consider that traditional CanLit is no more.
Canada has grown up, they will tell you. What has taken the place of
traditional CanLit? Turmoil. In February 2018, the *Globe and Mail*
described CanLit as a "grudge match that has blown up into an all-out
war."[193] Political correctness is on the march. Blood is on the field. The
right of the literary establishment to interpret Canada freely, as they see

191 "What Was Canadian Literature?" *Partisan Magazine*, 13 April 2015 http://www.par-
    tisanmagazine.com/blog/2015/3/17/what-was-canadian-literature (accessed 19 July
    2017).
192 Nick Mount, *Arrival: The Story of CanLit*, (Toronto: Anansi, 2017). See also Anna
    Porter, *In Other Words: How I Fell in Love with Canada One Book at a Time* (Toronto:
    Simon & Schuster, 2018).
193 Marsha Lederman, "Wading into the choppy waters of CanLit," https://www.
    theglobeandmail.com/arts/books-and-media/twitterature-wading-into-the-choppy-
    waters-of-canlit/article37838912/ (accessed 19 February 2018).

fit, dully if they wish, has come under fire and is badly damaged. The unwilling and central figures in this dramatic development are another trio—Steven Galloway, Joseph Boyden, and Hal Niedzvicki.

STEVEN GALLOWAY

Steven Galloway is a respected writer best known for his 2008 best-selling book *The Cellist of Sarajevo*. He was chair of the Creative Writing Program at the University of British Columbia and a tenured associate professor. He became romantically involved with a middle-aged female student; the relationship lasted several years but apparently ended badly. His former lover and other women students—how many is not clear—complained to the university about Galloway, alleging sexual harassment, bullying, playing favourites, and general bad behaviour. He was suspended by UBC in November, 2015. A university statement cited only "serious allegations" made against him. A month later, the university commissioned a retired judge to investigate the accusations. The judge's findings, given to the university at the end of April 2016, were not made public, but it is believed she rejected the majority of the allegations. In June 2016, UBC fired Galloway, issuing another vague statement, this time citing "irreparable breach of trust" by him. The whole process lacked transparency by any standard.

The CanLit establishment rallied to Galloway's defense. In November 2016, more than eighty Canadian writers signed a letter to the university (the "Open Letter") complaining about lack of due process in the Galloway case.[194] The letter requested, "that the University of British Columbia establish an independent investigation into how this matter has been handled by the Creative Writing Program, the Dean of the Faculty of Arts and the senior administration at UBC." The signatories of the Open Letter included well-known names—James Boyden (the principal organizer and drafter), Michael Ondaatje, Susan Swan, Jane Urquhart, Margaret Atwood, and others.

---

194 The complete text of the letter and a list of the signatories can be found at *UBC Accountable*, http://www.ubcaccountable.com/open-letter/steven-galloway-ubc/

The Open Letter quickly came under attack. The signatories were accused of favouring Galloway rather than sympathizing with the female complainants. Ludicrously, the signatories were described as supporters of rape culture. An "Open Counter-Letter," signed by a fewer number of lesser-known authors, many of them Québecois, expressed anger "because no support was expressed for the female complainant or for the other female students who felt it was safe to make complaints after Steven Galloway was suspended. We are furious that there is only support for Galloway himself because he is a fellow writer, and because he is friends with many who signed the letter."[195]

There were still angry Tweets attacking the Open Letter a year later under the hashtag "ubcaccountable." Margaret Atwood, presumably because of her prominence, was a particular target of angry supporters of Galloway's accusers. Attacks against Atwood continued over a long period. She published an article in the *Globe and Mail* in 2018 entitled "Am I a bad feminist?"[196] She wrote: "My fundamental position is that women are human beings, with the full range of saintly and demonic behaviours this entails, including criminal ones. They're not angels, incapable of wrongdoing. If they were, we wouldn't need a legal system." She focused on the Galloway affair and the appalling conduct of UBC, and criticized the #MeToo movement, calling it "a symptom of a broken legal system."

Once again Twitter erupted. On the day following the article's publication, Atwood sent out more than thirty tweets defending her position, finishing with "Taking a break from being Supreme Being Goddess, omniscient, omnipotent, and responsible for all ills. Sorry I have failed the world so far on gender equality. Maybe stop trying? Will be back later. (Next incarnation maybe.)" As this was happening, venerable Canadian cultural institutions and personalities were engulfed by charges of sexual impropriety, adding fuel to the CanLit flames. Albert Schultz, founder and artistic director of Soulpepper Theatre Company,

195 For the full text of the Open Counter-Letter, see https://www.change.org/p/ubc-accountable-open-counter-letter-about-the-steven-galloway-case-at-ubc (accessed 26 July 2017).
196 13 January 2018 https://www.theglobeandmail.com/opinion/am-i-a-bad-feminist/article37591823/ (accessed 15 January 2018).

resigned. Concordia University's English Department was roiled by allegations from former students about professors' conduct. A member of the poetry board of Coach House Press was accused of sexual harassment and Coach House suspended its poetry publishing program.

The criticisms of the Open Letter were completely unjustified. To insist on due process and transparency is to argue for the justice system in general and not for any one participant. Unaccountably, thirteen signatories of the Open Letter were spooked by the attacks and, not to their credit, formally and quickly withdrew their support.[197] Sometime later, an additional ten writers removed their names from the letter, and there were still calls on Twitter for those who had left their names on the letter to "unsign."[198] The *Guardian* newspaper reported: "The issue has divided Canada's literary scene between the more established authors who signed the letter and the many young, emerging authors who took to social media—and letters in response—to criticise them, arguing that the prestige of the authors would deter those wanting to report possible sexual harassment and assault."[199]

The lack of due process in UBC's handling of the Galloway case was indefensible. Galloway's legal and moral rights to fair treatment were ignored. There are three reasons why this happened. First, UBC was in a governance crisis. Arvind Gupta, who had been president for only a year, mysteriously resigned in the summer of 2015. Shortly afterwards, the chairman of the board of governors, John Montalbano, also resigned. Governance turmoil impeded strong and resolute handling of the crisis. Second, the Galloway case followed on the heels of the 2014 Jian Ghomeshi affair. There was a pervasive hypersensitivity to allegations of sexual misconduct, particularly misconduct by a powerful man directed towards less powerful women. A measured and careful response to such allegations no longer seemed adequate or even possible. An important

---

197 They were Kathryn Kuitenbrouwer, Wayne Johnston, Jean Baird, George Murray, Carrie Snyder, Sheila Heiti, Saleema Nawaz Webster, Camilla Gibb, Miriam Toews, Andrew Westoll, John K. Samson, Erik Rutherford, and Christine Fellows.

198 Those who subsequently "unsigned" included Madeliene Thien, Rawi Hage and Lisa Moore.

199 "Canadian literary world divides over sex charges against novelist," 29 November 2016 https://www.theguardian.com/books/2016/nov/29/canadian-literary-world-sex-charges-against-novelist-steven-galloway (accessed 24 July 2016).

public institution could not be seen to be dragging its heels in such a matter. Third, all of this occurred in the context of the capitulation of universities to political correctness that I have already described.

By the end of 2017, Stephen Galloway was said to be unemployed, living at an unknown location, and—so gossip had it—suffering a mental breakdown. In a 2018 interview with Gary Mason of *The Globe*, Galloway said, "I still think about killing myself on a daily basis. I just don't see much of a future for myself. I'm trying. I'm fighting it. But it's hard."[200] In a lengthy article in the *National Post* in July 2018, giving a plausible and sad account of what happened, Galloway was insistent: "What I must reject is the notion that I am guilty of appalling crimes because someone said that I am. I am not. I did not commit the crime I was accused of. This is not a question of differing interpretations of events: The events alleged against me simply did not happen."[201] Galloway's comment on CanLit: "Recently, 'CanLit' has been described as a dumpster fire. Though juvenile, the description is apt. I've watched what I always imagined to be a kind, inclusive, supportive community turn against itself. The cruelty some people have displayed has been shocking. There have always been those who seek to build themselves up by tearing others down, but I'd never seen so much of it until recently. We have been taken over by a bloodlust in a search for targets of indignation."

An arbitrator awarded Galloway $167,000 in damages in 2018, finding "that certain communications by the University contravened the Grievor's [Galloway's] privacy rights and caused harm to his reputation." On 26 October 2018, Galloway struck back against his accusers, filing a defamation lawsuit against the woman who first accused him of

---

200 "Galloway opens up, says 'life is destroyed'," 11 June 2018 http://globe2go.news-paperdirect.com/epaper/viewer.aspx?noredirect=true (accessed 20 June 2018). For a very detailed account of the Galloway matter (sympathetic to Galloway), see Brad Cran, "A Literary Inquisition: How Novelist Steven Galloway Was Smeared as a Rapist, Even as the Case Against Him Collapsed," *Quillette*, 21 June 2018 https://quillette.com/2018/06/21/a-literary-inquisition-how-novelist-steven-galloway-was-smeared-as-a-rapist-even-as-the-case-against-him-collapsed/ (accessed 23 June 2018).

201 "Steven Galloway in his own words: I'm not a monster. I won't let false allegations define me," 13 July 2018 https://nationalpost.com/opinion/steven-galloway-in-his-own-words-exclusive (accessed 16 July 2018).

sexual assault, two UBC professors (including the well-known novelist Annabel Lyon) who had described him as a "rapist," and a number of people who "recklessly repeated" the woman's allegations on social media.[202] Galloway's attack on those who allegedly defamed him on social media is particularly significant, reminding everyone that social media cannot be used with impunity. The law still counts for something.

JOSEPH BOYDEN

The dumpster fire was soon to engulf Joseph Boyden, the architect of the Open Letter. Boyden went from defending Steven Galloway to defending himself.

Joseph Boyden is a prominent Canadian novelist of undisputed talent. He won the Giller prize in 2008 for his novel *Through Black Spruce*. His books are centered on the culture of Indigenous People. He lectured in the University of British Columbia's Creative Writing Program in 2014-15 when Steven Galloway was chair of the program. He claims Nipmuc and Ojibway heritage and in the past has also claimed Mi'kmaq and Metis antecedents. Many regard him as an Indigenous author. He has been called the face of the country's Indigenous awakening. Not everyone loves him. A Giller prizewinner described him to me as "a piece of work."

Just before Christmas 2016, Boyden's claimed Indigenous ancestry was suddenly challenged in a series of tweets from an account shared by Indigenous writers and journalists. It's unclear why this happened— there has been talk of a mysterious "dossier" exposing Boyden that had been circulating for months and finally came into the open. Then, on December 23, 2016, Jorge Barrera of the Aboriginal Peoples Television Network published a lengthy article skeptical of Boyden's Indigenous identity and detailing the confused and conflicting claims made by Boyden over many years.[203] Boyden responded on Twitter, saying that

202 See Galloway's Statement of Claim https://ubyssey.storage.googleapis.com/media/files/2018/10/Notice_of_Civil_Claim_S-1811588.PDF (accessed 1 November 2018)
203 "Author Joseph Boyden's shape-shifting Indigenous identity," 23 December 2016, *aptn national news* http://aptnnews.ca/2016/12/23/author-joseph-boydens-shape-shifting-indigenous-identity/ (accessed 26 July 2017).

said he was of "mostly Celtic heritage," but also had Nipmuc roots on his father's side and Ojibway roots on his mother's. A public debate began, particularly involving Indigenous writers and artists. It was suggested that Boyden had profited in a variety of ways from asserting a spurious Indigenous identity, including receiving the 2005 $5,000 McNally Robinson Aboriginal Book of the Year award for *Three Day Road*. He was described as a "shape shifter." He was called a "cultural tourist." Boyden's responses to these charges were vague and inconsistent.

This attack led to a separate but related criticism that Boyden, not really an Indigenous person, had unacceptably "appropriated" the Indigenous voice in his fiction. It was said that some of his fiction was "not original" but improperly repeated "traditional tales" that were part of an oral tradition. This, it was argued, amounted to plagiarism. The claim was hard to take seriously. If Boyden used traditional tales in his writing, is that any different, for example, from a composer drawing on folk melodies, something done freely by Dvořák, Smetana, Grieg, Rimsky-Korsakov, Brahms, Liszt, de Falla, Wagner, Sibelius, Vaughan Williams, and Bartók? Was black music improperly appropriated by Bob Dylan, Eric Clapton, the Beatles and the Rolling Stones? What about pictures by Matisse, Braque, and Picasso, inspired by African sculpture? "J.C." of the *Times Literary Supplement* has commented, "It's a dismal, dystopian thought, that artists henceforth are entitled to fashion only works inspired by their own experience–a fallacious notion anyway, since monocultural purity is impossible."[204] J.C. has quoted Bernard Lewis, a scholar of Middle Eastern studies who was accused of cultural appropriation by Edward Said: "If westerners cannot legitimately study the history of Africa or the Middle East, then only fish can study marine biology."[205]

Sponsoring groups cancelled some scheduled Boyden appearances and he withdrew from others. "It's a salacious story, riven with serious

204 "NB," *The Times Literary Supplement*, 12 January 2018, p. 40. I am indebted to J.C. for some of the examples of historic "cultural appropriation" that I mention. He gives many more, and writes, "No great artist appropriated more from other cultures than Shakespeare." In an April 13, 2018 column, J.C. quotes Toni Morrison when asked whether William Styron had the right to write about Nat Turner in *Confessions of Nat Turner*: "He has the right to write about whatever he wants. To suggest otherwise is outrageous."
205 "NB," *The Times Literary Supplement*, 15 June 2018, p. 44.

implications, and yet unavoidably sad," journalist Terry Glavin wrote. "A kind of consensus is emerging among white people around the proposition that Boyden is being cruelly drowned in a well of faddish and poisonous aboriginal identity politics."[206] The opposite view was forcefully expressed by Robert Jago, an Indigenous journalist. "While he may self-identify as one of us, he has yet to point to a community that recognizes him as such, though he has tried to point to many different communities. . . For non-Natives to call this investigation a "lynching" or a racial witch hunt is the epitome of colonial arrogance. . . When we Indigenous people present pointed questions to what is in effect, a shady politician, we're treated to grade-school lectures about bad form. We're told to accept someone as one of us who doesn't meet our standards of belonging, because he meets a non-Native standard for a type of race-based identity that we don't recognize."[207]

Boyden published a lengthy justification of his position in *Maclean's* magazine in August 2017.[208]

I, along with others in my family who were so inclined, have spit into plastic tubes and sent our mucus off for DNA testing. And guess what? The verdict is: we're mutts. Celtic DNA. Check. Native American DNA. Check. DNA from the Arctic. Cool. I didn't know that. Explains my love for winter. Some Ashkenazi Jew? I love it. . . Those who were most vocal in their arguments against me and my family over the holidays last year were adamant, though, that it wasn't about DNA at all when they spoke about my right to call myself an Indigenous person. It's about whom you claim, and who claims you. If I am accepted by people in Indigenous communities, if I have been traditionally adopted by a number of people in Indigenous communities, if my DNA test shows I have

206 "Glavin: The many twists and turns of the Joseph Boyden controversy," *Ottawa Citizen*, 4 January 2017 http://ottawacitizen.com/opinion/columnists/glavin-the-many-twists-and-turns-of-the-joseph-boyden-controversy (accessed 31 July 2017).

207 "The Boyden Controversy Is Not about Bloodline," *Walrus*, 10 January 2017 https://thewalrus.ca/the-boyden-controversy-is-not-about-bloodline/ (accessed 2 August 2017).

208 "My name is Joseph Boyden," *Maclean's*, 2 August 2017 http://www.macleans.ca/news/canada/my-name-is-joseph-boyden/ (accessed 6 August 2017).

Indigenous blood, if I have engaged my whole career in publicly defending Indigenous rights as well as using my public recognition as an author to shine light on Indigenous issues, am I not, in some way, Indigenous?

The consensus seemed to be that the *Maclean's* article was weakly argued, and that by publishing it Boyden did himself more harm than good.

Why does anyone care about Boyden's cultural claims? Eric Andrew-Gee has written that the debate raises questions important to all Canadians. "What does being Indigenous entail? Is it an ethnicity? A culture? A polity? A worldview? Even something like a religion, or spiritual practice? And then, who gets to claim the mantle? Who is Indigenous and who isn't?"[209] Views differ on whether this debate is important or not, and on whether Joseph Boyden is an exemplary bridge between two cultures or an opportunistic self-promoter. One thing that is absent in the argument is cogent, even-handed criticism of Boyden's books. On social media, some have said that they won't buy or read his books anymore because of what, in their eyes, is his reprehensible behaviour.

The cultural appropriation debate staggered on. In July 2018, the Montreal Jazz Festival cancelled Robert Lepage's show SLAV, which featured a largely white cast singing songs composed by black slaves, because of criticism that it was an example of cultural appropriation. Said Lepage of theatre: "This ancient ritual requires that we borrow, for the duration of a performance, someone else's look, voice, accent and at times even gender. . . But when we are no longer allowed to step into someone else's shoes, when it is forbidden to identify with someone else, theatre is denied its very nature, it is prevented from performing its primary function and is thus rendered meaningless."[210]

209 "The making of Joseph Boyden," *Globe and Mail*, 4 August 2017 https://www.theglobeandmail.com/arts/books-and-media/joseph-boyden/article35881215/ (accessed 6 August 2017).
210 See "Robert Lepage says decision to cancel SLAV show a 'blow to artistic freedom'," *Globe and Mail*, 7 July 2018 http://globe2go.newspaperdirect.com/epaper/viewer.aspx?noredirect=true (accessed 10 July 2018).

Lepage subsequently cancelled the production in Paris of *Kanata*, a play about the relationship between whites and Aboriginal Peoples, which had no Indigenous actors and was attacked as culturally insensitive (later the show went ahead at Paris's Théâtre du Soleil). Eventually, Lepage, it seems, felt repentant—sort of. In December 2018, in a public letter, he acknowledged "clumsiness and misjudgments."

HAL NIEDVICKI

The Writers' Union of Canada (TWUC) is a venerable institution. It was founded in 1973 by a group of about a hundred writers who wanted to lobby government on cultural policy matters and generally promote the interests of those who wrote for a living. The prime movers included Graeme Gibson, Margaret Atwood, Margaret Laurence, and Marian Engel. By 2017, about two thousand professional writers, with diverse interests and backgrounds, and differing degrees of eminence, belonged to TWUC.[211]

Hal Niedzviecki is a Canadian novelist. In 2017, he was editor of *Write*, TWUC's quarterly magazine for its membership. In the spring issue of the magazine, which featured Indigenous writers, Niedzviecki wrote an editorial about cultural appropriation. It said, in part: "I don't believe in cultural appropriation. In my opinion, anyone, anywhere, should be encouraged to imagine other peoples, other cultures, other identities. I'd go so far as to say that there should even be an award for doing so—the Appropriation Prize for best book by an author who writes about people who aren't even remotely like her or him."

Pandemonium ensued. Other contributors to the *Write* Indigenous issue expressed outrage on Twitter and elsewhere. Several members of the magazine's editorial board resigned. Something called the TWUC Equity Task Force issued a statement about the Niedzviecki column which said in part, "We are angry and appalled by the publication. . . In the context of working to recruit writers historically marginalized in the union, this essay contradicts and dismisses the racist systemic

---

211 I have been a member of TWUC for a number of years.

barriers faced by Indigenous writers and other racialized writers. This is especially insulting given that this issue features the work of many Indigenous writers." Niedzviecki had little choice but to resign quickly as *Write*'s editor.

On May 10, TWUC issued a formal apology to the world. "The Writers' Union of Canada deeply regrets the pain and offence caused by an opinion article in our member publication, *Write* magazine. The Writers' Prompt piece offended and hurt readers, contributors to the magazine and members of the editorial board. We apologize unequivocally."

There was some backlash to the apology, seen by some as craven and ill judged, and to Niedzviecki's treatment by TWUC. Jonathan Kay wrote in the *National Post*, "TWUC's over-the-top apology describes the 'pain' that the article allegedly caused. It's part of what may be described as the medicalization of the marketplace of ideas: It is no longer enough to say that you merely disagree with something. Rather, the author must be stigmatized as a sort of dangerous thought criminal."[212] Two days after his article was published, Kay resigned as editor of *Walrus* magazine, although he says his resignation was not directly related to the cultural appropriation debate. Kenneth Whyte, former editor of *Maclean's*, Steve Ladurantaye, managing editor of CBC's The National, and other prominent journalists, expressed support for Niedzviecki, and even said they would help fund an Appropriation Prize (later, under fire, outgunned, many of these commentators backed off).

Cultural appropriation had been a sensitive subject in Canada, and for the Writers' Union, for some time. It was a subject of controversy as early as 1989 at the Union's Annual General Meeting in Kitchener, Ontario. It is a real and complex issue calling for thoughtful and dispassionate debate. The intense Niedzviecki controversy, much of it not thoughtful and not dispassionate, was made possible by the advent of social media. On Twitter, once again, anyone could express an instant opinion in extreme terms and expect wide and gratifying

212 "Cultural appropriation should be debated. Too bad Canada's Writers Union instead chose to debase itself," 12 May 2017 http://nationalpost.com/opinion/ jonathan-kay-cultural-appropriation-should-be-debated-too-bad-canadas-writers-union-instead-chose-to-debase-itself (accessed 2 January 2018).

circulation. There was no need to await the ponderous pronouncement of an establishment professor in a learned journal. Those who before had been largely voiceless could now confront the literary and media establishment head on. It was a CanLit version of the Arab Spring.

The Niedzviecki affair was different from the Galloway and Boyden imbroglios. In the Galloway matter, there were distracting allegations of sexual misbehaviour and breach of trust on the one side, and a plausible charge of lack of due process on the other. In Boyden, the main issue was alleged personal deception about spurious Indigenous roots (although that charge intersected with the cultural appropriation issue). In Niedzviecki, a writer was, quite simply, pilloried for an opinion that was seen to be out of tune with the times.

WHO CARES?

Now the CanLit community is divided and the division is bitter. It is between the establishment, older and successful writers, your smartest aunt in her favourite sweater, who may have signed the Galloway Open Letter, and have some sympathies for Joseph Boyden and Hal Niedzviecki, and younger writers, thirty-two-year-old men who go to work by skateboard, who see the establishment as stuck in the old image of CanLit, too quick to defend the bad behaviour of their own, and ignorant of what is politically correct. CanLit is no longer the cutting edge of blandness but a sea of turmoil. Passion and pressure has frightened some writers, who are now reluctant to voice views that they think might get them into trouble. Ideas involved in the CanLit debate, particularly the idea of cultural appropriation, are being used to shut people up.

ONLY TWO HUNDRED?

A senior CanLit observer, someone who signed the Open Letter, said to me, "You know, there's only two hundred people in Canada who care about this stuff." That's true if what you're doing is making a list of those who sign open letters and letters attacking open letters, who investigate the cultural provenance and purity of writers, and who are determined to find a politically incorrect comment around every literary corner. It's not true if you accept that writers are the prime interpreters and historians of our age. Then, it matters enormously if they are badgered, harassed, and intimidated. If that happens we all lose, for our freedom to memorialize, understand and reform our society is diminished.

PART FOUR

PUBLIC SPACE

We need the police to keep order and shield us from harm but they themselves can be a threat to freedom, particularly in the counter-terrorism state.

Privacy is a chimera. There is almost nothing about ourselves that we are able hide, and there is little information about others that we can avoid. It is impossible to be left alone.

Sometimes it seems as if we have the worst of all possible worlds, a toxic mixture of no personal privacy and excessive government secrecy.

CHAPTER NINE

POLICE

WHO WILL PROTECT US?

As we have seen, it can be dangerous to rely on non-elected officials—judges—to protect us from those we have voted into office. The police present a similar danger. We need them to keep order and shield us from harm but they can be a threat themselves. Justice Ian Binnie of the Supreme Court of Canada caught part of the predicament in *R. v. Grant* (2009): "While the uniformed police embody society's collective desire for public order and livable and safe communities, they also present a serious and continuing risk to the individual's right to be left alone by the state.[213]

The police are the most visible manifestation of the state and its power. Most of those who work for the state are tucked away in remote office buildings in distant cities and cannot be reached easily even by telephone or email. The police are not tucked away. They may no longer walk the beat as they once did, but they drive the streets in intimidating automobiles tricked out with lights, sirens, radios, and computers and, in most parts of Canada, can be summoned quickly. Police stations occupy prime real estate, often dominating the streetscape. Ordinary citizens may never meet a cabinet minister, senior government bureaucrat, or judge, but will probably see a policeman every day, certainly if they live in a city. And they will have feelings about the police, perhaps negative; after all, you're more likely to be handed a speeding ticket by a surly constable, or be carded if you're Black, than be rescued from distress by a polite policeman. (A number of studies have shown that politeness and consideration by the police enhance their moral credibility and the likeliness of citizen cooperation. What a surprise!) And the police exercise the state's monopoly on legitimate violence in a civilian context. Only a policeman—in some circumstances—can hit you over the head with a stick without breaking the law.

Almost every day, the newspapers give us examples of poor police organization or general incompetence, sometimes eye popping. These examples have a pernicious effect, encouraging a debilitating loss of confidence in the constabulary and the legal system in general. Anyone who reads Justice John Major's 2010 fine report on the hapless Royal Canadian Mounted Police conduct surrounding the 1985 Air India bombing,[214] or considers the Toronto police bumbling investigation into serial killings over many years in Toronto's gay village,[215] will wonder about the safety of our society and the ability of the police to protect citizens. When the police behave with distinction, as they did in the April 2018 Yonge Street van killings in Toronto, the community heaves a collective sigh of relief and gratitude.[216] But my concern here is not so much police competence, or lack of it, as police culture and rules.

---

214 *Air India Flight 182: A Canadian Tragedy,* Report of the Commission of Inquiry into the Investigation of the Bombing of Air India Flight 182 http://publications.gc.ca/collections/collection_2010/bcp-pco/CP32-89-4-2010-eng.pdf (accessed 28 March 2018). This report has not been given the attention it deserves.

215 See, for example, Justin Ling, "Are police doing enough to find missing people in Toronto's Gay Village?" *Maclean's,* 15 December 2017 http://www.macleans.ca/news/canada/are-police-doing-enough-to-find-missing-people-in-torontos-gay-village/ (accessed 16 April 2018).

216 Betsy Powell, "'Cop deserves a medal': Toronto officer praised for cool response in tense standoff with van suspect," *Toronto Star,* 24 April 2018 https://www.thestar.com/news/gta/2018/04/23/cop-deserves-a-medal-cool-response-from-toronto-officer-at-tense-standoff-wins-praise.html (accessed 24 April 2018).

ADAM NOBODY AND OFFICER BUBBLES

The biggest policing event in Canadian history was the June 2010 Toronto meeting of the G20 heads of government. The Toronto Police Service, the Royal Canadian Mounted Police, the Ontario Provincial Police, the Peel Regional Police Service, and the Canadian Forces, were all on duty. The event was a policing disaster. The financial cost was enormous. The relevant law was never explained to the general public or anyone else. There was violence between police and demonstrators. Heads were broken. Later, heads rolled.[217]

One G20 demonstrator, Adam Nobody (his real name), was beaten by a policeman on the lawn of Queen's Park, an incident videotaped by another demonstrator.[218] The policeman, Constable Babak Andalib-Goortani, the only law enforcement officer involved in the G20 imbroglio to be criminally charged, was found guilty of assault and received a suspended sentence. Constable Andalib-Goortani was also docked five-days' pay by a police disciplinary tribunal. Another policeman, who became known as Officer Bubbles, was caught on a YouTube video threatening a G20 protester who blew bubbles at him (the protestor was later arrested).[219] G20 policing, encapsulated in the stories of Adam Nobody and Officer Bubbles, was a public relations disaster for the police and government. Litigation and public inquiries ensued. The calamity exemplifies Canada's issue with the police. They are there to protect and serve us. But what if, out of control, they become the enemy?

Nathalie Des Rosiers, who succeeded Alan Borovoy as general counsel of the Canadian Civil Liberties Union and is now Master of Massey College in Toronto, together with Graeme Norton, a Vancouver lawyer who worked for the CCLU, has described the G20 Summit as a critical

---

217 For a compelling, if perhaps biased, account of this fiasco, see Alok Mukherjee (with Tim Harper), *Excessive Force: Toronto's Fight to Reform City Policing*, (Madeira Park, BC: Douglas and McIntyre, 2018), chapter 3. Mukherjee is a former chair of the Toronto Police Services Board, the body that provides civilian oversight of the Toronto police. His book is an interesting, if self-serving, account of relations between the police, the Police Services Board, and City Hall.

218 See https://www.youtube.com/watch?v=NI2b8igEYc8

219 See https://www.youtube.com/watch?v=PGMTm3QRwEc

moment in Canadian policing. "It saw the largest number of mass arrests in Canadian history outside of war time, left many Torontonians feeling as if their city had been temporarily turned into a police state. . . Many of those arrested were rounded up in indiscriminate mass arrests, while others alleged they had been subjected to excessive police force, verbal and physical threats, and significant violations of their personal dignity and constitutional rights."[220] Well over a thousand people were arrested. One of the best-known incidents, leading to mass arrests and arbitrary detentions, many of them unlawful and unconstitutional—often, for example, detainees were denied access to legal counsel—was the highly aggressive police kettling of protestors and journalists at the major Toronto downtown intersection of Queen and Spadina. Kettling, a controversial tactic formally forbidden by RCMP policy, is the forcible containment of a crowd within a confined area.

The G20 affair led to multiple investigations of police conduct and several court cases. Des Rosiers and Norton list ten official reviews of police action and note that there were also investigations by Ontario's Special Investigations Unit (responsible for investigating incidents of serious injury or death involving police officers), by the Ontario Office of the Independent Review Director which considers individual police misconduct complaints, and also observation reports by various civil society groups. The most important review was conducted by Justice John Morden for the Toronto Police Services Board.[221] Kent Roach has written that the Morden Report "revealed in unequivocal terms the democratic deficit that besets policing."[222] This democratic deficit extends to a broad range of policing policies, including training, deployment, stop policies, use of weapons, and conditions of police custody. Roach writes, "The lack of engagement with democratic control and

---

220 "Civilian Oversight and the 2010 G20 Summit in Toronto," in Ian D. Scott (editor), *Issues in Civilian Oversight of Policing in Canada*, (Toronto: Canada Law Book, 2014), p. 111. This collection of essays is the most thorough and comprehensive study available of civilian oversight in Canada. Scott is a former Director of Ontario's Special Investigations Unit.

221 *Independent Civilian Review in Matters Relating to the G20 Summit*, June 2012 http://www.tpsb.ca/g20/ICRG20Mordenreport.pdf (accessed 28 March 2018).

222 "Models of Civilian Police Review: The Objectives and Mechanisms of Legal and Political Regulation of the Police," in Scott, note 217, p. 302.

responsibility of the police reflects a deeper malaise about the state of democracy."[223]

The general public's abhorrence over what happened was not assuaged by inquiries and reports. Des Rosiers and Norton concluded in their analysis of G20 policing:

> There is little accountability for the long-term damage done to freedom of association, freedom of expression, and public trust in police. On a systemic level, there has been little done to heal the relationship between protesters and police or to ensure that public confidence in the policies regained. There is no guarantee that the types of police excesses that happened during the G20 could not happen again.
>
> On the law reform side, some of the key issues that remain unresolved include the broad discretion afforded to police through breach of the peace arrest powers, the scope of expression-restricting bail conditions, the constitutionality of "kettling," the legality of undercover police informers' illegal actions, and the surveillance of dissenting groups.[224]

In March 2018, the *Safer Ontario Act* (Bill 175), put forward by the doomed Wynne Liberal government, came into force. Much of the Bill dealt with police accountability. So, for example, a new office, the Inspector General of Policing, was created. The official Explanatory Note to the legislation explained, "Any person may complain to the Inspector General that a member of one of the boards regulated under the Act is not complying with the applicable code of conduct. Complaints may also be made about various other policing matters. The Inspector General is to consider the complaints and, if there are grounds for investigation, investigate them." The existing Special Investigations Unit, Office of the Independent Police Review Director, and Ontario Civilian Police Commission, were given a limited overhaul and expanded mandates. Reaction to Bill 175, from both police associations and critics of

223 p. 304.
224 pp. 133–4.

the police, ranged from indifferent to tepid to hostile. On June 7, 2018 Ontario elected a new Conservative government, with Doug Ford as premier. A month later, the Ford government's Throne Speech said that the government intended to "free police from onerous restrictions that treat those in uniform as subjects of suspicion and scorn." Bill 175 was characterized as "anti-police." In 2019, the Comprehensive Ontario Police Services Act (COPS) was introduced to replace Bill 175. COPS narrowed the role of the Special Investigations Unit, and replaced the Office of the Independent Police Review Director with a new Law Enforcement Complaints Agency with limited powers. Strangely, given the official rhetoric, COPS kept much of the maligned Bill 175 intact. ·

CARDING

"Carding," sometimes called "street checks" or (absurdly) "community contacts policy," is the police practice of stopping a person on the street, requesting identification, and asking questions about what that person is doing, where he lives, where he's been, the names of his friends, and anything else that tickles the policeman's fancy.[225] The encounter is documented, originally on a card, now in a computer database. Typically, documentation includes comments on the person's appearance, including his ethnicity. Justice Michael Tulloch of the Ontario Court of Appeal, in a 2018 report to the Ontario Minister of Community Safety and Correctional Services,[226] defined carding as when "a police officer randomly asks an individual to provide identifying information when there is no objectively suspicious activity, the individual is not suspected of any offence and there is no reason to believe that the individual has any information on any offence."

225 For a detailed account of carding across Canada, and its deleterious effects, see Robyn Maynard, *Policing Black Lives: Violence in Canada from Slavery to the Present*, (Nova Scotia: Fernwood Publishing, 2017), pp. 88–91.
226 *Report of the Independent Street Checks Review*, https://www.mcscs.jus.gov.on.ca/english/Policing/StreetChecks/ReportIndependentStreetChecksReview2018.html (accessed 26 March 2019).

In various forms, carding has been and still is (at the end of 2018) used in Toronto, Hamilton, Halifax, Ottawa, Windsor, London, Saskatoon, Edmonton, Calgary, Vancouver, and other Canadian cities. Many studies and investigative reports have concluded that it informally incorporates a form of racial profiling, primarily targeting non-white males.[227] Some attempts have been made in some jurisdictions to mitigate the policy by ending arbitrary or race-based stops,[228] with limited success.

Journalist and Black activist Desmond Cole published an influential article in 2015 about carding in *Maclean's* magazine.[229] Cole wrote with passion: "I have been stopped, if not always carded, at least fifty times by the police in Toronto, Kingston, and across southern Ontario. By now, I expect it could happen in any neighbourhood, day or night, whether I am alone or with friends. These interactions don't scare me anymore. They make me angry. Because of that unwanted scrutiny, that discrimi-

---

227 See, for example, a series of articles in the *Toronto Star* – https://www.thestar.com/ news/gta/knowntopolice.html (accessed 27 March 2018). See also Sunny Dhillon, "Vancouver Police Department's use of carding disproportionately targets Indigenous people," *Globe and Mail*, 4 June 2018 https://www.theglobeandmail.com/canada/ british-columbia/article-vancouver-police-departments-use-of-carding-disproportion-ately/ (accessed 8 June 2018). Dhillon reported: "Street checks conducted by the Vancouver Police Department disproportionately involved people who were Indigenous, according to data released by the force. . . The data, recently posted to the department website, said 16 per cent of those who were subjected to street checks last year were Indigenous people, who make up about 2 per cent of Vancouver's population. The data said people who were black, about 1 per cent of Vancouver's population, were also disproportionately stopped. About 5 per cent of street checks last year were of black people."

228 New Ontario rules on carding, which came into force in January 2017, can be found at https://www.ontario.ca/laws/regulation/160058 (accessed 27 March 2018). Under these rules, a police officer who stops someone and requests information has to explain why he is asking and is obliged to tell the person he can refuse the request. There has been pushback by some police. In June 2018, Peel Region Police Chief Jennifer Evans publicly blamed the new carding rules for a rise in violent crime, saying it has "empowered" criminals. See Molly Hayes and Jeff Gray, "Police chief slams crackdown on carding, *Globe and Mail*, 29 June 2018 http://globe2go.newspaperdirect.com/ epaper/viewer.aspx?noredirect=true (accessed 29 June 2018).

229 "The Skin I'm In: I've been interrogated by police more than 50 times—all because I'm black," 21 April 2015 https://torontolife.com/city/life/skin-im-ive-interrogated-police-50-times-im-black/ (accessed 29 March 2018).

natory surveillance, I'm a prisoner in my own city." Alok Mukherjee, once chair of the Police Services Board, later wrote that Cole's article "changed the debate, and suddenly the fight against profiling and carding was no longer limited to community activists, lawyers and a handful of reporters."[230]

Those who support carding point to its usefulness in solving crimes and suppressing criminality. They argue that a certain amount of police intrusion into citizens' lives is necessary and is accepted by society. For example, closed circuit television cameras can be found almost everywhere and are routinely used, without controversy, to discourage and solve crime. And it is provable that certain groups—young men in particular—are more likely to be involved in crime, and it is therefore not unreasonable for the police to pay them especial attention.

Professors Anthony Doob and Rosemary Gartner, of the University of Toronto's Centre for Criminology & Sociolegal Studies, published in January 2017 an extensive study of the effects of police stops for the Toronto Police Services Board.[231] A key point in the paper is the difficulty in scientifically evaluating the evidence on police crackdowns. The Doob/Gartner conclusion was muted but it generally opposed carding.

> Looking at the issue that we started with–street stops by the police of people who have not apparently committed an offence–it is quite clear to us that it is easy to exaggerate the usefulness of these stops, and hard to find data that supports the usefulness of continuing to carry them out.
>
> This is not to say that the police should not be encouraged to continue to talk to people on the street. But the evidence that it is useful to stop, question, identify, and/or search people and to record and store this information simply because the police and citizens "are there" appears to us to be substantially outweighed by convincing evidence of the harm of such practices both to the

---

230 Note 214, p. 140.
231 *Understanding the Impact of Police Stops* http://criminology.utoronto.ca/wp-content/uploads/2017/03/DoobGartnerPoliceStopsReport-17Jan2017r.pdf (accessed 27 March 2018). Among other things, the Doob/Gartner study presents the evidence for disproportionate carding of racialized groups.

person subject to them and to the long term and overall relationship of the police to the community.[232]

Carding sows social dissension. In can easily be seen as discriminatory oppression of racialized groups. There is little, if any, evidence that carding reduces crime. There is evidence that it does harm. The December 2018 Tulloch Report to the Ontario government, thoughtful and far-reaching, found no evidence of carding being a useful investigative tool and recommended that the practice be ended. The government has shown little interest in the report. Meanwhile, a 2019 report to the Nova Scotia Human Rights Commission showed that in Halifax, Black Nova Scotians are stopped five times more than their white counterparts.[233]

RACIALIZED GROUPS

Carding is only one example of how Canadian police treat racialized groups. These groups include Indigenous people, African-Canadians, those of Asian background, and other non-whites. Evidence of a systemic problem is overwhelming.

The *Toronto Star* reported in 2017 that for the decade ending in 2014 the Toronto police arrested three times as many Black people as white people per capita for possession of marijuana.[234] "The disparity is largely due to targeting of Black people by Toronto police, according to criminologists and defence lawyers interviewed by the *Star*, who note that surveys show little difference in marijuana use between Black and white people." The marijuana statistics mirror those for carding. The Toronto Police Accountability Coalition has commented, "One gets the sense that the [Toronto Police Services] Board does not place racial

232 p. A22.
233 *Halifax, Nova Scotia: Street Checks Report*, March 2019 https://humanrights.novascotia. ca/sites/default/files/editor-uploads/halifax_street_checks_report_march_2019_0.pdf (accessed 28 March 2019).
234 Jim Rankin and Sandro Contenta, "Toronto marijuana arrests reveal 'startling' racial divide," 6 July 2017 https://www.thestar.com/news/insight/2017/07/06/toronto-marijuana-arrests-reveal-startling-racial-divide.html (accessed 26 April 2018).

discrimination by officers, and how this might be curtailed, anywhere near the top of its agenda. Disgraceful."[235]

In April 2018, the Canadian Broadcasting Corporation made public a study of four hundred and sixty-one deaths during police interventions from 2000 to 2017.[236] "Nationally," the study reports, "the vast majority of victims of police shootings are Caucasian, which is not surprising given that this is the largest racial group in the country. However, when taking into account the racial and ethnic composition of the overall population, two distinct groups are overwhelmingly over-represented in these encounters: black and Indigenous people. For example, black people in Toronto made up on average 8.3 per cent of the population during the seventeen-year window, but represent nearly 37 per cent of the victims. In Winnipeg, Indigenous people represent on average 10.6 per cent of the population, but account for nearly two thirds of victims."

In December 2018, an interim report released by the Ontario Human Rights Commission found that black people were "grossly overrepresented" in about four hundred and thirty cases, reviewed by the Special Investigations Unit, in which force was used by Toronto police.[237] The first two paragraphs of the interim report's executive summary told a bleak story:

> Between 2013 and 2017, a Black person in Toronto was nearly 20 times more likely than a White person to be involved in a fatal shooting by the Toronto Police Service (TPS). Despite making up only 8.8% of Toronto's population, data obtained by the Ontario Human Rights Commission (OHRC) from the Special Investigations Unit (SIU) shows that Black people were over-represented in use of force cases (28.8%), shootings (36%), deadly encounters (61.5%) and fatal

235 Toronto Police Accountability Bulletin No. 108, 26 April 2018.
236 Jacques Marcoux and Katie Nicholson, *Deadly Force*, https://newsinteractives.cbc.ca/longform-custom/deadly-force (accessed 6 April 2018).
237 See *A Collective Impact: Interim report on the inquiry into racial profiling and racial discrimination of Black persons by the Toronto Police Service*, http://www.ohrc.on.ca/en/public-interest-inquiry-racial-profiling-and-discrimination-toronto-police-service/collective-impact-interim-report-inquiry-racial-profiling-and-racial-discrimination-black (accessed 26 March 2019).

shootings (70%). Black men make up 4.1% of Toronto's population, yet were complainants in a quarter of SIU cases alleging sexual assault by TPS officers.

SIU Director's Reports reveal a lack of legal basis for police stopping or detaining Black civilians in the first place; inappropriate or unjustified searches during encounters; and unnecessary charges or arrests. The information analyzed by the OHRC also raises broader concerns about officer misconduct, transparency and accountability. Courts and arms-length oversight bodies have found that TPS officers have sometimes provided biased and untrustworthy testimony, have inappropriately tried to stop the recording of incidents and/ or have failed to cooperate with the SIU.

Also in December 2018, the Ontario Office of the Independent Police Review Director (abolished in 2019 by the Doug Ford government) reported that systemic racism permeated the Thunder Bay police service,[238] just days after the Ontario Civilian Police Commission issued a report on its investigation of the Thunder Bay Police Service Board[239] which concluded that the board had failed to recognize and address a pattern of violence and racism against Indigenous people in Thunder Bay. This led to the disbanding of the board and the appointment of a temporary administrator.

Robyn Maynard has written that, although Canada is known as a land of multiculturalism and relative racial harmony, "Black lives in Canada have been exposed to a structural violence that has been tacitly or explicitly condoned by multiple state or state-funded institutions."[240] Maynard documents this violence in impressive scholarly detail. Structural violence extends far further than the country's black population. "In a society like Canada that remains stratified by race, gender,

---

238 *Broken Trust: Indigenous People and the Thunder Bay Police Service*, http://oiprd.on.ca/ wp-content/uploads/OIPRD-BrokenTrust-Final-Accessible-E.pdf (accessed 26 March 2019).

239 https://slasto-tsapno.gov.on.ca/ocpc-ccop/wp-content/uploads/sites/5/2018/12/ TBPSB_Investigation_Final_Report_-_EN-FINAL-1.pdf (accessed 26 March 2019).

240 Note 222, p. 4. Maynard has a broad view of the "policing" concept that goes far beyond the criminal justice system.

class and citizenship," Maynard writes, "state violence acts to defend and maintain inequitable social, racial and economic divisions. As such, the victims of this violence have been the dispossessed: primarily but not exclusively people who are Indigenous, Black, of colour, particularly those who are poor, women, lacking Canadian citizenship, living with mental illness or disabilities, sexual minorities and other marginalized populations."[241] State violence against dispossessed groups goes far beyond policing. It includes policing, of course, but may encompass almost all state activity.

However bad things may seem in Canada, they are far worse in the United States. In April, 2018, Howard French, a black man, once a reporter at *The New York Times* and now a professor of journalism at Columbia University, published a review of two important books in the *Times Literary Supplement*, entitled "The crime of being black."[242] After being abroad, French returned to New York in 1986. "Mostly invisible to the general public," he wrote, "which in any case broadly supported 'tough' policing, and far more insidious, were the tactics just then coming into widespread use by the New York Police Department and police forces in many other cities around the country, whereby black men were regularly stopped for hostile questioning and searched for drugs, contraband or weapons, without any obvious cause for suspicion beyond race and age." Both books, he said, "launch into an extended history of how municipal police departments normalized practices that involved the unprovoked stopping of black men in the street, followed by aggressive questioning and humiliating public body searches–a set of behaviours that has kept this segment of the population in a state of what might be called provisional liberty, and inflicted not only routine indignities but lasting psychological wounds."

The situation in the United Kingdom is much the same. A 2018 study by the London School of Economics found that Black Britons are

---

241 p. 6.
242 https://www.the-tls.co.uk/articles/public/the-crime-of-being-black/ (accessed 18 May 2018). French was reviewing two books – *Chokehold: Policing black men* by Paul Butler, and *I Can't Breathe: The Killing that Started a Movement* by Matt Taibbi. (Taibbi is also the author of the brilliant and poignant *The Divide: American Injustice in the Age of the Wealth Gap*.)

nine times more likely to be stopped and searched for drugs than white people.[243] *The Guardian* reported early in 2019: "Black people make up 15.6% of London's population while white people make up 59.8%. In 2018, 43% of searches were of black people, while 35.5% were of white people, according to official figures from the London Mayor's Office for Policing and Crime (MOPAC). A briefing note for senior officials, seen by *The Guardian*, says "disproportionality has increased", with the likelihood of black people being stopped 4.3 times higher than white people in 2018, compared with 2.6 times more likely in 2014, according to figures from MOPAC, which oversees the Met."[244]

THE COUNTER-TERRORISM STATE

My first plane trip, on a Trans-Canada Airlines Douglas DC-8, was in 1962, from Winnipeg to Montreal. More than fifty years later, aircraft look much the same and fly at more or less the same speed, but everything else is completely different. In 1962, there was no airport security. You could stroll on and off your aircraft at the airport, and relatives and friends could freely come to the gate to wave goodbye or greet you upon arrival. The first whiff of trouble was the May 1, 1961 hijacking to Cuba of a flight from Miami bound for Key West, Florida. From a security point of view, things then went rapidly downhill. Now airports are an armed camp, the romance and pleasure squeezed out of them by security procedures and surly, ill paid, and poorly-educated security staff who mechanically and humourlessly administer pointless protocols.

In the autumn of 1966, Harold Wilson, prime minister of the United Kingdom, came to Exeter College, Oxford, for dinner. The then-Rector

243 Mark Townsend, "Racial bias in police stop and search getting worse, report reveals," *The Guardian*, 13 October 2018 https://www.theguardian.com/law/2018/oct/13/racial-bias-police-stop-and-search-policy-black-people-report?CMP=Share_iOSApp_Other (accessed 14 October 2018).

244 Vikram Dodd, "Met police 'disproportionately' use stop and search powers on black people," 26 January 2019 https://www.theguardian.com/law/2019/jan/26/met-police-disproportionately-use-stop-and-search-powers-on-black-people?CMP=share_btn_link (accessed 27 March 2019).

of Exeter, Sir Kenneth Wheare, was an old friend of Wilson. I was a student at the College. The prime minister, sitting in the front passenger seat, arrived in an ordinary Rover sedan driven by a plainclothes police officer. There was nobody else with him—no police on motorcycles, no motorcade, no helicopters, no snipers positioned on nearby buildings, no police shooing rubberneckers away. Today, the UK prime minister travels in a specially manufactured car that cost over half-a-million dollars and features an explosive resistant steel plate underneath the body, a titanium and Kevlar lined cabin, armoured windows with bullet-resistant glass, run-flat tires, gun ports enabling bodyguards to return fire at any attackers, and a mechanism for releasing tear gas. The prime minister's car is normally escorted by several unmarked Range Rovers. Who knows what other security precautions are taken. Ask about them, and you may be taken in for questioning.

In the UK, in those days, the archetypal police officer was Dixon of Dock Green, a fictional police constable in a popular BBC TV series. Dixon, friendly and gentle, yet firm, would stroll the beat, unarmed and alone, offering his famous greeting, "Evening, all." If you took the train from Oxford to London's Paddington Station in the late 1960s, there were no police to be seen when you arrived. Now when you arrive at Paddington there are often groups of police dressed in black, wearing large lace-up military boots and dark glasses, with miniature receivers in their ears, carrying automatic weapons, with the word POLICE in big letters on the back of their jackets. (By the way, in Greater London there are about 500,000 CCTV cameras. The UK has about one CCTV camera for every fourteen people.)

What's changed? Terrorism arrived, that's what. A small number of people, motivated by ideology or political belief or personal grievance, or driven by mental illness, have upended the world with indiscriminate violence and have inflicted huge, multifarious costs on society. Terrorism has been spectacularly successful. One consequence has been to give the police and other institutions of government a more prominent but paradoxically more secret role in the community. Another has been legislation that threatens human and civil rights. All this has been made possible by an absurd and incoherent overreaction to the so-called "terrorist threat." Harvard psychologist Steven Pinker has pointed out that terrorism poses a miniscule threat—you're more likely to die from drowning in the bathtub than at the hands of a terrorist—and that, in general, the world has been getting far safer.[245]

In the United States, the legislative movement to restrict freedom in the name of safety began just a few weeks after 9/11 with the October 2001 Patriot Act. Law professor Jeffrey Rosen has written, "From the beginning, Democratic and Republican critics of the Patriot Act warned that its extraordinary surveillance powers would be used to investigate political dissent or low-level offenses rather than terrorism. And their fears were soon vindicated."[246] The UK had a multi-faceted legislative response to terrorism, leading Maria Norris to write in a damning *New Statesman* article, "The United Kingdom is now a counter-terrorism state, where the duty to prevent terrorism encompasses almost every facet of our lives, from nurseries, to schools, hospitals, and the posters on bus stops telling us all to be vigilant. . . Counter-terrorism legislation relies on a bevy of administrative and executive measures that effectively sidestep the rule of law, deploying punitive measures before the criminal justice system becomes involved."[247] Every citizen has become a potential informant, urged on by the oft-repeated chilling injunction from anonymous authorities, "If you see something, say something," an instruction that is endlessly repeated all over the globe, including over tiny loudspeakers in the Toronto subway system.

Canada enacted its own Anti-Terrorism Act in December 2001. This was followed by a host of other related legislation, culminating in the controversial Bill C-51, which became law in June 2015. Bill C-51 has been widely criticized for having a chilling effect on free speech, promoting increased surveillance and eroding privacy, dangerously increasing the powers of the Canadian Security Intelligence Service

---

245 Pinker's most recent book is *Enlightenment Now: The Case for Reason, Science, Humanism, and Progress* (New York: Viking, 2018).

246 "The Patriot Act Gives Too Much Power to Law Enforcement," *New York Times*, 8 September 2011 https://www.nytimes.com/roomfordebate/2011/09/07/do-we-still-need-the-patriot-act/the-patriot-act-gives-too-much-power-to-law-enforcement (accessed 13 April 2018).

247 "Fifteen years on from 9/11, how the UK bypassed justice to become a counter-terrorism state," 11 September 2016 https://www.newstatesman.com/politics/uk/2016/09/fifteen-years-911-how-uk-bypassed-justice-become-counter-terrorism-state (accessed 14 April 2018).

(turning CSIS into a dreaded "secret police"), facilitating preventive arrest and detention, and diminishing Charter rights.[248] The Liberals when in opposition voted for Bill C-51 (a prominent Liberal member of parliament who later became a senior cabinet minister told me the "people wanted C-51," but how she knew that, I've no idea). The Liberals expressed reservations in the subsequent 2015 election campaign and introduced Bill C-59 late in 2017 to change some parts of Bill C-51. Bill C-59 was given Royal Assent in June 2019.

Equally pernicious are the attitudes and beliefs of the people, encouraged by the authorities, permitting these laws, regulations, and institutions to stand and expand. Citizens will almost always trade freedom for safety. An Egyptian acquaintance who lived in Cairo said, "My children's security when they walk to school matters more to me than being able to vote in a fair election." Who would disagree? Steven Levitsky and Daniel Zitblatt, both professors of government at Harvard University, have written in their book *How Democracies Die,* "Major security crises . . . are political game changers. Almost invariably, they increase support for the government. Citizens become more likely to tolerate, and even endorse, authoritarian measures when they fear for their security."[249]

DANGER

We need the police, but they can threaten us. There is a "democratic deficit" in Canadian policing. The most shameful example is the practice of carding. Some of the danger can be mitigated by tough rules, by formal government and citizen oversight bodies, and by a vigilant and independent Fourth Estate with a liking for investigatory journalism. Meanwhile, ham-handed official attempts to prevent terrorism have created their own threats to freedom.

---

248 See, for example, Canadian Civil Liberties Association, "Understanding Bill C-51: The Anti-Terrorism Act, 2015," 19 May 2015 https://ccla.org/understanding-bill-c-51-the-anti-terrorism-act-2015/ (accessed 14 April 2018).

249 Steven Levitsky and Daniel Zitblatt, *How Democracies Die* (New York: Crown Publishing, 2018), p. 192.

CHAPTER TEN

PRIVACY, SURVEILLANCE, SECRECY

LEAVE ME ALONE

I had to change doctors recently. I had an introductory meeting with my new physician. "A few months ago I had blood tests," I told him. "I suppose you'd like me to get the results from my old doctor and give them to you." "That's not necessary," he said, turning on his laptop computer and tapping away at the keys. "I've got the results right here. Now let's see. . ."

How did he do that? Nonplussed at the time, I didn't ask. Later I did ask a friend who'd been a senior hospital administrator and knew the Ontario health system inside out. He told me about something called an Electronic Medical Record (EMR), which can access the Ontario Laboratories Information System (OLIS), a provincial laboratory result database maintained by eHealth Ontario.[250] Clinicians using an EMR

---

250 "OLIS is a system that connects hospitals, community laboratories, public health laboratories and practitioners to facilitate the secure, electronic exchange of laboratory test orders and results. As a province-wide, integrated repository of tests and results, OLIS contributes to fundamental improvements in patient care by providing practitioners with timely access to information that is needed at the time of clinical decision making." See https://www.ehealthontario.on.ca/for-healthcare-professionals/

can access patients' lab data outside of hospital settings through the laboratory company or OLIS. True, there are some safeguards. The 2004 Ontario Personal Health Information Protection Act (known as "PHIPA") contains rules for the collection, use and disclosure of personal health information to protect confidentiality and privacy. Other provinces have enacted similar legislation. The federal Personal Information Protection and Electronic Documents Act ("PIPEDA") applies to the collection, use or disclosure of personal information in the course of a commercial activity. It has a broad scope, applies to medical information, and buttresses provincial legislation. Yet, despite these safeguards, how private are medical records? My experience suggested, not as much as you might assume.[251] The average citizen would probably not expect or want their medical records to be easily or widely accessible.[252]

It has long been argued that freedom requires privacy, and—a stronger claim—that privacy is itself an independent freedom that should be protected. In 1890, prompted by the growing popularity and sophistication of photography, and a new, aggressive, and prurient journalism, the future Supreme Court Justice Louis Brandeis and a lawyer called Samuel Warren published an article together in the *Harvard Law Review* which

ontario-laboratories-information-system-olis (accessed 23 April 2018). In the US, more than half the population has their health information stored in a computer system called Epic. See Atul Gawande, "The Upgrade," *The New Yorker*, 12 November 2018, p. 62.

251 It has been known for some time that Canadians' mental health records are routinely shared with the US customs officials and the Federal Bureau of Investigation. Some Canadian with a history of mental-health issues have been denied entry into the US. See, e.g., "Police sharing of mental health information is a nightmare," *Globe and Mail* 17 April 2014 https://www.theglobeandmail.com/opinion/editorials/the-police-database-that-shared-too-much-about-mental-health/article18060176/ (accessed 8 May 2018). In Ontario, the Police Record Checks Reform Act came into force on November 1, 2018. This statute severely limits disclosure by police of so-called "non-conviction" records, including mental health records.

252 A particularly egregious breach of privacy recently occurred in Nova Scotia. A pharmacist used the provincial Drug Information System to obtain medical information about friends, acquaintances, and friends of her children. See Office of the Information and Privacy Commissioner for Nova Scotia, Investigation Report IR18-01, August 1, 2018 https://oipc.novascotia.ca/sites/default/files/reports/IR18-01%20DHW%20(01%20Aug%202018).pdf (accessed 19 August, 2018). "This is a case of a pharmacist accessing highly sensitive personal health information over a two-year period to satisfy personal curiosity."

argued for the recognition of a new legal right "to be let alone."[253]
More than a hundred years later, in 1998, Orlando Patterson, a Harvard
University sociologist, wrote in the *New York Times*, "Our privacy is not
simply a privilege derived from our freedom. Far more important, it is
an integral element of our liberty, 'the most comprehensive of rights,'
as Justice Louis D. Brandeis recognized, 'and the right most valued by
civilized man'."[254]

Professor Thomas Emerson of the Yale Law School presciently
argued in 1979, "The constantly increasing scope of governmental
intercession in most areas of national life, the development of modern
technology for ferreting out and monitoring everyone's affairs from
womb to tomb, the closing in of physical and psychic space for the average person, all make the need for creation of an adequate law of privacy
imperative for the future health of our society."[255] The United States
Supreme Court, among other courts around the world, has repeatedly
and robustly endorsed the right to privacy as a fundamental freedom.
In 1965, in *Griswold v. Connecticut*, the Court ruled that a state's ban
on the use of contraceptives violated the right to marital privacy. The
apogee in the US was the 1973 case of *Roe v. Wade*. The Supreme Court
held that the right to privacy was broad enough in certain circumstances
to encompass a woman's decision to have an abortion. This was a decision of great legal and political significance, controversial to this day.

Privacy has now pretty much gone for good, despite a desperate and bally-hooed rearguard action often employing legislation of
limited scope (PHIPA and PIPEDA are examples) and other forms
of government intervention. The "right to privacy," discussed and
promoted for decades, is dying if not dead. It cannot withstand the
juggernauts of technology and social media. It cannot withstand an
intrusive state—think, for example, of the tracking implications of Social

---

253 "The Right to Privacy," (1890) IV *Harvard Law Review* http://groups.csail.mit.edu/mac/
classes/6.805/articles/privacy/Privacy_brand_warr2.html (accessed 23 April 2018).

254 "What Is Freedom Without Privacy?" 15 September 1998 https://www.nytimes.
com/1998/09/15/opinion/what-is-freedom-without-privacy.html (accessed 23 April
2018).

255 "The Right of Privacy and Freedom of the Press," 14 *Harvard Civil Rights – Civil
Liberties Law Review*, p.329 http://digitalcommons.law.yale.edu/cgi/viewcontent.
cgi?article=3789&context=fss_papers (accessed 23 April 2018).

Security Numbers—and prying corporations.[256] Technology has created the ability to accumulate huge amounts of information in digital form, manipulate it in a variety of interesting and lucrative ways, and make it widely and easily available, legally and illegally. Social media, with its hundreds of millions of colluders, has provided a hugely attractive recipient and powerful salesman of staggering amounts of personal information.[257] And, anyway, privacy is a complicated and elusive concept, hard to use effectively, and often invoked for dubious purposes.[258]

ONCE MORE UNTO THE BREACH

Data security breaches are major factors in the death of privacy. These breaches have been many and varied, and there will be more.

The biggest data breach so far happened in 2013 when three billion Yahoo email accounts were compromised. The breach was not announced by Yahoo until 2016. *The New York Times* reported:

> Digital thieves made off with names, birth dates, phone numbers and passwords of users that were encrypted with security that was easy to crack. The intruders also obtained the security questions and backup email addresses used to reset lost passwords—valuable information for someone trying to break into other accounts owned by the same user, and particularly useful to a hacker seeking to break into government computers around the world.[259]

256 See Sarah E. Igo, "The Naked Society," *Times Literary Review*, 9 November 2018, p. 23.
257 And it's not just social media. Insurance companies, for example, have vast amounts of personal information. See Ed Leefelt, "Your insurance company knows more about you than Facebook," *Moneywatch*, 27 April 2018 https://www.cbsnews.com/news/your-insurance-company-knows-more-about-you-than-facebook/ (accessed 5 May 2018). And then there's the government, particularly the tax department.
258 See Sarah Igo, *The Known Citizen* (Boston: Harvard University Press, 2018), reviewed extensively by Louis Menand, "Why Do We Care So Much About Privacy?" *New Yorker*, 18 June 2018 . https://www.newyorker.com/magazine/2018/06/18/why-do-we-care-so-much-about-privacy?mbid=social_tablet_e (accessed 14 June 2018). Menand points out that privacy is particularly valuable to criminals.
259 Nicole Perlroth, "All 3 Billion Yahoo Accounts Were Affected by 2013 Attack," *New York Times*, 3 October 2017 https://www.nytimes.com/2017/10/03/technology/yahoo-hack-3-billion-users.html (accessed 23 April 2018).

This breach dramatically reduced the commercial value of Yahoo, which became a shell of its former self. Equifax, a major American consumer credit reporting agency, revealed in September 2107, "hackers had gained access to company data that potentially compromised sensitive information for 143 million American consumers, including Social Security numbers and driver's license numbers."[260] This was not the first breach of Equifax data security. In September 2018, Facebook discovered an attack on its computer network had exposed the personal information of about 30 million users. Other significant breaches of private sector data have happened to (among others) Heartland Payment Systems (2008), Sony's PlayStation Network (2011), LinkedIn (2012), MySpace (2013), Target Stores (2013), Adobe (2013), Neiman Marcus (2013), eBay (2014), JP Morgan Chase (2014), Home Depot (2014), Adult Friend Finder (2016), Uber (2016), Pizza Hut (2017), Delta Airlines (2017), Under Armour (2018), Fed Ex (2018), Amazon (2018), Marriott International (the 2018 Marriott hack was second in size only to the 2013 attack on Yahoo), and Capital One bank (2019). In Canada, major data breaches have affected Ashley Madison (2015), Bell Canada (2018), and Hudson's Bay Company (2018). Nor are governments immune. A recent Wikipedia entry lists several hundred private and public data breaches since 2005, each involving the theft or compromise of thirty thousand or more records.[261]

BARGAINING WITH THE DEVIL

The greatest threat to privacy comes from the bargain between social media and its users. Many commentators have pointed out that modern surveillance depends to a large extent on the willing participation of those being surveilled, so-called "user-generated surveillance."[262]

---

260 Tara Siegel Bernard, Tiffany Hsu, Nicole Perlroth and Ron Lieber, "Equifax Says Cyberattack May Have Affected 143 Million in the U.S." *New York Times*, 7 September 2017 https://www.nytimes.com/2017/09/07/business/equifax-cyberattack. html?mcubz=1 (accessed 23 April 2018).

261 https://en.wikipedia.org/wiki/List_of_data_breaches (accessed 11 November 2018).

262 See, e.g., David Lyon, *The Culture of Surveillance* (Cambridge: Polity Press, 2018).

Facebook is the biggest and most powerful social media site with more than two billion participants worldwide (there are about twenty-five million Facebook users in Canada). About one-and-a-half billion users visit the site daily.[263] Facebook's network of data centres houses hundreds of thousands of servers. In recent times, the company's market capitalization has ranged between $400 and $600 billion. It employs over thirty thousand people. In 2017 Facebook's cost of operations was more than $20 billion. Its revenue was almost $41 billion.

Where does Facebook's huge revenue come from? Users do not pay in coin to visit the site. Almost all revenue comes from advertisers who pay to have targeted digital advertisements published. Facebook tells potential advertisers that advertisements can be targeted according to demographics, location, interests, and "behaviours." Its website explains:

> Demographics: Find people based on traits like age, gender, relationship status, education, workplace, job titles and more. Location: Reach people in areas where you want to do business. You can even create a radius around a store to help create more walk-ins. Interests: Find people based on what they're into, like hobbies, favorite entertainment and more. Behaviors: Reach people based on their purchase behaviors, device usage and other activities.[264]

The information that permits such targeting comes, of course, from users who voluntarily, even joyfully, provide details about themselves and their lives, which are then sliced and diced and supplied to advertisers who exploit individual user profiles. Facebook users pay for their participation with information rather than money. It is disingenuous for them to complain about the bargain they have made. In exchange for the information they give, they receive the chance to participate, responsibly or not, but pleasurably, in a huge community.

---

263 The other two major social media sites are Twitter and Instagram. Twitter has about three hundred and fifty million users (seven-and-a-half million in Canada). Instagram has almost a billion users (twelve million in Canada).

264 *Facebook business*, https://www.facebook.com/business/products/ads/ad-targeting (accessed 27 April 2018).

That is why the 2018 Cambridge Analytica scandal was a misguided tempest in a teapot. Cambridge Analytica is a UK data mining company (there are many such companies around the world) that worked for presidential candidate Donald Trump. In 2018, the *New York Times* reported that, starting in 2014, Cambridge Analytica had acquired the private Facebook data of about eighty-seven million users.[265] Facebook's data-sharing policies at the time, and data-sharing partnerships particularly with device makers like Apple and Samsung, made this kind of data collection possible.[266] There was nothing illegal about it despite subsequent squeals of outrage and distress that hysterically invoked the right to privacy.

The data was used to target voters with "hyper-specific appeals" on Facebook and elsewhere. In the fevered atmosphere of Trump's Washington, swirling with accusations of Russian collusion, this was seen as a scandalous breach of privacy. The founder and chief executive of Facebook, Mark Zuckerberg, testified before Senate and House committees in April 2018. Many of the senators and congress members who questioned Zuckerberg later made clumsy Facebook posts about the hearing. In the days following Zuckerberg's testimony the value of Facebook shares increased by more than five percent. At Facebook's May 2018 developer conference, Zuckerberg unveiled a new privacy control called "clear history" that allows a user to clear his Facebook browsing history within the Facebook app. Facebook started aggressively policing and significantly limiting access to Facebook data by third-party developers, the source of the problem in the first place.[267]

---

265 The technique was described by *Fortune* magazine, "Facebook Cambridge Analytica Scandal: 10 Questions Answered," 10 April 2018 http://fortune.com/2018/04/10/facebook-cambridge-analytica-what-happened/ (accessed 27 April 2018): "During the summer of 2014, the U.K. affiliate of U.S. political consulting firm Cambridge Analytica hired a Soviet-born American researcher, Aleksandr Kogan, to gather basic profile information of Facebook users along with what they chose to "Like." About 300,000 Facebook users, most or all of whom were paid a small amount, downloaded Kogan's app, called This Is Your Digital Life, which presented them with a series of surveys. Kogan collected data not just on those users but on their Facebook friends, if their privacy settings allowed it."

266 See Gabriel J.X. Dance, Nicholas Confessore and Michael LaForgia, "Facebook's Device Partnerships Explained," *New York Times*, 4 June 2018 https://www.nytimes.com/2018/06/04/technology/facebook-device-partnerships.html (accessed 9 June 2018).

267 "Tinder, the dating app, discovered that its users were no longer able to log into the

Cambridge Analytica went into liquidation. What happened to its data is not clear. As one cybersecurity specialist put it, data is "sticky"; once it's out there, "it doesn't go away."

Europe seems more agitated by privacy issues than North America. In May 2018, the European Union General Data Protection Regulation ("GDPR") came into force. The Regulation emphasizes privacy, aims primarily to give individuals more control over their personal data (companies must get consent to harvest a user's data), and gives them greater ability to require companies like Facebook to reveal personal information they hold and to insist that they delete that information if requested to do so. The GDPR has been described as "the most significant change to digital privacy since the internet was invented . . . a watershed for the digital economy."[268] Towards the end of May 2018, Zuckerberg spoke informally to the European parliament. Several parliamentarians suggested that Facebook was abusing its dominant position, and amounted to a monopoly that should be broken up.

It is not just social media platforms that sell or distribute personal data. Canadian banks may have the ability to sell customer data without customer consent to so-called "fintechs" which are not subject to federal financial regulation. Provisions in the 2018 federal omnibus budget bill seemed to expand this possibility. Representatives of the banks appeared before the Senate banking committee on May 24, 2018 and sought to reassure the public. Bank officials said "that customer consent is required and that information sharing contracts with third parties have strong privacy and security safeguards. . ."[269]

---

app using their Facebook accounts. Pod, a calendar syncing app, found that its users could no longer see Facebook events within their calendars. And Job Fusion, a jobs app that allowed users to see where their Facebook friends worked, announced that it was no longer able to offer its services within Facebook." See Sheera Frenkel, "Facebook's Privacy Changes Leave Developers Steaming," *The New York Times*, 30 April 2018 https://www.nytimes.com/2018/04/30/technology/facebook-privacy-developers. html (accessed 4 May 2018).

268   Tamsin McMahon, "The European data-privacy rules that change the game," *Globe and Mail*, 25 May 2018 https://www.theglobeandmail.com/world/article-what-new-european-data-privacy-rules-could-mean-for-canadian-companies/ (accessed 25 May 2018).

269   Bill Curry, "Customer info sharing is safe, banks tell senators," *Globe and Mail*, 25 May 2018 https://www.theglobeandmail.com/politics/article-customer-info-shared-with-fintechs-is-secure-bank-executives-tell/ (accessed 25 May 2018).

THE MAN WHO KNEW TOO LITTLE

When people talk about privacy, they almost always talk about their ability, or inability, to shield their personal information from others, particularly from "powerful others" such as government institutions, big media, and large corporations. But equally intrusive—the flip side of privacy loss—is our inability to avoid being bombarded with often unwanted information generated by those powerful others, particularly media operating on a twenty-four-hour news cycle. This information carpet-bombing can be as destructive and degrading as loss of our own personal information. It flies in the face of our right to be left alone.

Erik Hagerman has been called the most ignorant man in America.[270] He was living alone on a pig farm in Ohio in 2018. He is an artist as well as a pig farmer. He studied at Oxford University as a Marshall Scholar. He was a corporate executive at Nike, Disney, and Walmart. He appears to have significant private investments. When Donald Trump was elected president, in November 2016, a disgusted Hagerman decided to do whatever he could to avoid national and international news (local news is ok). He put in place something he calls The Blockade. One important part of The Blockade is avoiding social media. *The New York Times* reported in March 2018, "he is now more than a year into knowing almost nothing about American politics. He has managed to become shockingly uninformed during one of the most eventful chapters in modern American history. He is as ignorant as a contemporary citizen could ever hope to be." Hagerman says he has never felt healthier emotionally.[271]

The Blockade has been controversial. Is it a stunt? One commentator called Hagerman "the most selfish man in America," writing, "If everyone did what Hagerman did, there would be no United States. There would be no democracy. There would be no forward progress

270 See Sam Dolnik, "The Man Who Knew Too Little," *The New York Times*, 10 March 2018 https://www.nytimes.com/2018/03/10/style/the-man-who-knew-too-little.html (accessed 4 May 2018).

271 It is reported that, despite The Blockade, Hagerman read the article about him in *The New York Times*. But concerned friends who gave it to him redacted references to current events.

or people helping others in times of need. There would be nothing but complacency in the suffering and exploitation of others."[272] Some agree with this tough criticism. Others, overwhelmed and revolted by the political situation in the United States and the world beyond, profess sympathy and support for Hagerman. After all, all Hagerman wants is to be left alone. Don't we all have the right to be left alone, as part of our right to privacy and freedom?

Is privacy an independent freedom whose loss we should mourn? Are other freedoms weakened by the loss of privacy? Without privacy, personal autonomy is exposed and diminished. There is little about us that we can hide and there is little information about others that we can avoid. It is impossible to be left alone.

SURVEILLANCE

A leader in *The Economist* painted the grim picture: "They're watching you. When you walk to work, CCTV cameras film you and, increasingly, recognize your face. Drive out of town, and number-plate-reading cameras capture your journey. The smartphone in your pocket leaves a constant digital trail. Browse the web in the privacy of your home, and your actions are logged and analysed." [273]

In Toronto, there are surveillance cameras all over the place. There are police cameras on poles (mostly downtown). In 2018 The Toronto Police Services Board asked the city for money to more than double the number of public CCTV cameras, from thirty-four to seventy-four, and install a system called ShotSpotter to pinpoint gunshot locations and send alerts to police. Later it was decided not to deploy ShotSpotter for fear that it contravened constitutional provisions forbidding unreasonable search and seizure. Toronto Transit Commission cameras, lots of them, are on buses, streetcars, subway cars, and in stations. There are cameras in banks, stores, office buildings, malls, and other places of business. It is the same in other major Canadian cities, and in many

---

272 Kellen Beck, *Mashable*, 10 March 2018 https://mashable.com/2018/03/10/new-york-times-selfish-man/#0SkAVgHiauqp (accessed 4 May 2018).

273 *The Economist*, "Perfected in China, a threat in the West," 2 June 2018.

smaller communities as well—Sturgeon Falls, Ontario, for example, or Antigonish, Nova Scotia. (Why do Sturgeon Falls and Antigonish need surveillance cameras?)

Anyone can buy and install his own closed circuit television camera. Amazon offers an "Analog Camera Home Security Systems With HD Night Vision" for $32.99. Signs alerting the public to the presence of surveillance cameras permit the fiction of informed consent and in theory encourage freedom of information applications and formal privacy complaints. But many cameras have no such signage, even though such absence is sometimes contrary to the federal Personal Information Protection and Electronic Documents Act and similar privacy legislation found in several provinces.

Those in favour of surveillance cameras say their presence discourages and helps fight crime and terrorism. But the cameras do not know why they are there and can be used for any purpose, good or bad. They can be used, for example, to spy on the innocent and unsuspecting. And studies strongly suggest that the role of cameras as both a forensic instrument, gathering evidence, and as a deterrent, have been seriously exaggerated.[274]

The UK leads in the use of closed circuit television surveillance. I have mentioned already that the UK has an estimated six million surveillance cameras, with about five hundred thousand in London. On the morning of July 7, 2007, four terrorists detonated three bombs on London Underground trains and, later, a fourth bomb on a double-decker bus. Fifty-two people, including the terrorists, were killed. Police immediately examined about two-and-a-half thousand pieces of CCTV footage. They quickly found footage of the four suspects at King's Cross railway station, which has seventy-six surveillance cameras. Tapes showed that the four men, after leaving King's Cross, split up and went in different directions through London's Underground system. Police found earlier footage of the men buying supplies to build the bombs at a hardware store and a supermarket. Two weeks later, on July 21, around midday, there were four attempted bomb attacks on the London public transport system. The bombs failed to explode and the suspects fled the

---

274 See Surveillance Camera Awareness Network, *A Report on Camera Surveillance in Canada*, January 2009 http://www.sscqueens.org/sites/default/files/SCAN_Report_Phase1_Final_Jan_30_2009.pdf (accessed 5 May 2018).

scene. The following day, CCTV images of four suspects were released. They were soon arrested.

In Chicago, a relatively new system of over thirty thousand linked surveillance cameras "can deliver the license plate of every passing vehicle, a photo of every area resident with an arrest record, gang boundaries, 911 reports and more, right to a patrol officer's cellphone."[275] In Newark, New Jersey, the police "have opened up feeds from dozens of closed-circuit cameras to the public, asking viewers to assist the force by watching over the city and reporting anything suspicious."[276] In China, about two hundred million surveillance cameras (it is estimated that there will be three hundred million by 2020) use advanced facial recognition technology to identify a person from a database of more than two billion people in seconds.[277]

Electronic surveillance has spread to offices and factories around the world, monitoring workers' productivity and bathroom breaks.[278] But the biggest threat of all comes from commonplace internet-enabled devices found in the home and the pocket and used with enthusiasm. Smartphones (above all else), televisions, activity trackers and fitness devices, toothbrushes, refrigerators, cameras, sex toys, robot vacuum cleaners—indeed, all "smart devices," sometimes also known as "soft surveillance" devices—collect and transmit data to an extraordinary extent, with the willingness of the user, often with no attempt to keep that data secure.[279]

275 Timothy Williams, "Can 30,000 Cameras Help Solve Chicago's Crime Problem?" *The New York Times* 26 May 2018 https://www.nytimes.com/2018/05/26/us/chicago-police-surveillance.html (accessed 27 May 2018).

276 Rick Rojas, "In Newark, Police Cameras, and the Internet, Watch You," *The New York Times*, 9 June 2018 https://www.nytimes.com/2018/06/09/nyregion/newark-surveillance-cameras-police.html (accessed 11 June 2018).

277 See Paul Mozur, "Inside China's Dystopian Dreams: A.I., Shame and Lots of Cameras," *New York Times*, 8 July 2018 https://www.nytimes.com/2018/07/08/business/china-surveillance-technology.html (accessed 10 July 2018).

278 See Emine Saner, "Employers are monitoring computers, toilet breaks – even emotions. Is your boss watching you?" *The Guardian*, 14 May 2018 https://www.theguardian.com/world/2018/may/14/is-your-boss-secretly-or-not-so-secretly-watching-you?CMP=Share_iOSApp_Other (accessed 17 May 2018).

279 See Alex Hern, "UK homes vulnerable to 'staggering' level of corporate surveillance," *The Guardian*, 1 June 2018 https://www.theguardian.com/technology/2018/

SECRECY

In the midst of plenty, there is scarcity. There is so much information, outgoing (our personal information) and incoming (everything else), and yet information we really want is often unavailable. That information is secret. Who keeps it secret? The worst offender is the government. Sometimes it seems as if we have the worst of all possible worlds, a toxic mixture of no personal privacy and excessive government secrecy.

In a democracy, most information must be freely available if citizens are to enjoy freedom and fulfill their responsibilities to the state and their fellow citizens, including reining in government when necessary. Some information, of course, cannot be revealed on national security or similar grounds, although as many have pointed out "national security" is an imprecise and often abused concept. We must know the facts, directly from government, or indirectly from an independent press. The US Supreme Court said in the 1936 case of *Grosjean v. American Press*, "an informed public is the most potent of all restraints upon misgovernment."[280] (*Grosjean* struck down as unconstitutional a Louisiana state tax on newspaper advertisements, a type of tax "with a long history of hostile misuse against the freedom of the press.") Courts and commentators in many countries—in Canada as much as anywhere else—have made similar comments. Hortatory statements on the subject can be found all over the place, many made by parliamentarians and judges. One Canadian commentator, listing many of these statements, has written, "It has become trite to argue that access to information is an essential attribute of democracy."[281] Legislation has attempted to enshrine some of these high-flown principles—for example, in Canada, the 1985 Access to Information Act, with its many exemptions and exclusions, frustrations and delays.

jun/01/uk-homes-vulnerable-to-staggering-level-of-corporate-surveillance?utm_source=esp&utm_medium=Email&utm_campaign=GU+Today+main+NEW+H+categories&utm_term=276854&subid=20125188&CMP=EMCNEWEML661912 (accessed 3 June 2018).
280 *Grosjean v. American Press Co.*, 297 U.S. 233, at p. 250.
281 Craig Forcese, "Clouding Accountability: Canada's Government Secrecy and National Security Law 'Complex'", (2004) 36 *Ottawa Law Review* 49, at 53. Professor Forcese gives an important, although now dated, analysis of the issues.

In Chapter Three, I described some of the ways in which the government of Stephen Harper sought to deprive the citizenry of information, for example, by muzzling government scientists. It has often been said that the Harper government had a "cult of secrecy" or "love affair with secrecy." Despite the promise of sunny ways, the Justin Trudeau government has behaved no better. Notwithstanding a specific promise made by Justin Trudeau in the 2015 campaign, the Access to Information Act has not been amended to make the Prime Minister's Office and cabinet ministers' offices subject to the statute (yes, another broken promise). The number of senior public servants subject to lifetime gag orders, so-called "persons permanently bound to secrecy" or "PPBSs", has increased significantly. The total is not known for certain, but it is in the many hundreds. The Auditor General of Canada has strongly criticized the federal government for denying him access to information on the formulation of government policy. The former Information Commissioner of Canada, Suzanne Legault, who left office at the end of February 2018, on her way out the door accused the Liberal government "of reneging on its promise to bring a new era of openness to Ottawa and of failing to defend the 'Charter right' of Canadians to quick and easy access to federal documents and data."[282]

GOING, GOING, GONE

Privacy, or the right to be left alone, is going. Information about individuals is everywhere, much of it handed over with a smile by the individuals themselves for the sake of efficiency and sociability. Multiplying surveillance cameras are popping up on poles, allegedly to protect us and society from criminals and terrorists. Secrecy, particularly governmental secrecy, burgeons. There's not much citizens can safely be told. It is a matter of good government and national security. That's what they say.

---

282 Daniel LeBlanc, "Information watchdog blasts Liberals ahead of her retirement," *Globe and Mail*, 21 February 2018 https://www.theglobeandmail.com/news/politics/information-watchdog-blasts-liberals-ahead-of-her-retirement/article38060282/ (accessed 20 May 2018).

Freedom requires personal privacy and government transparency. We have neither. Much of our privacy has been freely given away, mostly through voluntary participation in social media. What remains has been snatched away by surveillance and data breaches. And government tells us only what it wants us to know.

PART FIVE

CRISES

It is hard to feel free if every day is an economic struggle, if you cannot buy much more than second-rate food and rudimentary shelter, if your economic future is irreparably bleak. It is hard to feel free if you are poor.

The Indigenous People of Canada have been and are badly treated. It is a wound that never heals. Until history is overcome and ceases to determine the present and future, our country falls short of freedom.

How much freedom will we have when fires sweep across our country, the seas rise relentlessly, the animals die, and the beauty of nature is gone? How much freedom will we have when there are vast migrations of people across continents, fleeing natural disasters, ignoring national borders, fighting for scarce resources?

CHAPTER ELEVEN

ECONOMIC INEQUALITY

THE SIDE HUSTLE

I graduated from the University of Manitoba with a Bachelor of Arts degree in 1965. In those days, if you had done reasonably well in a university undergraduate program (not necessarily an A average; a B would do), the world was your oyster. Well-paying careers that lasted a lifetime would be on offer. All you had to do was choose. Would you like to work for the government? That was the first choice of many. What about a bank, or some other great capitalist enterprise? That did not seem like a bad idea. Or perhaps a professional school—law, medicine, or engineering—followed by a satisfactory and lucrative professional career? Freedom from money worries, stability, status in the community, a nice house, perhaps a cottage on a lake, an ability to accumulate personal capital over the years (not a fortune, but something), an indexed defined-benefit pension when your career was over, a fulfilling retirement, financial legacies for your children, a gold watch at age sixty-five, cruises in the Caribbean, the good life—all beckoned, all were virtually guaranteed, provided you did not do something stupid along the way or have some very bad luck. Am I remembering those halcyon days correctly? I think so (although one reader of this manuscript in draft commented, "that was only true if you were a white male").

Today, in downtown Toronto where I live for part of the year, the streets are full of Uber and Lyft cars picking people up and dropping them off and food couriers (Uber Eats, Foodora, DoorDash, SkipTheDishes) whizzing about on bicycles with thermal food carriers strapped to their back taking fast food to fast folks. Many people lucky enough to have an apartment in the city centre rent a bedroom out now and then, for a night or two, on sites like Airbnb or VRBO. If you have a spare parking spot, you can rent that out too for a few hours using an app called Rover Parking. You can provide (or get) cleaning services and home cooking and hair styling, and just about anything else, using online platforms. If you need an office to work in, you can rent space during the day in what is a restaurant by night, provided you clear out when it has to start getting ready to serve dinner (for some reason, this is known as "co-working").[283]

Welcome to the "gig" or "side hustle" or "sharing" or "on demand" economy, full of mostly young or fairly young people, many with a post-secondary education that they once thought— because their university or college or parents told them so—would lead to decent and secure employment, often dragging big debt behind them because of the absurdly-inflated cost of that education. Members of the gig economy work as risk-taking independent contractors for organizations minimally regulated by government, for close to the minimum wage and with no benefits, without the benefit of labour laws and with no fixed place of work. They will almost certainly always be poor or near poor, with no prospect of a comfortable retirement based on a pension plan or the increase in value of personal real estate. They are almost certainly much worse off than their parents, and will remain so. They are not happy, although some pretend to be, desperately invoking, ironically, the "freedom" of their situation. They are not economically free. They are the serfs of cyber-feudalism.[284] They are victims of a breakdown of the generational contract, "the tacit deal in which the young look after

---

283   See Nellie Bowles, "Sorry, Power-Lunchers. This Restaurant Is a Co-Working Space Now," *The New York Times,* 8 July 2018 https://www.nytimes.com/2018/07/08/technology/restaurants-co-working-areas.html (accessed 9 July 2018).

284   See, e.g., Peter Fleming, *The Death of Homo Economicus: Work, Debt and the Myth of Endless Accumulation,* (London: Pluto Press, 2017).

the old and the old help the young have a better life than the generation before."[285]

Mind you, not every commentator is critical of the gig economy. In an unconvincing 2018 article, *The Economist* concluded that worries about the rise of the gig economy are mostly overblown.[286] Said the newspaper: "The advantages for consumers are clear. With a swipe or a click, almost anyone can get Rover walked in the park. . . Critically, benefits also accrue to workers. The algorithms that underpin gig-economy platforms improve the 'matching' between giggers and jobs, leading to less dead time. The evidence that gig workers face a pay penalty compared with conventional employees is patchy."[287]

Hardly overblown, according to most who have studied or thought seriously about the phenomenon. A 2017 report on the Greater Toronto Area (GTA) sharing economy by the Canadian Centre for Policy Alternatives comments: "People who have worked in this sector of the economy have a variety of reasons for doing so: sixty-four per cent agree that they do it to make extra money, sixty-three per cent because they like it, fifty-five per cent because it's the only way to make a living right now, and fifty-three per cent say it's something to do until they can find something better. These answers are indicative of overall labour market conditions in the GTA, with the rise in precarious work and with barriers to young workers' ability to find secure, full-time jobs."[288] Andrew Cash, the musician and former member of parliament, says this about gig economy workers: "They fix our leaky roofs, walk our dogs, look after our seniors, tutor our children and drive us to the airport,

---

285 See Robert Booth, "Give millennials £10,000 each to tackle generation gap, says think-tank," *The Guardian*, 8 May 2018 https://www.theguardian.com/money/2018/may/08/give-millennials-10000-each-to-tackle-generation-gap-says-thinktank (accessed 5 June 2018). The report referred to is Resolution Foundation, *A New Generational Contract: The final report of the Intergenerational Commission*, https://www.resolutionfoundation.org/advanced/a-new-generational-contract/ (accessed 5 June 2018).

286 See "Serfs up," 6 October 2018, p. 64.

287 "Workers on tap," 6 October 2018, p. 14.

288 Sheila Block and Trish Hennessey, *"Sharing economy" or on-demand service economy? A survey of workers and consumers in the Greater Toronto Area* https://www.policyalternatives.ca/sites/default/files/uploads/publications/Ontario%20Office/2017/04/CCPA-ON%20sharing%20economy%20in%20the%20GTA.pdf (accessed 22 May 2018).

do our bookkeeping and write this article. They work on Sundays and statutory holidays; they work when others play; they work when they have the flu or are on chemo. When they do take a week's holiday, well, that's a week where they simply don't get paid."[289]

It's not just strapping young men delivering food on bicycles or cash-strapped millennials renting out a room in their apartment for a few days. It's interns who are paid little or nothing by the companies or institutions they work for; freelance journalists, who despite great skill and commitment, are paid a pittance (and sometimes nothing); writers who cannot earn a living from writing[290]; musicians, and others in the cultural sector, doomed to live in basement apartments; and underpaid part-time and sessional college professors who have been steadily replacing full-time teachers. According to StatsCan, says Andrew Cash, "ninety per cent of all jobs created in Canada in 2015 and 2016 were temporary, and they paid on average thirty per cent less than corresponding permanent positions." In Britain, the gig economy has more than doubled in size since 2016, with one in ten working-age adults (four million seven hundred thousand workers) now working on gig economy platforms.[291]

The gig economy bleeds into the professions. The *Star* newspaper reported in August 2018, "A survey . . . of 1,000 professionals across

289 "The Gig Economy," *albertaviews*, 24 April 2018 https://albertaviews.ca/the-gig-economy/ (accessed 22 May 2018).

290 If you have any doubt, see Danuta Kean, "Publishers are paying writers a pittance, say bestselling authors," *The Guardian*, 27 June 2018 https://www.theguardian.com/books/2018/jun/27/publishers-pay-writers-pittance-philip-pullman-antony-beevor-sally-gardner?CMP=share_btn_link (accessed 29 June 2018). Kean quotes Philip Pullman: "Many of us are being treated badly because some of those who bring our books to the public are acting without conscience and with no thought for the future of the ecology of the trade as a whole. . . This matters because the intellectual, emotional and artistic health of the nation matters, and those who write contribute to the task of sustaining it." In October 2018, the Writers' Union of Canada released a survey of its members' incomes and reported a 27 percent decrease in writing income over the past three years and a 78 percent decrease over the last twenty years. See *Diminishing Returns: Creative Culture at Risk* https://www.writersunion.ca/sites/all/files/DiminishingReturns-Web.pdf (accessed 28 October 2018).

291 Richard Partington, "Gig economy in Britain doubles, accounting for 4.7 million workers," *The Guardian*, 28 June 2019 https://www.theguardian.com/business/2019/jun/28/gig-economy-in-britain-doubles-accounting-for-47-million-workers?CMP=Share_iOSApp_Other (accessed 16 August 2019).

the country found that one in five are in precarious jobs, working con-
tract-to-contract, part-time, or freelance. More than half of those in
insecure employment said their income varied significantly, and sixty
per cent said they don't have pension plans or sick pay."[292] The survey
found that "precarious professionals are in all professions, but they're
concentrated in three occupational categories: education (twenty-eight
per cent), health care (eighteen per cent), and business, finance and
administration (nineteen per cent). The majority of precarious professionals are women (sixty per cent) and there is a higher incidence among
professionals aged 55 and up."[293]

There are a lot of these people around. They do not have the
hopes and expectations, and corresponding commitment to society,
of previous generations. They do not have the economic freedom of
previous generations. They are dispossessed and disaffected. They have
what some US doctors call "shit-life syndrome." They are prone to
depression and anxiety.[294] They can become dangerous. It's one of the
reasons for the great political upheavals we now witness. As Will Hutton
explained in *The Guardian*: "Poor working-age Americans of all races
are locked in a cycle of poverty and neglect, amid wider affluence. They
are ill-educated and ill-trained. The jobs available are drudge work
paying the minimum wage, with minimal or no job security. They are
trapped in poor neighbourhoods where the prospect of owning a home
is a distant dream. There is little social housing, scant income support
and contingent access to healthcare. Finding meaning in life is close

292 Sara Mojtehedzadeh, "Growing number of professionals face job insecurity, study finds,"
21 August 2018 https://www.thestar.com/news/canada/2018/08/21/growing-
number-of-professionals-face-job-insecurity-study-finds.html (accessed 22 August
2018). The study was by the Canadian Centre for Policy Alternatives.
293 Trish Hennessy and Ricardo Tranjan, "No Safe Harbour: Precarious Work and Economic
Insecurity Among Skilled Professionals in Canada," 21 August 2018 https://www.
policyalternatives.ca/publications/reports/no-safe-harbour (accessed 22 August 2018).
294 See Jeffrey C. Martin and Wayne Lewchuk, *The Generation Effect: Millennials, employment precarity and the 21st century workplace*, McMaster University, September 2018
https://pepso.ca/documents/the-generation-effect-full-report.pdf (accessed 2
September 2018). This reports on a survey of millennials in Hamilton, Ontario. It con-
cludes: "Millennial workers in general have a high prevalence of less than good mental
health. Those in precarious employment show an even higher prevalence of mental health
concerns, depression and anger than millennials in secure employment." (p. 8)

to impossible; the struggle to survive commands all intellectual and emotional resources."[295]

Yuval Noah Harari wrote, "The technological revolution might soon push billions of humans out of the job market and create a massive new "useless class," leading to social and political upheavals that no existing ideology knows how to handle." In the long run, says Harari, no job will be safe from automation. The brilliant criminologist Jeff Ferrell has written of low-end retail and service workers, "For them, the Fordist model of occupational stability and advancement is finished; their work lives are now defined by the uncertainty of part-time and temporary employment, flex scheduling, missing medical and retirement benefits, and aborted careers. For them the old social contract has been annulled. . . And so, a lesson we're meant to miss amidst the giltz of fancy shops and valet parking: accompanying ever 'successful' urban redevelopment scheme, every old factory converted into high-end lofts and retail spaces, is an increase of the number of workers left with few options but to drift between unstable employment, unaffordable housing, and economic failure. These are the members of the new "precariat."[296]

EXCESSIVE WEALTH DISORDER

It is hard to feel free if every day is an economic struggle, if you cannot buy much more than second-rate food and rudimentary shelter and only that with difficulty. It is hard to feel free if you cannot afford "wellness," a state of being that Barbara Ehrenreich has recently reminded us mainly belongs to the rich.[297] It is hard to feel free if you are on the wrong end of economic inequality.

295 "The bad news is we're dying early in Britain – and it's all down to 'shit-life syndrome'," 19 August 2018 https://www.theguardian.com/commentisfree/2018/aug/19/bad-news-is-were-dying-earlier-in-britain-down-to-shit-life-syndrome?CMP=Share_iOSApp_Other (accessed 19 August 2018).

296 *Drift: Illicit Mobility and Uncertain Knowledge*, (Oakland: University of California Press, 2018), pp. 34-5. "Fordism" has been defined as "a manufacturing system designed to spew out standardized, low-cost goods and afford its workers decent enough wages to buy them."

297 In *Natural Causes: Life, death, and the illusion of control* (London: Granta, 2018).

Of course, some might say that fighting for economic survival, or caring nothing for it, is to be freer than working long albeit lucrative hours in an office or on a factory floor, committed to one demanding and unreasonable employer. Maybe a trapper off the grid in northern Canada is freer than a corporate lawyer on Toronto's Bay Street. Economists are increasingly criticized for not attributing quantitative value to happiness and quality of life. The significance of inequality as an impediment to well-being and freedom can be overstated. Does inequality of income (or education, or anything else) always harm the disadvantaged? Not necessarily. It may not matter, for example, if there is no relationship or interaction between unequal parties.[298]

But in most instances, inequality does matter. Quite apart from its practical consequences, it creates psychological distress. Two UK psychologists have observed, "Inequality increases our insecurities about self-worth because it emphasizes status and strengthens the idea that some people are worth much more than others."[299] And inequality corrupts democracy. One would expect that a true democracy would work to redistribute wealth downwards. There are many more poor people than rich people, and in a true democracy each person has only one vote. You might expect the poor majority to send wealth in its direction, through tax policy and social programs. Yet, by and large, this does not happen. One explanation is that political power goes hand-in-hand with riches; those with money can thwart the popular will and protect themselves. *The Economist* commented, "The rich have many means to shape public opinion. . . Although their power may sometimes be used to influence the result of a particular vote, it is often deployed more subtly, to shape public narratives about which problems deserve attention."[300] Paul Krugman, who won the Nobel Prize for Economics in 2008, wrote: "Through a variety of channels—media ownership, think tanks, and the

---

298 See T.M. Scanlan, *Why Does Inequality Matter?* (London: Oxford University Press, 2018).

299 Richard Wilkinson and Kate Pickett, "Inequality breeds stress and anxiety. No wonder so many Britons are suffering," *Guardian*, 10 June 2018 https://www.theguardian.com/commentisfree/2018/jun/10/inequality-stress-anxiety-britons?CMP=Share_iOSApp_Other (accessed 11 June 2018).

300 "Free exchange: The ballot or the wallet," 21 July 2018, p. 58.

simple tendency to assume that being rich also means being wise—the 0.1 percent has an extraordinary ability to set the agenda for policy discussion, in ways that can be sharply at odds with both a reasonable assessment of priorities and public opinion more generally."[301]

Inequality in income in Canada, as elsewhere, varies according to geographic region, age, education, gender, ethnicity, indigenous status, and other factors. Different ways of measuring inequality produce different conclusions as to its severity and effect. The Gini index, which considers the distribution of a nation's income or wealth with zero representing complete equality and one hundred total inequality (one person possesses all the wealth), is widely used. Canada does not do well on this index, with a Gini rating of about thirty-four, about the same as Britain. But many important factors are not reflected in such an index. For example, *how* inequality is reduced may be as important as the reduction itself. In a 2017 study, Canada's Institute for Research in Public Policy (IRPP) observed:

> Many people form their notion of the fairness of society and self-respect based on their role relative to that of others in the productive system. Accordingly, a more unequal distribution of rewards in the labour market can challenge this notion of fairness and be detrimental to both the self-respect of those at the bottom of the pay scale and the respect they get from others, despite subsequent income redistribution through taxes and transfers. It is, after all, one thing to obtain one's share of the pie as remuneration for work and quite another to obtain it as a combination of low remuneration and government transfers.[302]

There is a difference between inequality and poverty. In a rich country, even one with a high Gini rating, you can have an income towards the

301 "Notes on Excessive Wealth Disorder," *The New York Times*, 22 June 2019 https://www.nytimes.com/2019/06/22/opinion/notes-on-excessive-wealth-disorder.html (accessed 16 August 2019).

302 David A. Green, W. Craig Riddell and France St-Hilaire, *Income Equality in Canada*, Institute for Research in Public Policy 2017 http://irpp.org/research-studies/aots5-intro/ (accessed 25 May 2018). This is a valuable and detailed analysis. It contains an extensive discussion of various policies that might mitigate income inequality.

bottom of the scale but still not be poor. Some argue that governments should worry about poverty, not about inequality. But then, as
we have seen, inequality produces unhappiness. Should governments
worry about unhappiness?

We all know about the "One Percent," the small number of people
who accumulate and control vast and disproportionate wealth bringing
with it great economic and political power. Less than one percent of
the world's adult population holds almost half of all global wealth. In
Russia and India, the top one percent holds more than half the wealth.
In Canada, the top one percent holds about twenty-four percent of the
country's wealth.[303] It was the Occupy Movement, which began on Wall
Street in September 2011, that brought attention to this worldwide
phenomenon. The 2017 IRPP study of income inequality described the
situation in Canada in detail:

> Apart from temporary setbacks associated with recessions, the
> share of income received by those at the top of the distribution
> has increased steadily over time. Based on data from income tax
> files, the share of market income received by the top one percent
> increased from 7.6 percent in 1982 to 13.6 percent in 2006, before
> declining slightly to twelve percent in 2011. Increases in income
> shares were even more pronounced at the very top of the income
> distribution, with the share of the top 0.1 percent more than dou-
> bling from around two percent in the early 1980s to around five
> percent in recent years. In other words, the income of this small
> group (one tax-filer out of a thousand) went from twenty times
> average income to fifty times average income over this period. Much

303 See Credit Suisse Research Institute, *Global Wealth Report 2018*, http://publications.
credit-suisse.com/index.cfm/publikationen-shop/research-institute/global-wealth-
report-2018-en/ (accessed 20 October 2018). "Wealth per adult in Canada, at USD
288,260, is 29% lower than that in the United States. Wealth is more equally distributed
than in the United States, which accounts for the much higher median wealth in Canada
– USD 106,340 compared with USD 61,670 in the United States. Relative to the United
States, Canada has both a smaller percentage of people with less than USD 10,000, and
a larger percentage above USD 100,000. It has 1.3 million millionaires, and accounts
for 3% of the top 1% of global wealth holders, despite having only 0.6% of the world's
adults." (p. 54)

of the surge in top incomes occurred in the 1990s, but the trend was evident starting in the 1980s.

The IRPP study comments that inequality trends "have the potential over time to tear at the fabric of our society, not just economically but also in terms of the strength of our democracy and the quality of social interactions."

In the US, earning discrepancies between senior executives and the average worker are extraordinary. In 2018, publicly-traded corporations in the US were required to start revealing their pay ratios, comparisons between the pay of their chief executive and the median compensation of other employees at the company. What was discovered?

A Walmart employee earning the company's median salary of $19,177 would have to work for more than a thousand years to earn the $22.2 million that Doug McMillon, the company's chief executive, was awarded in 2017. At Live Nation Entertainment, the concert and ticketing company, an employee earning the median pay of $24,406 would need to work for 2,893 years to earn the $70.6 million that its chief executive, Michael Rapino, made last year. And at Time Warner, where the median compensation is a relatively handsome $75,217, an employee earning that much would still need to work for 651 years to earn the $49 million that Jeffrey Bewkes, the chief executive, earned in just 12 months.[304]

It was reported in 2019 that US chief executives earned an average of US$17.2 million each in 2018, two hundred and seventy-eight times the salary of the average worker in their company.[305]

The situation in Canada is similarly stark, although not as dramatic. A January 2016 report from the Canadian Centre for Policy Alternatives

304 David Gelles, "Want to Make Money Like a C.E.O.? Work for 275 Years," *The New York Times*, 25 May 2018 https://www.nytimes.com/2018/05/25/business/highest-paid-ceos-2017.html (accessed 26 May 2018).

305 Dominic Rushe, "Top US bosses earn 278 times more than their employees, *The Guardian*, 14 August 2019 https://www.theguardian.com/us-news/2019/aug/14/ceo-worker-pay-gap?CMP=Share_iOSApp_Other (accessed 16 August 2019).

("CCPA") noted, "the average top-100 CEO will have earned the average worker's pay by 12:18 p.m. on January 4, 2016—the second paid day of the year—and the average minimum-wage worker's pay by 2:07 p.m.—on New Year's Day."[306] A July 2018, CCPA report[307] focused on inequality in Canada in relative wealth or net worth, defined as the sum of individual or family assets minus debts. It found "that while the average net worth of Canada's wealthiest families rose by 37% between 2012 and 2016—from $2.2 billion to $3.0 billion, for a gain of $806 million in inflation-adjusted dollars per family—the net worth of middle class families increased by 16%, or $41,000, over the same period (from $264,000 to $305,000)." The Report continued: "Canada's wealthiest eighty-seven families now have 4,448 times more wealth than the average Canadian family, and they collectively own the same amount as the lowest-earning twelve million Canadians. At present, the wealthiest eighty-seven families have a net worth of $259 billion, which is about what everyone in Newfoundland and Labrador, Prince Edward Island and New Brunswick collectively owns ($269 billion)." Another driver of increasing economic inequality is the fact that most people do not participate in the stock market in a significant way; only those already wealthy have benefited from the extraordinary post-2008 bull market, once more highlighting the fact that capital will always produce more economic gains than labour.

A PICKET FENCE

Once upon a time, every youngish Canadian with a job, almost any kind of job, could reasonably expect, fairly early in life, to buy a house. Not necessarily a fancy house, but a decent house, a detached house, with a backyard and perhaps a picket fence, a backyard where the kids could play and the dog could run around. This expectation was reasonable

306 Hugh Mackenzie, *Staying Power: CEO Pay in Canada*, p. 7 https://www.policyalternatives.ca/sites/default/files/uploads/publications/National%20Office/2016/01/Staying_Power_CEO_Pay.pdf (accessed 27 May 2018).
307 David Macdonald, "Born to Win: Wealth concentration in Canada since 1999," https://www.policyalternatives.ca/publications/reports/born-win (accessed 31 July 2018).

because the youngish person had a secure career with a predictable income, not a series of precarious side hustles. He functioned in an economy with a reasonable distribution of wealth and income rather than one where a handful of people hoovered up most of the cash. He lived in a place where house prices reflected a sensible local economy, not one driven by investment bankers and offshore investors and money-launderers seeking a haven for their wealth. A related expectation was inter-generational: children would eventually be at least as well off as their parents, and their parents would help them get to that point, in part by gifts and bequests (the generational contract). These expectations created peace and happiness and freed people to do valuable non-economic things for themselves and their community. It is worth remembering as well that this was a time when most households had only one income.

RBC Economics Research publishes quarterly reports on Canadian homeownership affordability. Its "Housing Affordability Measure" is based on the cost of owning a detached bungalow: the higher the reading, the less affordable a home. So, for example, a reading of thirty-two means that the cost of owning such a home, including mortgage payments, utilities and property taxes, would take up thirty-two percent of a typical household's monthly pre-tax income, considerably more after tax. (RBC does not define a "typical household.") The September 2018 RBC Report[308] analyzed the second quarter of 2018. It found the national aggregate measure for that quarter to be fifty-four percent, the worst since 1990. The aggregate measure in Toronto was seventy-six percent; in Vancouver it was a staggering eighty-eight percent (the worst housing affordability ever recorded in Canada)[309]; in Victoria,

---

308 http://www.rbc.com/economics/economic-reports/pdf/canadian-housing/house-sep2018.pdf (accessed 1 October 2018).

309 The Report is particularly gloomy about Vancouver: "The word 'crisis' is often being used these days to describe the affordability situation in the Vancouver area. And why not—RBC's aggregate measure is at a never-seen-before level (88.4%) anywhere in Canada, and continuing to rise rapidly (up 8.2 percentage points in the past year, including a 1.6 percentage point rise in the second quarter). Buying a single-detached home is for the rich only (it would take almost 120% of a typical household's income to cover ownership costs). And settling for a condo also increasingly looks like a luxury for many. Worse, the situation is poised to deteriorate further as interest rates continue to rise."

it was sixty-five percent; Calgary was forty-four percent; Montreal, forty-four percent; St. John had the lowest affordability measure of any major city at twenty-seven percent. The RBC Report predicted that the situation would worsen, if only because of expected interest rate increases. The International Monetary Fund calculates that Canada's home-prices-to-income ratio is the fourth highest among thirty-three countries (the highest is New Zealand, the lowest is Poland).[310]

The causes of this dramatic lack of affordability are not clear. Some point to an influx of offshore money, particularly from China and Russia. This theory leads to the imposition of foreign-buyer taxes, higher property taxes on second homes, and special taxes on empty homes. Taxes like these do have an effect: in Vancouver, they appear to have reduced house prices significantly.[311] Other theories point to speculators, reckless mortgage lending, an inadequate supply of housing, and zoning that favours low-density housing.

The situation for renters is also dire. The 2018 Canadian Rental Housing Index concluded, "Over 1.7 million renter households spend over the recommended affordability benchmark of thirty per cent of gross income on rent and utilities. Of those, 795,000 renter households spend over half of their income on housing costs."[312] The PadMapper Canadian Rent Report tells us that in March 2019 the median monthly rent in Toronto for a one bedroom apartment was $2,260, up $650 in two years.[313]

MEANWHILE, DOWN HERE IN THE COUNTRY

For several months of the year I live on the edge of a small fishing village in Queens County, Nova Scotia. Queens County is one of the

310 See International Monetary Fund, *Global Housing Watch*, 1 May 2018 http://www.imf. org/external/research/housing/ (accessed 24 June 2018).

311 See Kerry Gold, "Recycled listings around Vancouver obscure a major market correction," *Globe and Mail*, 6 July 2018 http://globe2go.newspaperdirect.com/epaper/ viewer.aspx?noredirect=true (accessed 6 July 2018).

312 See www.rentalhousingindex.ca (accessed 3 June 2018).

313 https://blog.padmapper.com/canadian-rent-trends (accessed 31 March 2019).

poorest places in Canada. It has a dwindling population (now about ten thousand), and few employment opportunities. The paper mill, once the biggest employer by far, closed years ago. Most young people leave. They have no choice.

I go from an apartment in downtown Toronto, surrounded by gleaming bank towers and shining high-rise condominiums, to an old house looking across a wide estuary with an abandoned fish processing plant on the distant other side, its night-time lights still glowing mysteriously across the water. Our house, sitting on a rudimentary pot-holed road, has well water and a septic field. The village has a volunteer fire department. About the only visible municipal service is fortnightly garbage collection. A home-made sign down the road warns, "Danger. 20-year-old potholes ahead." In a hot summer, wells can run dry and you realize how difficult life becomes without an adequate supply of water. (A history professor who spends the summer in the village pointed out to me that in Canada the water supply is only reliable in cities.) Hurricanes in the fall and nor'easters in the winter can bring down power lines and sometimes there is no electricity for days.

More than eighty percent of Canadians live in cities. There's a big divide between them and those who live in the country. There's a huge difference in services available, both public and private. There's a big disparity in income: rural work is generally low-paid work, often seasonal or part-time. Much rural housing is inadequate, medical facilities are scarce and there is little to no public transportation. Often there is no high-speed internet. The political influence of rural communities is slight.

MONEY

Money can't buy happiness. Some disagree. Money doesn't buy love. Is that true? It has been argued that in an age of increasing misery and deprivation, citizens self-medicate with love.[314] Does money buy freedom? Maybe not, but it is hard to be free if you are poor.

---

314 See Laurie Essig, *Love, Inc.: Dating Apps, the Big White Wedding, and Chasing the Happily Neverafter* (Oakland: University of California Press, 2019).

CHAPTER TWELVE

INDIGENOUS PEOPLE

A WOUND THAT NEVER HEALS

The plight of Canada's Indigenous People is a wound that never heals. Any mention of it easily evokes pain, misunderstanding, resentment, and anger.

In the Foreword I noted that an early draft of this book was criticized by an anonymous academic reader on the grounds that my "voice" was one of "a dominant culture man speaking to other dominant culture men." The anonymous reader was particularly critical of this chapter on Indigenous People. "There is no evidence in this manuscript that Mr. Slayton is speaking with indigenous people—just about them."

My response is simple. Like everyone else, I am a creature of my time, circumstances, and history. My point of view necessarily incorporates and expresses these constraints. But people of good faith try and transcend the limits of their point of view when commenting on the circumstances of others, and I have tried to do that.

OH, TO BE FREE!

There are about a million and a half Indigenous People (First Nations, Métis and Inuit) in Canada. Their history, since Europeans came to North America is one of suffering. Their current plight is abject. They are an oppressed minority, fighting an indifferent and ignorant, sometimes hostile, majority for rights and respect. Their traditional lands have been taken from them, and generations are condemned to a cycle of poverty and illness. Because they must constantly fight for rights and respect, Indigenous People lack freedom in an essential sense. But so does the majority that requires them to fight in this way. To carelessly deny freedom to others is to lose self-respect and the respect of those others. To live in a country where a minority is denied freedom is to be less free even if you are in the majority.

WINNIPEG

My family came to Winnipeg in 1954, by train from Montreal where the ship from England had docked, arriving at the old Canadian Pacific station in Winnipeg's North End in late October just as the Winnipeg winter was beginning. I was ten years old. Years later my mother told me that the first thing we did when we left the station was go to a nearby diner for something to eat. "I asked for a cup of tea," she said. "They gave me a mug of hot water and a teabag. I thought I'd died and gone to hell." My mother was unpretentious and from an ordinary family, but she had strict English views about the proper way to make tea.

In those days, north Winnipeg—particularly along Main Street—was seedy. Not hell, perhaps, but decrepit and depressing for sure. Arriving at the Canadian Pacific station in north Winnipeg and getting tea at a nearby diner was not a good introduction to a new life in Canada. A lot of Indians (they were commonly called that then) hung out in the north end, apparently without much to do. The common opinion of white people was that many of them were drunk most of the time. I don't know if this was true. There was a lot of casual prejudice in Winnipeg against Indigenous People then. Epithets were hurled. Jokes were cracked. It was a part of a general attitude that you quickly absorbed, particularly if you were only ten years old.

More than sixty years later, the aboriginal situation in Winnipeg, home to Canada's largest urban indigenous population (seventeen percent of Manitoba's population is indigenous, the highest percentage of any province), is still dire. Casual prejudice and violence remain. In 2014, the Winnipeg journalist, Bartley Kives, wrote an article in

The Guardian newspaper about an imminent Winnipeg mayoralty election:[315]

> Winnipeg votes on a new mayor on Wednesday, and indigenous relations have dominated the race. By any metric you choose–income, education, employment, health, life expectancy, access to housing, incarceration and above all exposure to violent crime –Winnipeg's roughly 80,000 First Nations, Métis or Inuit residents are worse off, on average, than the other 620,000 city dwellers. Closing this "great divide," as it's coming to be known in Winnipeg, has emerged as the city's crucial obstacle. . .
>
> Much of the city's aboriginal community . . . remains underemployed, undereducated and relegated to relatively impoverished neighbourhoods in Winnipeg's inner city and North End. Two of the three poorest postal codes in Canada are in Winnipeg. Both are predominantly indigenous neighbourhoods. They are plagued by substandard housing, inadequate financial and retail services and higher-than-average levels of violent crime, mostly because of the domestic violence associated with poverty but also because of the presence of indigenous gangs.

On October 23 2014, Brian Bowman, a Métis (an indigenous person of mixed European and First Nations ancestry), was elected mayor of Winnipeg. A story in *Maclean's* early in 2015 claimed racism in Canada was at its worst in Winnipeg.[316] "The Manitoba capital is deeply divided along ethnic lines. It manifestly does not provide equal opportunity

---

315 "The 'great indigenous divide': Winnipeg stares into an ethnic chasm," 21 October 2014 https://www.theguardian.com/cities/2014/oct/21/winnipeg-election-indigenous-divide-aboriginal (accessed 2 July 2018).

316 Nancy Macdonald, "Welcome to Winnipeg: Where Canada's racism problem is at its worst," 22 January 2015 https://www.macleans.ca/news/canada/welcome-to-winnipeg-where-canadas-racism-problem-is-at-its-worst/ (accessed 2 July 2018). The *Maclean's* article received a lot of criticism. See, for example, Tom Brodbeck, "Many flaws in *Maclean's* story about Winnipeg's race problem," *Winnipeg Sun*, 26 January 2015 http://winnipegsun.com/2015/01/26/many-flaws-in-macleans-story-about-winnipegs-race-problem/wcm/5c50bbb9-aaf3-4bc6-a69d-b00ef8f3267f (accessed 4 July 2018).

for Aboriginals. And it is quickly becoming known for the sub-human treatment of its First Nations citizens, who suffer daily indignities and appalling violence." The article was particularly graphic about the North End where my family had arrived by train so many years before:

> Winnipeg is physically divided by the CP rail yards, which cut the primarily Aboriginal North End from the rest of the city. North End Winnipeg looks nothing like the idyllic, tree-lined, middle-class neighbourhoods to the south. It is the poorest and most violent neighbourhood in urban Canada.
>
> The neighbourhood is home to two of the country's three poorest postal codes—the median household income in the North End is $22,293, less than half that of the wider city at $49,790. The homicides that plague the city, earning it the nickname "Murderpeg" and the country's highest rate of violent crime, are a primarily North End phenomenon. . .
>
> One in three North End residents drop out of school before Grade 9, leaving huge swaths of young residents wholly disconnected from the labour market. One in six children are apprehended by Manitoba's Child and Family Services. Girls as young as 11 or 12 routinely work the stroll. On North Main Street, traffic slows to a stall when intoxicated residents stumble across the street. Solvent abuse is as common as alcoholism here, and rising.

TINA FONTAINE

Tina Fontaine was an Indigenous woman, born in 1999, from the Sagkeeng First Nation one hundred and fifteen kilometres north of Winnipeg. On about August 5, 2014 she went missing from downtown Winnipeg where she had been for several weeks. While she was in Winnipeg she had various contacts with the police, security officers, hospital staff and Child and Family Services. She twice visited city shelters asking for a place to sleep but was told there were no beds. Before she went to Winnipeg, Fontaine was much involved with Child and Family Services and the RCMP. She had a record of chronic absenteeism from school. She used drugs and was sexually exploited by adults. No one seemed to realize the amount of help she needed. No one took charge of her case.

On August 17, 2014 Tina Fontaine's seventy-two pound body was found in the Red River wrapped in a duvet cover and weighted down with rocks. She had been dead for several days. The cause of her death could not be determined. In December, Raymond Joseph Cormier was charged with her murder but there was little evidence against him. A three-week trial found Cormier not guilty. After the verdict, outside the courthouse, Manitoba Keewatinowi Okimakanak Grand Chief Sheila North, referring to the fate of Indigenous youth in general, in eloquent and tearful remarks, said, "This is not the Canada I want to be part of." Another Indigenous speaker angrily said, "Everyone in Canada should be ashamed at what happened to Tina Fontaine." After Fontaine's death, her cousin was shot in the back of the head and set alight in Winnipeg and her uncle committed suicide (these events were apparently not directly related to Fontaine's murder). Tina's father, Eugene, had been murdered in 2011 on the Sagkeeng First Nation, an event, it is said, that changed Tina's life. She received no grief counselling or other help from social services following her father's brutal death.

A special report on the Tina Fontaine case by the Manitoba Advocate for Children and Youth began, "To know Tina's story, to really understand how she came to symbolize a churning anger of a nation enraged, each of us can look as far back as the arrival of European settler. . . In order to understand the story of Tina's life and death it is important to first recognize the history of colonization. . . Like so many, Tina's parents were significantly impacted by historical traumas; their struggles with housing, intimate partner violence, addictions, and mental illness can be directly tied to Canada's history of colonial practices and the implications of this history that continue to exist today for so many Indigenous families."[317]

317 *A Place Where it Feels Like Home: The Story of Tina Fontaine*, March 2019, Executive Summary https://manitobaadvocate.ca/wp-content/uploads/MACY-Special-Report-March-2019-Tina-Fontaine-FINAL1.pdf (accessed 2 April 2019).

Has the situation improved since? The BBC seems to think so. BBC News reported in August 2018 that "Canada's most racist city" had made a comeback.[318] "Four years ago, the death of an indigenous teenager put Winnipeg on the map for all the wrong reasons. But instead of hiding in shame, the city— buoyed by its indigenous organisations—became a leader of Canada's reconciliation movement." But the BBC report was cautious and judged that, "Winnipeg still has a long way to go. Over the past two years, meth has flooded the streets, and it disproportionately affects vulnerable populations like the indigenous community. Many still live in poverty, and many children are still separated from their families in child services."

TRUTH AND RECONCILIATION

The Truth and Reconciliation Commission, established in 2008, was mandated by the Indian Residential Schools Settlement Agreement. The Commission's job was to inform Canadians about what had happened in Indian Residential Schools. Its December 2015 Final Report—comprehensive, heartfelt and hortatory, with sweeping "calls to action"—began: "Canada's residential school system for Aboriginal children was an education system in name only for much of its existence. These residential schools were created for the purpose of separating Aboriginal children from their families, in order to minimize and weaken family ties and cultural linkages, and to indoctrinate children into a new culture—the culture of the legally dominant Euro-Christian Canadian society. . . The Commission heard from more than 6,000 witnesses, most of whom survived the experience of living in the schools as students. The stories of that experience are sometimes difficult to accept as something that could have happened in a country such as Canada, which has long prided itself on being a bastion of democracy, peace, and kindness throughout the world. Children were abused, physically and sexually, and they died in the schools in numbers that would not

---

318 Robin Levinson-King, "Canada's 'most racist city' makes a comeback," 24 August 2018
     https://www.bbc.com/news/amp/world-us-canada-45215814?__twitter_impression=
     true (accessed 30 September 2018).

have been tolerated in any school system anywhere in the country, or in the world."[319]

The Commission's report describes the children's lot in painful detail. The educational experience at residential schools was extremely poor. Rote memory work and religious training were emphasized. The curriculum had racist overtones. Non-educational work, such as growing food, was important because the schools were supposed to be self-sufficient. The speaking of Aboriginal languages was suppressed. The diet was meager. Discipline was severe. Sexual and physical abuse was rampant. Illness was common and many children died, often of tuberculosis.

The legacy of the residential schools has been dire. It is detailed in the Commission's report. For example: "Current conditions such as the disproportionate apprehension of Aboriginal children by child-welfare agencies and the disproportionate imprisonment and victimization of Aboriginal people can be explained in part as a result or legacy of the way that Aboriginal children were treated in residential schools and were denied an environment of positive parenting, worthy community leaders, and a positive sense of identity and self-worth."[320] Residential schools harmed the ability of those who attended to be loving parents later on, leading to a child welfare crisis. The schools severely impeded the educational and economic potential of Indigenous people. The children's physical health was damaged. Justice was denied. The RCMP was compromised. There were few criminal prosecutions for abuse. White lawyers were unsympathetic or ignorant. Traditional legal regimes were ignored or suppressed. The damage done to Indigenous people was profound.

The Commission's work and its Final Report was well received. The report contained ninety-four "calls to action," seventy-six falling within federal jurisdiction. Prime Minister Justin Trudeau promised to implement all of the federal calls to action. But progress has been glacial. By early 2018, only three had been implemented, although a number of others were said to be "in the works." Little has been done since.

---

319 *Honouring the Truth, Reconciling for the Future*, https://nctr.ca/assets/reports/ Final%20Reports/Executive_Summary_English_Web.pdf (accessed 30 July 2018).
320 Note 316, p.135.

MISSING AND MURDERED

Since 1980 somewhere between 1,200 and 4,000 Indigenous women and girls have been murdered or have gone missing. No one knows the exact number.[321] In December 2014, when asked by the CBC's Peter Mansbridge about the possibility of an inquiry into missing and murdered aboriginal women, Prime Minister Stephen Harper said, "Um it, it isn't really high on our radar, to be honest, Peter. You know, our ministers will continue to dialogue ah with, ah, those who are concerned about this. They're studying it."[322] Thinking differently and in part reacting to the Tina Fontaine murder and pressure from a variety of groups, the Trudeau government in 2016 created the independent National Inquiry into Missing and Murdered Indigenous Women and Girls and gave it two years to report.[323]

The Inquiry was troubled from the start. Staff and commissioners resigned almost from the beginning. There was widespread criticism, particularly from the Indigenous community, and calls for the

321 The interim report of the Commission on Missing and Murdered Indigenous Women and Girls says "According to Statistics Canada, 9% of female homicide victims in 1980 were Indigenous. By 2015, Indigenous women made up nearly one-quarter (24%) of homicide victims in Canada. The same report shows that while homicide rates for non-Indigenous women have gone down over the decades, homicide rates for Indigenous women have been going up. The likelihood of violent death is significantly higher for Indigenous than for non-Indigenous women. . . Indigenous women are 12 times more likely to be murdered or missing than any other women in Canada, and 16 times more likely than Caucasian women. In Manitoba and Saskatchewan, they are 19 times more likely than Caucasian women to be murdered or missing." See http://www.mmiwg-ffada.ca/wp-content/uploads/2018/03/ni-mmiwg-interim-report.pdf (accessed 30 July 2018), pp. 7-8.
322 Full text of Peter Mansbridge's interview with Stephen Harper, 17 December 2015 http://www.cbc.ca/news/politics/full-text-of-peter-mansbridge-s-interview-with-stephen-harper-1.2876934 (accessed 29 July 2018).
323 The Commission defines its mandate thusly: "The National Inquiry must look into and report on the systemic causes of all forms of violence against Indigenous women and girls, including sexual violence. We must examine the underlying social, economic, cultural, institutional, and historical causes that contribute to the ongoing violence and particular vulnerabilities of Indigenous women and girls in Canada. The mandate also directs us to look into and report on existing institutional policies and practices to address violence, including those that are effective in reducing violence and increasing safety." See http://www.mmiwg-ffada.ca/mandate/ (accessed 29 July 2018).

resignation of the Chief Commissioner, Marion Buller. Progress was very slow. The communications and media strategy was a shambles. In September 2017, a *Maclean's* article commented that from the day the Inquiry was created, it "has been plagued by internal power struggles, high profile resignations, leaks, and lost friendships. . ."[324]

The Commission published its Interim Report in November 2017.[325] "As Commissioners," it began, "we acknowledge and honour the memory of all Indigenous women and girls—including those who are Two-Spirit, lesbian, gay, heterosexual, bisexual, transgender, queer, or non-binary, and those with disabilities or special needs—who are missing or who have lost their lives to violence." It continues:

> In all that we do, we are guided by the National Inquiry's overarching principle—that our women and girls are sacred. This informs our vision: helping Indigenous women and girls reclaim their power and place. . . . To bring this vision to life, the National Inquiry has set out on a three-part mission: finding the truth, honouring the truth, and giving life to the truth. This is our path to healing. . . For the violence against Indigenous women and girls to end, the ongoing colonial relationship that facilitates it must end. . . Our vision is to see Indigenous women and girls restored to their rightful power and place. This is based on our guiding principle: that all Indigenous women and girls are sacred.

The Interim Report offered sobering statistical evidence of the perilous life often led by Indigenous women and girls. It exhaustively reviewed previous studies and the work of prior commissions and summarized their recommendations. It described in detail the way in which the Commission process sought to respect and incorporate Indigenous practices and ways of thinking. It made no findings or definitive recommendations.

In 2018, the government rejected a request for a two-year extension of the Commission's mandate, set to expire on November, 1 2018,

---

324 Nancy Macdonald and Meagan Campbell, "Lost and Broken," 13 September 2017 https://www.macleans.ca/lost-and-broken/ (accessed 29 July 2018).
325 See note 318.

and an additional $50 million (the original budget was $54 million). The Commission was given an extra six months instead, which it clearly regarded as hopelessly inadequate. The final hurried report was published in June 2019.[326] It contained two-hundred-and-thirty-one individual "Calls for Justice" directed at governments, institutions, social service providers, industries and all Canadians. It controversially described the murder of Indigenous women as a "genocide." It called for major reforms of the criminal justice system and of policing. We wait to see what action the government will take.

IDLE NO MORE

It started in 2012 with another Stephen Harper omnibus budget bill, this one Bill C-45, the so-called Jobs and Growth Act. Buried in Bill C-45 were amendments to Indian Act provisions dealing with voting and approval procedures in relation to proposed land designations, and other provisions, particularly amendments to the Navigable Waters Protection Act and the Fisheries Act, thought to be adverse to the rights of Indigenous People.

Four women from Saskatchewan were particularly upset. Part of their problem was the government's use of omnibus legislation, an unlikely but legitimate trigger for a broad protest movement. In November 2012, the four women created Idle No More, a First Nations protest movement seeking government guarantees for treaties and an end to what they saw as a legislative erosion of First Nations rights. The movement's mission statement said, "Idle No More calls on all people to join in a revolution which honors and fulfils Indigenous sovereignty which protects the land and water."

Protests were held and road and rail-line blockades took place. There were flash mobs, round dances and singing. There was no violence. The movement quickly gained remarkable strength and staying power, using social media skillfully. Justin Trudeau, then leader of the opposition,

326 *Reclaiming Power and Place,* https://www.mmiwg-ffada.ca/final-report/ (accessed 16 August 2019).

expressed sympathy, as did the Assembly of First Nations. Idle No More attracted a lot of attention and, despite peaking in 2012–13, was still active years later, with an increasingly international aspect. In March 2015, for example, it demonstrated on Parliament Hill against proposed anti-terror legislation, Bill C-51, saying that some of its provisions threatened freedom of speech. Ken Coats has written, "The collective events and gatherings that gained the nation's attention in 2012–2013 represent, in my mind, the largest and most sustained demonstration of Indigenous identity and cultural determination in Canadian history."[327]

FREEDOM FOR ALL

We measure the freedom of a democratic society by the extent to which all of its members are free. A free society is one where those who are less fortunate and more vulnerable are respected and helped by all so that they enjoy almost as much liberty as the person who lives in the big house on the hill. While the Indigenous People of Canada are badly treated, until history is overcome and ceases to determine the future, while we ignore what we see around us, our country falls short of freedom.

---

327 *#Idlenomore and the Remaking of Canada,* (Regina: University of Regina Press, 2015), p. XIII.

CHAPTER THIRTEEN

WORLD ON FIRE

FIRE

In the summer of 2018, I got an email from an English cousin who had just arrived in Calgary. "Calgary is full of smoke," the email said. "I can't breathe properly. What should I do?" I checked the news. "The smoke is moving in from northern Alberta and the mountain parks," the *Calgary Herald* reported. "For some people, the thickening smoke will bring on coughing, throat irritation, headaches and shortness of breath. Children, seniors and those with cardiovascular or lung disease, such as asthma, are especially at risk."[328] I had no useful advice for my cousin.

When I got my cousin's email, I was at my house on Nova Scotia's south shore where we were experiencing the third year of a drought. Wells were running dry. People were going to community centres for a shower. Municipalities were handing out jugs of drinking water. My pond, which for twenty years had been a sylvan haven for ducks, herons and otters, had gone dry for the second year in a row, and was now just a bowl of mud. Extreme storm surges leading to flooding were becoming routine, and wild winds (hurricanes, sometimes) frequently knocked out power. Shorebirds and bats were disappearing, replaced by deer ticks and mosquitoes.

---

328 "The smoke is back: Alert issued for Calgary," 22 August 2018 https://calgaryherald. com/news/local-news/the-smoke-is-back-alert-issued-for-calgary (accessed 24 August 2018).

Later that year, my close friend Jean, who lived in Malibu, California, was visiting San Francisco for the weekend. While she was there a wildfire of gigantic proportions, the Woolsey Fire, propelled by the Santa Ana winds, leapt across the Pacific Coast Highway and burnt her house (and many others) to the ground. Jean had lived in that house for over fifty years. Further north in California another huge wild fire, the Camp Fire, raged at the same time. Many were killed trying to flee these fires. The consensus of experts was that climate change had exacerbated if not caused these conflagrations and things would get worse. Year-after-year, average temperatures have been rising and annual rainfall declining. Robinson Meyer in the *Atlantic* magazine wrote about what this means for the lives of people in California: "Millions of people have gotten used to living near big fires—sniffing the smoke when they open their door every morning, seeing the somber pink circle of sun in the sky every evening. A smaller number have fled homes in the middle of the night or driven through a storm of embers."[329]

The world is burning. In North America, in the summer of 2018, forest fires were out of control in British Columbia, Alberta, Ontario, Quebec, and California. Bush fires ravaged Australia and New Zealand. Wildfires swept through parts of Russia, Greece and Portugal. Temperatures never before experienced were recorded throughout Europe, the Middle East, Africa and Asia. The hottest July ever recorded was in 2019: the ten hottest years throughout the world since record keeping began have all occurred in the past two decades.[330] Extreme weather events, from floods to droughts, were becoming the norm. Weather commentators ran out of extravagant adjectives to describe what was happening.

329 "The Worst Is Yet to Come for California's Wildfires," 11 November 2018 https://www.theatlantic.com/science/archive/2018/11/californias-deadly-wildfires-worst-yet-come/575590/ (accessed 13 November 2018).

330 Brady Dennis and Andrew Freedman, "Here's how the hottest month in recorded history unfolded around the world," *Washington Post,* 5 August 2019 https://www.washingtonpost.com/climate-environment/2019/08/05/heres-how-hottest-month-recorded-history-unfolded-around-globe/ (accessed 18 August 2019).

ICE

Land-based ice is melting. It is melting much faster than experts predicted it would a decade ago. If all the land-based ice in Antarctica melts, the sea level worldwide will rise by at least 200 feet.[331] The Arctic ice cap has shrunk to less than half its size of forty years ago. Soon, in the summer and autumn, there will be no sea ice at all.[332] Sea ice melting does not directly raise water levels, but contributes to temperature increase which has the same effect.

The melting process is accelerating and likely unstoppable. No one knows how long it will take until the ice is all gone and no one knows how fast the sea level will rise. Inevitably, shorelines will move dramatically inland around the world. The process has already begun, its effect exacerbated by bad development decisions.[333] It is unnecessary to predict the apocalyptic consequences in detail. Every coastal community in the world, including dozens of major cities, will become uninhabitable. There will be hundreds of millions of climate refugees, angry and displaced, gravely threatening the established order, leading to a wholly

331 See Kendra Pierre-Louis, "Antarctica Is Melting Three Times as Fast as a Decade Ago," *New York Times,* 13 June 2018 https://www.nytimes.com/2018/06/13/climate/antarctica-ice-melting-faster.html (accessed 26 August 2018). And see "Mass balance of the Antarctic Ice Sheet from 1992 to 2017," *Nature* 13 June 2018 https://www.nature.com/articles/s41586-018-0179-y (accessed 26 August 2018)/

332 Elizabeth Kolbert writes: "Sea ice reflects sunlight, while open water absorbs it, so melting ice leads to further warming, which leads to more melt, and so on. . . Arctic soils contain hundreds of billions of tons of carbon, in the form of frozen and only partially decomposed plants. As the region heats up, much of this carbon is likely to be released into the atmosphere, where it will trap more heat—another feedback loop. In the Arctic Ocean, vast stores of methane lie buried under frozen sediments. If these stores, too, are released, the resulting warming is likely to be catastrophic." "How to Write About a Vanishing World," *The New Yorker,* 15 October 2018 https://www.newyorker.com/magazine/2018/10/15/how-to-write-about-a-vanishing-world?mbid=social_tablet_e (accessed 10 October 2018).

333 See Christian Aid, *Sinking Cities, Rising Seas A perfect storm of climate change and bad development choices,* 5 October 2018 https://www.christianaid.org.uk/sites/default/files/2018-10/Christian-Aid-Sinking-cities-rising-seas-report.pdf (accessed 5 October 2018). This report singled out, as particularly vulnerable even today, the cities of Jakarta, Bangkok, Lagos, Manila, Dhaka, Shanghai, London, and Houston.

different and much worse way of life for all of humanity.[334] Where will
the refugees go? Many areas not affected by rising sea levels will be too
hot to support ordinary life. Other areas will have no water, as drought
spreads.[335]

THE SIXTH EXTINCTION

The natural world is a vanishing world. Biodiversity, all living flora and
fauna, is disappearing. We are facing the Sixth Extinction (the first was
450 million years ago). There is no coming back from extinction. The
Sixth Extinction is the first to be caused by human activity. A principal
cause is climate change. Other causes include habitat loss, pollution,
unsustainable harvesting, and the introduction of invasive species, all
the work of humans. The Fifth Extinction, 66 million years ago, had
nothing to do with human activity. It was caused by the impact of a
giant asteroid landing in the Yucatán Peninsula.

The Canadian World Wildlife Fund (WWF) 2017 *Living Planet
Report* said, "From 1970 to 2014, half (451 of 903) of monitored wildlife species in Canada declined in abundance. This is true for all wildlife
groups: approximately half of the mammals (54 per cent), fish (51 per
cent), birds (48 per cent), and amphibians and reptiles (50 per cent)
included in the analysis exhibited declining trends during this time"[336]
The 2018 WWF *Living Planet Report* reported an overall, worldwide
decline of sixty percent in the population sizes of vertebrates between

334 See Eric Holthaus, "Ice Apocalpyse," *Grist*, 2 November 2017 https://grist.org/
   article/antarctica-doomsday-glaciers-could-flood-coastal-cities/ (accessed 26 August
   2-18). For a visual representation, see Science Insider, "What Europe Would Look
   Like If all the Earth's Ice Melted," https://www.youtube.com/watch?annotation_id=
   annotation_465221637&feature=iv&src_vid=VbiRNT_gWUQ&v=FuNggCNVUf4 ,
   and "How Earth Would Look if All The Ice Melted," https://www.youtube.com/
   watch?v=VbiRNT_gWUQ (9 October 2018).
335 See Bill McKippen, "How Extreme Weather is Shrinking the Plant," *The New Yorker*, 26
   November 2018 https://www.newyorker.com/magazine/2018/11/26/how-extreme-
   weather-is-shrinking-the-planet?mbid=social_tablet_e (accessed 3 April 2019).
336 See http://assets.wwf.ca/downloads/WEB_WWF_REPORT_v3.pdf?_ga=2.119256
   201.1693506105.1542123855-1082962237.1542123855 (accessed 13 November
   2018).

1970 and 2014.[337] In March 2018, the UN-funded Intergovernmental Science-Policy Platform on Biodiversity and Ecosystem Services reported that "exploitable fisheries in the Asia-Pacific, the world's most populous region, are on course to decline to zero by 2048; that freshwater availability in the Americas has halved since the 1950s; and that 42% of land species in Europe have declined in the past decade."[338] In 2019, the journal *Science* reported that nearly three billion North American birds, twenty-nine percent of all birds in Canada and the United States, have disappeared since 1970.[339] Throughout the world, insects are disappearing. A German study found that, measured by weight, the overall abundance of flying insects in German nature reserves had decreased by seventy-five percent over twenty-seven years.[340] These kinds of results have been replicated for many insects (there are millions of species) across a multitude of countries. And there are severe knock-on effects of insect depletion. Many birds, for example, rely on insects for food. If there are not enough insects, birds will starve.

FAILURE

The world has failed to address these crucial issues and will continue to fail with calamitous consequences. We can only be saved now by some fantastical geoengineering technology—for example, deployment of a gigantic manmade atmospheric sunshade, or pumping reflecting particles into the atmosphere to block some of the sun's energy, or filling the oceans with silver ping pong balls.

---

337 https://wwf.panda.org/knowledge_hub/all_publications/living_planet_report_2018/ (accessed 13 November 2018). A major UN report on biodiversity (from the Intergovernmental Science-Policy Platform on Biodiversity and Ecosystem Services) is expected in late 2019.

338 Jonathan Watts, "Destruction of nature as dangerous as climate change, scientists warn," *Guardian,* 23 March 2018 https://www.theguardian.com/environment/2018/mar/23/destruction-of-nature-as-dangerous-as-climate-change-scientists-warn (accessed 13 November 2018).

339 "Decline of the North American avifauna," *Science*, 4 Oct 2019 https://science.sciencemag.org/content/366/6461/120 (accessed 9 October 2019).

340 Brooke Jarvis, "The Insect Apocalypse Is Here," *The New York Times*, 27 November 2018 https://www.nytimes.com/2018/11/27/magazine/insect-apocalypse.html (accessed 3 April 2019).

There are five principal reasons for the world's devastating failure to deal effectively with climate change. The first is the magnitude of the problem. The second is the widespread economic behaviour generally referred to as "the tragedy of the commons" (a nineteenth-century phrase, revived in 1968 by biologist Garrett Hardin).[341] The third is the political inability of democratic governments to take the strict and sweeping steps necessary to deal with the problem. The fourth is world disparities in economic development and the unwillingness of developing countries to do anything that will impede their own economic growth. The fifth is the absence of powerful international institutions with the ability to compel international cooperation on climate change.

First, the climate change problem is immense. The widely agreed upon goal, which would have seemed highly achievable a few years ago, is to limit global warming to one-and-a-half degrees Centigrade. Auden Schendler and Andrew P. Jones, writing in *The New York Times* in October 2018,[342] described what would be necessary to do this.

The world would need to reduce greenhouse gas emissions faster than has ever been achieved, and do it everywhere, for fifty years. Northern European countries reduced emissions about four to five percent per year in the 1970s. We'd need reductions of six to nine percent. Every year, in every country, for half a century.

We'd need to spread the world's best climate practices globally, like electric cars in Norway, energy efficiency in California, land protection in Costa Rica, solar and wind power in China, vegetarianism in India, bicycle use in the Netherlands.

---

341 "The Tragedy of the Commons," *Nature* 162, p. 1243. Hardin's article has been very influential, but not everyone agrees with his theory. For example, in 2018 historian Fabien Locher wrote, "Today, our historical perspective and improved understanding show this line of thinking for what it is: a misconception with no concrete basis, skewed by a highly ideological perception of social systems. Since the 1970s . . . the social sciences have empirically documented hundreds of cases of communities past and present that sustainably manage their resources as communal property." See "Debunking the Tragedy of the Commons," *CNRS News* https://news.cnrs.fr/opinions/debunking-the-tragedy-of-the-commons (accessed 9 September 2018).

342 "Stopping Climate Change Is Hopeless. Let's Do It," 6 October 2018 https://www.nytimes.com/2018/10/06/opinion/sunday/climate-change-global-warming.html (accessed 7 October 2018).

We'd face opposition the whole way. To have a prayer of 1.5 degrees Celsius, we would need to leave most of the remaining coal, oil and gas underground, compelling the Exxon Mobils and Saudi Aramcos to forgo anticipated revenues of over $33 trillion over the next twenty-five years.

In October 2018, a report by the UN Intergovernmental Panel on Climate Change, commissioned under the terms of the 2015 Paris Agreement, warned "there is only a dozen years for global warming to be kept to a maximum of 1.5C, beyond which even half a degree will significantly worsen the risks of drought, floods, extreme heat and poverty for hundreds of millions of people."[343] The report said that to prevent a catastrophic 2.7 degrees of warming, "greenhouse pollution must be reduced by forty-five percent from 2010 levels by 2030, and one hundred percent by 2050. It also found that, by 2050, use of coal as an electricity source would have to drop from nearly 40 percent today to between one and seven percent. Renewable energy such as wind and solar, which make up about twenty percent of the electricity mix today, would have to increase to as much as sixty-seven percent."[344] All this seems extremely unlikely if not impossible.[345] In September 2019, Climate Action Tracker warned, "Under the current course of policies, the world could reach the 1.5 degree C warming limit by 2035, 2 degrees by 2053 and 3.2 degrees by the end of the century."[346]

343 See Intergovernmental Panel on Climate Change, "Global Warming of 1.5°C: Summary for Policymakers," http://report.ipcc.ch/sr15/pdf/sr15_spm_final.pdf (accessed 8 October 2018). Jonathan Watts, "We have 12 years to limit climate change catastrophe, warns UN," *The Guardian*, 8 October 2018 https://www.theguardian.com/environment/2018/oct/08/global-warming-must-not-exceed-15c-warns-landmark-un-report?CMP=Share_iOSApp_Other (accessed 8 October 2018).

344 Coral Davenport, "Major Climate Report Describes a Strong Risk of Crisis as Early as 2040, *New York Times*, 8 October 2018 https://www.nytimes.com/2018/10/07/climate/ipcc-climate-report-2040.html (accessed 8 October 2018).

345 See Fourth National Climate Assessment, Volume II: Impacts, Risks, and Adaptation in the United States, a report issued by 13 U.S. Government agencies, November 2018 https://nca2018.globalchange.gov/ (accessed 3 April 2019). The Report says that climate change could cut U.S. Gross Domestic Product by ten percent by 2100.

346 https://climateactiontracker.org/publications/time-to-boost-national-climate-action/ (accessed 9 October 2019).

The second reason for failure is the tragedy of the commons. This phrase refers to selfish and ultimately irrational behaviour by individuals contrary to the common good.[347] Typically this behaviour involves individual exploitation of community-owned natural resources. The individual urge to behave this way is powerful if not irresistible. It is easy to determine and act on short-term selfish interest and difficult to grasp, let alone care about, the possible long-term consequences of everyone doing so. An example. If for personal convenience I travel by aircraft unnecessarily, with no thought of the aggregate consequences for the environment of air travel (severe pollution of the atmosphere), I am contributing to the tragedy of the commons. The free rider problem, the use of public goods by people who do not pay their share of the cost, is a related issue. And then there is disregard for unrepresented future generations which stand to lose more than we do. This problem is sometimes referred to as the "tragedy of the horizon." In a 2015 speech Mark Carney, then Governor of the Bank of England and former Governor of the Bank of Canada, said, "We don't need an army of actuaries to tell us that the catastrophic impacts of climate change will be felt beyond the traditional horizons of most actors–imposing a cost on future generations that the current generation has no direct incentive to fix."[348] As John Lanchester puts it, "The demand climate change makes on us is to feel empathy for the unborn poor of the global south, and change our economies to act on the basis of their needs."[349]

Thirdly, complex democratic governments cannot grapple effectively with climate change. In part this is because there is always a segment of the population, sometimes a substantial segment, sometimes a segment that controls government, that does not believe in climate change or

---

347 Marq de Villiers has argued that the tragedy of the commons argument is overstated. "A rational being, faced with the dilemma of the commons, would be able to calculate long-term prospects and conclude, rationally, that some sort of short-term limit arrived at through negotiation would be in his own interests . . . cooperation is a more rational decision than independence." *Our Way Out* (Toronto: McCLelland & Stewart), p. 314.

348 Larry Elliot, "Carney warns of risks from climate change 'tragedy of the horizon'", *The Guardian*, 29 September 2015 https://www.theguardian.com/environment/2015/sep/29/carney-warns-of-risks-from-climate-change-tragedy-of-the-horizon (accessed 4 October 2019)

349 "World on Fire," *New York Times Book Review*, 28 April 2019, p.1.

has a personal economic reason to ignore it (powerful corporations, or coal miners, for example), or espouses an incompatible philosophy (such as the libertarian gospel of Ayn Rand). This can lead to regulatory rollbacks reversing previous progress, such as the rollbacks of the US Environmental Protection Agency and the US Interior Department during the Trump administration, e.g., the Interior Department's loosening of safety regulations for offshore drilling that were issued by the Obama administration after the Deepwater Horizon disaster in the Gulf of Mexico in 2010.[350]

For a national democratic government, even one that truly believes in the need to combat climate change, to try and do decisively what should be done can easily create a level of discord that all but the most courageous democratic leaders will seek to avoid. Compounding the problem is conflict between different levels of government, each with its own jurisdiction, a conflict particularly acute in federal states. For example, the government of Justin Trudeau wisely pursued a national carbon tax as part of a Canadian climate plan. The Trudeau government required each province to enact a carbon pricing plan by the end of 2018, or have a national price imposed on it. The obvious idea was to discourage the use of fossil fuels by increasing the cost to the consumer of those fuels. Revenue raised would be returned to taxpayers in various ways (ideally, through improving public transportation). William Nordhaus, who won the 2018 Nobel Prize for Economics for demonstrating the efficacy of a carbon tax and the way it corrects market failure (the market left to itself ignores externalities such as pollution), has said, "I think the model is British Columbia. You raise electricity prices by $100 a year, but then the government gives back a dividend that lowers internet prices by $100 year. In real terms, you're raising the price of carbon goods but lowering the prices of non-carbon-intensive goods."[351] The only legitimate criticism of the Trudeau carbon tax was that it wasn't high enough.

---

350 See Coral Davenport, "Washington Rolls Back Safety Rules Inspired by Deepwater Horizon Disaster." *The New York Times,* 27 September 2018 https://www.nytimes.com/2018/09/27/climate/offshore-drilling-safety-deepwater-horizon.html?emc=edit_clim_20181003&nl=climate-fwd&nlid=8765915820181003&te=1 (accessed 3 October 2018).

351 Coral Davenport, "After Nobel in Economics, William Nordhaus Talks About Who's Getting

Initially, there was a widespread political consensus in Canada that a national carbon tax was a good idea. That consensus quickly disappeared, the victim of complicated politics and changes of provincial governments, and the political fact that many consumers irrationally object to the idea of paying more at the gas pump even if they get the money back later. Raising the price of energy is seldom popular. In the spring of 2019, the federal government was forced to impose a carbon tax on Ontario, Saskatchewan, Manitoba and New Brunswick, the dissenting provinces. British Columbia, Alberta and Quebec already had carbon tax plans, while Nova Scotia, Prince Edward Island and Newfoundland and Labrador voluntarily introduced their own version of the tax on January 1, 2019. Meanwhile, in April 2019, Environment Canada reported that Canada is warming twice as fast as rest of world and Northern Canada is heating up nearly three times as fast.[352]

Attempts by more local levels of governments, e.g., California under the governorship of Jerry Brown and certain municipal governments, private entities such as Google and Apple, and other civil society groups in the US, to collaborate and fill the void have been ineffective.[353] Good analysis, good intentions, and gradual measures are not enough. George Monbiot has written, "Only shifts commensurate with the scale of our existential crises have any prospect of averting them. Hopeless realism, tinkering at the edges of the problem, got us into this mess. It will not get us out."[354]

His Pollution-Tax Ideas Right," *The New York Times*. 13 October 2018 https://www. nytimes.com/2018/10/13/climate/nordhaus-carbon-tax-interview.html (accessed 13 November 2018). See David Leonhardt, "The Problem With Putting a Price on the End of the World," *The New York Times*, 9 April 2019 https://www.nytimes. com/interactive/2019/04/09/magazine/climate-change-politics-economics.html? smid=nytcore-ios-share (accessed 10 April 2019). And see Nordhaus, "Climate Change: The Ultimate Challenge for Economics," 2018 Nobel Prize Lecture https://www.nobel-prize.org/prizes/economic-sciences/2018/nordhaus/lecture/ (accessed 10 April 2019).

352   *Canada's Changing Climate Report*, https://changingclimate.ca/CCCR2019/ (accessed 4 April 2019).

353   See Brad Plumer, "They Defied Trump on Climate Change. Now, It's Their Moment of Truth," *The New York Times*, 11 September 2018 https://www.nytimes.com/2018/09/11/ climate/california-climate-summit.html?emc=edit_clim_20180912&nl=climate-fwd& nlid=8765915820180912&te=1 (accessed 13 September 2018).

354   "The Earth is in a death spiral. It will take radical action to save us," *The Guardian*, 14 November 2018 https://www.theguardian.com/commentisfree/2018/nov/14/earth-death-spiral-radical-action-climate-breakdown (accessed 14 November 2018).

Fourth, developing countries, often with autocratic governments, want to catch up economically with developed countries. They are not receptive to pleas from developed countries to limit their catch-up in order to protect the world environment. Often economic catch-up relies on old technologies, tools used by developed countries decades or centuries ago. Coal production and consumption is the most important energy-producing old technology. China and India, with a combined population of almost three billion, are the developing countries that matter the most. China has the largest coal production in the world, about fifty percent of the world's supply. Over four million Chinese work in the country's coal mines. About seventy percent of China's total energy consumption and nearly eighty percent of its electricity production come from coal. The amount grows year over year. China is the world's largest emitter of greenhouse gases, responsible for almost twenty-eight percent of global carbon dioxide emissions in 2017. China is also financing a number of new coal-fired power stations in Africa, particularly in sub-Saharan countries.

Coal is the principal source of energy in India, generating sixty-five percent of the country's power supply. India is the world's third-largest emitter of greenhouse gases. One expert wrote in 2016, "These are economic boom times in India. The government of Prime Minsiter Narenda Modi is presiding over seven-percent annual growth, fueled by the coal that generates most of the country's electricity and powers heavy industries like steel and motor manufacturing. . . To keep growth going, Modi last year called for the state-owned company Coal India . . . to double its production by 2020." Coal consumption in India increased by nine percent in 2018.[355]

Other Asian countries, particularly Japan, South Korea, Vietnam, and Indonesia, are major consumers of coal. The conservative government of Australia has rejected the phasing out of coal power. In 2018, the deputy prime minister, Michael McCormack, said Australia should "absolutely" continue to use and exploit its coal reserves.[356]

355 Fred Pearce, "The Human Cost of India's Push to Produce More Coal," *Yale Environment 360*, 15 March 2016 https://e360.yale.edu/features/on_burning_ground_human_cost_indias_push_produce_more_coal (accessed 13 September 2018).
356 Paul Karp, "Australian government backs coal in defiance of IPCC climate warning,"

Development of a major new Australian coal mine (the Carmichael mine) by an Indian company began in 2019.

At the end of the day, pollution, global warming, and the collapse of biodiversity, are international problems that have to be addressed internationally. In September 2018, António Guterres, the secretary general of the United Nations said, "The time has come for our leaders to show they care about the people whose fate they hold in their hands. We need to rapidly shift away from our dependence on fossil fuels." The Paris Agreement of 2015, which aimed to keep temperatures from rising more than two degrees Celsius from preindustrial levels (one-and-a-half degrees, if possible), has been the principal attempt at an international plan. It was signed by one hundred and seventy-four states and the European Union. Each signatory made a commitment, known formally as a Nationally Determined Contribution, to curtail its greenhouse gas emissions by a specific amount by 2030. The goals were inadequate to begin with, leaving the world on track for a catastrophic 2.7 degree warming this century. Even so, no major industrialized country, including Canada, has come close to meeting its modest Nationally Determined Contribution. The Paris Agreement asked signatories to revisit pledges before 2020 and then make new pledges every five years after. It recognized that developed nations must financially help developing countries with the costs of coping with the effects of climate change to an aggregate amount of at least $100 billion a year.

The US announced in June 2017 it would leave the Paris Accord by 2020. President Trump has said he intends to increase the burning of coal (he calls it, "clean, beautiful coal").[357] Brazil, the world's seventh-largest emitter of greenhouse gasses, under president Jair Bolsonaro, has announced plans to leave the Paris Accord and an intention to open up the Amazon rainforest to farmers and miners. Meanwhile, the

Guardian, 8 October 2018 https://www.theguardian.com/australia-news/2018/oct/09/australian-government-backs-coal-defiance-ipcc-climate-warning?CMP=Share_iOSApp_Other (accessed 10 October 2018).

357 See "Coal Is Killing the Planet. Trump Loves It," *The New York Times,* 8 October 2018 https://www.nytimes.com/2018/10/08/opinion/epa-climate-environment-trump.html (accessed 10 October 2018). Interestingly enough, despite Trump's enthusiasm, coal as a source of energy in America is diminishing as power plants switch to natural gas.

International Energy Agency reports that in 2018 Energy-related CO2 emissions rose by 1.7 percent to 33.1 billion tonnes from the previous year, the highest rate of growth since 2013.[358]

As for biodiversity, an issue always given second place after climate change, the situation is even worse. Eight years ago, under the Aichi Biodiversity Targets (agreed to in Aichi, Japan, following the 1992 UN Convention on Biological Diversity), nations promised to at least halve the loss of natural habitats, ensure sustainable fishing in all waters, and expand nature reserves from ten percent to seventeen percent of the world's land by 2020. Most have fallen far short of even these modest targets. The United States refuses to participate. Canada is a tepid supporter. It has committed, through Parks Canada, that "by 2020, at least 17% of terrestrial areas and inland water, and 10% of marine and coastal areas of Canada are conserved through networks of protected areas and other effective area-based measures."[359]

FREEDOM

How much freedom will we have when fires sweep across our country, the seas rise relentlessly, the animals die, and the beauty of nature is gone? How much freedom will we have when there are vast migrations of people across continents, fleeing natural disasters, ignoring national borders, fighting for scarce resources? No wall or national laws can contain hundreds of millions of desperate people on the move. The era of climate migration and mass death will soon be upon us. Climate change and its consequences, and the collapse of biodiversity, now seeming inevitable, dwarf all other dangers to freedom. Is there nothing that can be done?

---

358 "Global Carbon Emissions Hit Record High in 2018-IEA," *The New York Times*, 26 March 2019 https://www.nytimes.com/reuters/2019/03/26/us/25reuters-iea-emissions.html (accessed 3 April 2019).

359 See http://www.conservation2020canada.ca/the-pathway/ (accessed 13 November 2018)

PART SIX

THE SOLUTION

There is no freedom without selfless, principled and courageous leaders. There is no freedom without selfless citizens committed to civic engagement and willing to pay substantial taxes to promote the common good. The general welfare must trump personal interest if we are to survive, let alone prosper. We have moral agency; we are capable of making the right choices; we fail to make them at our peril.

Our evaluation of the state in Canada of the conditions for freedom tells us what must be done. The final chapter offers a Citizens Manifesto.

CHAPTER FOURTEEN

LEADERS AND CITIZENS

'TIS NOT TOO LATE TO BUILD A BETTER WORLD

Democracy only works if leaders and citizens care for the general welfare at least as much as they care for their personal interests. Do I really have to make this point? I think so. Many reject the argument on principle. Some people believe that pursuing personal advantage to the exclusion of all else, no questions asked, is a God-given right. Others, disciples of Adam Smith's invisible hand, think that pursuing personal advantage conveniently benefits the public good as well, so there's nothing to worry about.[360] And, of course, views substantially and legitimately differ as to what is the general welfare. But, regardless of these complications, if political leaders care mostly for themselves and their personal political ambition, and average citizens care mostly for themselves and their immediate families, the result is societal and state dysfunction, a pointless and unproductive butting of heads leading eventually to a dystopia where freedom is sidelined and social progress stalls or reverses.

---

360 The theory that individuals pursuing their economic self-interest benefit society more than they would if they tried to intentionally benefit society. Adam Smith was an eighteenth century Scottish economist and moral philosopher.

LEADERS

Democratic political leadership properly begins with big ideas carefully conceived to promote and increase the general good. Four things are then required to push ahead. First, conviction. The leader must believe, to the tips of his toes, that his big ideas are worthy. Second, his big ideas must have sufficient support from others, both in the political sphere and in the general population, to make progress possible; the leader's eloquence and capacity to persuade matter greatly. Third, the leader must have the ability to execute his program once it is broadly accepted. Fourth, and this is essential, the leader must have courage, for there will always be fierce opposition to big ideas and their implementation.

Franklin Roosevelt and Tommy Douglas (but not Barack Obama) are examples of political leaders who exemplified these leadership traits. On October 31, 1936, three days before a presidential election that saw him elected for a second term with a big majority, Franklin Roosevelt, in a speech at Madison Square Gardens in New York City, announced the Second New Deal. The First New Deal, social legislation designed to deal with the Great Depression and its consequences, had been savagely attacked from the right. In his Madison Square Gardens speech, Roosevelt defended the First New Deal ferociously: "We had to struggle with the old enemies of peace—business and financial monopoly, speculation, reckless banking, class antagonism, sectionalism, war profiteering. They had begun to consider the Government of the United States as a mere appendage to their own affairs. We know now that Government by organized money is just as dangerous as Government by organized mob. Never before in all our history have these forces been so united against one candidate as they stand today. They are unanimous in their hate for me—and I welcome their hatred."[361] Roosevelt went on, in the Second New Deal, still facing violent opposition, to introduce further landmark social legislation including the Social Security Act.

Tommy Douglas, New Democratic Party politician and premier of Saskatchewan from 1944 to 1961, was responsible for the creation

---

361 For the full text of this speech, see http://docs.fdrlibrary.marist.edu/od2ndst.html (accessed 7 October 2018).

of Medicare, a highly-popular government program first enacted in Saskatchewan in 1962 and now regarded as a defining characteristic of Canada. Initially, Medicare faced strong opposition, particularly from the medical profession itself. Tommy Douglas was burnt in effigy, and was confusingly called both a communist and a Nazi. He was uncowed. "Courage, my friends," he said. "'Tis not too late to build a better world."

President Barack Obama was eloquent but fearful. Psychologist Drew Westen has compared Obama unfavourably with Franklin Roosevelt and referred to Obama's "deep-seated aversion to conflict and his profound failure to understand bully dynamics."[362] Writes Westen: "When faced with the greatest economic crisis, the greatest levels of economic inequality, and the greatest levels of corporate influence on politics since the Depression, Barack Obama stared into the eyes of history and chose to avert his gaze. Instead of indicting the people whose recklessness wrecked the economy, he put them in charge of it. He never explained that decision to the public, a failure in storytelling as extraordinary as the failure in judgment behind it." Obama did not measure up to Roosevelt. He was short on big ideas and lacked political courage. His personal grace, integrity, and attractive style were only partial recompense.

The greatest challenge that now faces us is climate change with its apocalyptic implications. In an earlier chapter I discussed the obstacles that stand in the way of a solution to this problem, even a partial solution. The problem is far greater than the Depression of the 1930s or the inadequacy and unfairness of Canadian medical care in 1950s. We face an end to the world as we know it. A resolution is only possible if we summon up the greatest reserves of political leadership. As we have seen, there is no sign of this happening, in Canada or in the world – quite the opposite. Canada is far from meeting its Paris Accord commitments, and recently has fallen even further behind those commitments. The federal and provincial governments cannot even all agree on something as obvious as a carbon tax. The Climate Action Tracker,

---

362 "What Happened to Obama?" *New York Times*, 6 August 2011 https://www.nytimes.com/2011/08/07/opinion/sunday/what-happened-to-obamas-passion.html (accessed 7 October 2018).

offering independent scientific analysis, in September 2018, and again in January 2019, rated Canada's effort as "highly insufficient," the second-lowest rating.[363] Federal government representatives say the right things but do little. Most provincial government representatives do not even bother to say the right thing. Political leadership on the biggest issue of our times is an abject failure.

CITIZENS

A citizen's merit can be judged by how they meet two tests. First, do they embrace civic engagement? There are many ways to engage and to be an enthusiastic participant in civil society.[364] You can support charities according to your means. You can be a participant in politics and be sure to vote. The good citizen should not care exclusively, or even mostly, for themselves and their family. This is sometimes called civic humanism, "a variant of republicanism indicating active, participatory, patriotic citizenship as well as the ethos and educational ideal that goes with it." In recent times, Hannah Arendt restated the Aristotelian ideal of participatory citizenship. "Arendt defends the *vita activa* as a life of public engagement, and opposes it to a life that reduces the pursuit of happiness to individual, selfish, and for the most part acquisitive private undertakings."[365] The second test of a citizen's merit, related to the first,

---

363 "Canada's Pan-Canadian Framework on Clean Growth and Climate, announced in 2016, is an overarching strategy document for emission reductions, containing proposals for economy-wide measures, including a carbon pricing plan and a plan to phase-out traditional coal plants. Based on the implemented policies under this framework, Canada is likely to miss its Paris Agreement (NDC) target to reduce economy-wide GHG emissions by 30% below 2005 levels by 2030." See Climate Action Tracker, https://climateaction-tracker.org/countries/canada/ (accessed 8 October 2018).

364 Some of the activities of civil society include: "holding institutions to account and promoting transparency; raising awareness of societal issues; delivering services to meet education, health, food and security needs; implementing disaster management, preparedness and emergency response; bringing expert knowledge and experience to shape policy and strategy; giving power to the marginalized; and encouraging citizen engagement." See World Economic Forum, "Who and what is 'civil society?" 23 April 2018 https://www.weforum.org/agenda/2018/04/what-is-civil-society/ (accessed 15 October 2018).

365 *Stanford Encyclopaedia of Philosophy*, https://plato.stanford.edu/entries/humanism-civic/ (accessed 29 October 2018).

is whether they are willing (perhaps even happy) to pay taxes, including new taxes. Does the citizen accept that taxes are the price, the mark even, of civilization? Taxes finance the great common enterprise.

In 1762, Jean-Jacques Rousseau published *The Social Contract*. Rousseau was following in the philosophical footsteps of Thomas Hobbes and John Locke. The details of the theory of social contract, reiterated for centuries and still expounded in the present day, are complicated (and there remains controversy—feminists, for example, are suspicious about the theory's details) but Rousseau's general idea, as summarized by a modern expert on social contract theory, is simple enough.

> Since a return to the State of Nature is neither feasible nor desirable, the purpose of politics is to restore freedom to us, thereby reconciling who we truly and essentially are with how we live together. So, this is the fundamental philosophical problem that *The Social Contract* seeks to address: how can we be free and live together? Or, put another way, how can we live together without succumbing to the force and coercion of others? We can do so, Rousseau maintains, by submitting our individual, particular wills to the collective or general will, created through agreement with other free and equal persons. . .
>
> The sovereign is thus formed when free and equal persons come together and agree to create themselves anew as a single body, directed to the good of all considered together. So, just as individual wills are directed towards individual interests, the general will, once formed, is directed towards the common good, understood and agreed to collectively.[366]

Civic engagement and the payment of taxes can be thought of as creatures of the general will directed towards the common good. This is how we can be free and yet live together.

Taxes must be paid if we want to accomplish things together that we cannot accomplish individually. Regrettably the mindless and

366 Celeste Friend, "Social Contract Theory," *Internet Encyclopaedia of Philosophy*, https://www.iep.utm.edu/soc-cont/#H2 (accessed 15 October 2018).

destructive "no new taxes" movement seems vast, particularly in North America. It is routine, almost obligatory, for politicians to pander to this movement. "Read my lips: no new taxes," said George H.W. Bush, accepting the presidential nomination at the 1988 Republican National Convention. The slogan "no new taxes" is often fuelled by a perception of government corruption and incompetence. Why pay money if it will be misspent? It is odd that politicians so often endorse a way of thinking that presumes they cannot be trusted or are incompetent.

Avoiding taxes is seen by many citizens as a mark of cleverness. Smart people, often helped by overpaid lawyers and accountants, pay little or no taxes. This has been exemplified in the US by the Trump family. The Trump family has a long history, through the generations, of moving heaven and earth to avoid paying their fair share to government. In October 2018, *The New York Times*, in a remarkable thirty-four thousand-word feature article, set forth chapter and verse of the Trumps' tax avoidance, rampant illegal tax evasion, and money-laundering.[367] A few days later, the newspaper reported that Donald Trump's son-in-law, Jared Kushner, with a net worth estimated at more than $300 million, had almost certainly paid no tax for years.[368] Paul Krugman has called the Trump administration a "government of tax cheats, by tax cheats, for tax cheats."[369]

The attempt in Canada to levy a nationwide carbon tax is a good example of the failure both of political leadership and sound citizenship. I have already mentioned William Nordhaus, winner of the 2018 Nobel Prize in Economics, who said, "In other countries [other than the U.S.], people are grown-up, and they can live with taxes. The problem is political, rather than one of economics or feasibility. . . At some

367 David Barstow, Susanne Craig and Russ Buettner, "Trump Engaged in Suspect Tax Schemes as He Reaped Riches From His Father," 2 October 2018 https://www. nytimes.com/interactive/2018/10/02/us/politics/donald-trump-tax-schemes-fred-trump.html?module=inline (accessed 14 October2018).

368 Jesse Drucker and Emily Flitter, "Kushner Paid No Federal Income Tax for Years, Documents Suggest," 13 October 2018 https://www.nytimes.com/2018/10/13/business/jared-kushner-taxes.html (accessed 14 October 2018).

369 "Trump and the Aristocracy of Fraud," *The New York Times*, 4 October 2018 https://www.nytimes.com/2018/10/04/opinion/donald-trump-fred-taxes-fraud.html (accessed 14 October 2018).

point, I'm hopeful that grown-ups will take over and we will do what is necessary. I hope so."[370] But Nordhaus's hope is misplaced when it comes to Canada. The grown-ups have not taken over. The carbon tax should be easy to swallow, particularly a version that in some way returns to the individual taxpayer the extra tax he pays when he buys fossil fuel. But, as we have seen, in Canada the idea of a carbon tax has evoked a furious negative response, particularly by so-called "leaders" at the provincial level who believe that voters just don't want to pay any new tax no matter what it is about.

FREEDOM

There is no freedom without selfless, principled and courageous leaders. We need such leaders more than we ever did, particularly to confront the new and existential threats of global warming and biosphere collapse. There is no freedom without selfless citizens committed to civic engagement, and willing to pay substantial taxes to promote the common good. The general welfare must trump personal interests if we are to survive, let alone prosper. We have moral agency and, therefore, we are capable of making the right choices.

370 Coral Davenport, "After Nobel in Economics, William Nordhaus Talks About Who's Getting His Pollution-Tax Ideas Right," *The New York Times*, 13 October 2018 https://www. nytimes.com/2018/10/13/climate/nordhaus-carbon-tax-interview.html (accessed 13 November 2018).

CHAPTER FIFTEEN

A CITIZENS' MANIFESTO

THE NECESSARY CONDITIONS AGAIN

In Chapter One, I listed the necessary conditions for freedom. They are, in summary: an alert and skeptical citizenry willing to challenge authority; a fair electoral system; a strong legislature and legislative process; an appropriate apportionment of power between the executive and legislative branches which does not disproportionately favour the executive; a traditional and restrained judiciary that understands and reflects the will of the people; a vigorous, independent, diverse and disciplined press; a strong and independent secondary and post-secondary education system; an effective justice system accessible to all; a rejection of political correctness and simplistic ideas of human rights; effective civilian control of police; limits to government surveillance and loss of privacy; fair and just treatment of Indigenous People; the capacity and will to respond to the severe threats of climate change and loss of biodiversity; courageous political leadership; and a citizenry devoted to the common good. Most of this book has been devoted to showing in some detail the parlous state in Canada of these necessary conditions for freedom. Now, I ask: What is to be done?[371]

371 With thanks to Vladimir Lenin for the question.

A CITIZENS' MANIFESTO

An evaluation of the state in Canada of the conditions for freedom tells us what must be done. Action is every citizen's responsibility.

- Replace deference to establishment institutions and individuals with informed skepticism.

- Demand access to justice.

- Support reliable and unbiased sources of true news, including independent digital newspapers.

- Insist that universities reject a corporate consumer-driven model that emphasizes vocational training and instead teach critical thinking and good judgment.

- Be skeptical about the concept of human rights and their promotion by the human rights bureaucracy, recognizing that the idea of human rights can paradoxically be used to suppress freedom.

- Write and say what you want, however unpopular you think your views, and disregard concepts of political correctness.

- Hold politicians to their promises.

- Keep a close eye on the police.

- Don't worry about privacy (that battle is lost), but fight hard against excessive government surveillance and secrecy.

- Fight for greater economic equality.

- Engage on behalf of Indigenous People.

- Move heaven and earth to minimize global warming and the collapse of biodiversity.

- Be a good and altruistic citizen and support strong and wise political leadership.

- Hold hope close to your heart.

INDEX

p4